MANAGING LIMITED RESOURCES

MANAGING LIMITED RESOURCES
New Demands on Public School Management

Edited by

L. DEAN WEBB
Arizona State University
Tempe, Arizona

and

VAN D. MUELLER
University of Minnesota–Twin Cities
Minneapolis, Minnesota

Fifth Annual Yearbook of the
American Education Finance Association
1984

BALLINGER PUBLISHING COMPANY
Cambridge, Massachusetts
A Subsidiary of Harper & Row, Publishers, Inc.

Copyright © 1984 by American Education Finance Association. All rights reserved. No part of this publication may be reproduced, stored in a retrieval system, or transmitted in any form or by any means, electronic, mechanical, photocopy, recording or otherwise, without the prior written consent of the publisher.

International Standard Book Number: 0-88410-968-2

Library of Congress Catalog Card Number: 84-18415

Printed in the United States of America

Library of Congress Cataloging in Publication Data

Main entry under title:

Managing limited resources.

  (Fifth annual yearbook of the American Education Finance Association)
  Includes bibliographies and index.
  1. Public schools—United States—Business management—Addresses, essays, lectures. 2. Education—United States—Finance—Addresses, essays, lectures. 3. Educational accountability—United States—Addresses, essays, lectures. I. Webb, L. Dean. II. Mueller, Van D. III. Series: Annual yearbook of the American Education Finance Association ; 5th.
LB2823.5.M36 1984   379.1'54   84-18415
ISBN 0-88410-968-2

CONTENTS

List of Figures ix

List of Tables xi

Chapter 1
Public School Business Management:
Context and Future Directions
— Van D. Mueller and L. Dean Webb 1

Chapter 2
Accounting, Internal Control, and Auditing
— Suzette Pope and Stan Tikkanen 29

Chapter 3
Budgeting
— Charles H. Sederberg 59

Chapter 4
Fiscal Management — Investments
— Guilbert C. Hentschke 87

Chapter 5
Financing Public School Facilities:
Current Status and Trends
—Richard Salmon and William Wilkerson   111

Chapter 6
Sources of Alternative Revenue
—Lionel R. Meno   129

Chapter 7
Insurance and Risk Management:
Trends in Asset Protection and Fiscal Efficiency
—Bettye MacPhail-Wilcox   147

Chapter 8
Providing, Financing, and Managing
School Transportation
—Robert Gresham   165

Chapter 9
School Food Services:
Issues and Trends
—Lloyd E. Frohreich   179

Chapter 10
Managing Tomorrow's Facilities
—C. William Day   203

Chapter 11
Purchasing with Limited Resources
—Lloyd E. Frohreich and Joyce E. Ferguson   221

Chapter 12
Use of Computers in School Business Management
—E. Ronald Carruth and Gayden F. Carruth   247

Index	269
About the Editors	281
About the Contributors	283
American Education Finance Association Officers 1984-85	287

LIST OF FIGURES

2-1	The Financial Reporting "Pyramid"	36
3-1	The PPBADERS (PPBS) Cycle of Activities	65
3-2	Wildavsky's Political Process Orientation	66
4-1	Cash Flow Patterns in Two Districts	100
11-1	Purchasing Flow Diagram	224

LIST OF TABLES

1-1	Population of the United States: Age Cohorts, 1970-2000	3
1-2	Trends in Single-Parent Families and Married Working Women with Children	4
1-3	Revenue Receipts of Public Elementary and Secondary Schools, by Source, 1942-1979	14
1-4	Public Elementary and Secondary School Expenditures, 1959-60 to 1980-81	15
3-1	Centralization/Decentralization Continuums for Programs, Expenditure, and Revenue Planning Activities	76
4-1	The Cash-Flow Pattern of a Sample District	98
5-1	Capital Outlay and Debt Service Charges (in thousands) for Selected School Years, 1929-30 to 1982-83	113
5-2	Costs Per Square Foot for the Construction of Public School Facilities for Selected Years, 1976-1982	116
5-3	Public Elementary and Secondary School Bond Elections Held and Approved, and Par Values Proposed and Approved: Selected Years, 1965-1983	117
5-4	Summary of Municipal Bond Yield Averages by Moody Rating, United States, Selected Years, 1973-1983	118

LIST OF TABLES

8-1	Number and Percent of Public School Pupils Transported at Public Expense and Current Expenditures for Transportation: United States, 1929-30 to 1979-80	166
9-1	Per-Meal Federal School Lunch Reimbursement, FY82-FY84	181
9-2	School Breakfast Federal Reimbursement, FY82-FY84	183
9-3	Food Service Revenue: Percentage by Source	186

1 PUBLIC SCHOOL BUSINESS MANAGEMENT
Context and Future Directions

Van D. Mueller and L. Dean Webb

This book focuses on the business management of public elementary and secondary schools and only considers instruction, learning, and teaching incidentally or in relation to their management support-service needs. The book also examines the management of limited resources from the point of view of accountability to both the public and to the education professionals charged with the delivery of instruction to our children and youth.

The purpose of this introductory chapter is to discuss the larger political and social context in which public elementary and secondary schools exist; to examine the ways in which the education system responds to the impact of key events and movements in this larger context; to consider how the education system relates to, or perhaps even competes with, other public services and governmental agencies; and to provide observations and future directions for school business management. Selected demographic and political trends are developed in the first section of the chapter because it is important that the management of school business activities be viewed in its social and political context. For similar reasons, the second section includes a discussion of current issues in the governance and financing of schools. The final section presents a broad view of school organization and management; notes some of the specific issues associated with school site management, collective bargaining, and relations with the private sector; and offers some conclusions for policy consideration.

SOCIAL CONTEXT

The educational environment is rapidly changing, and if school systems are to survive intact, they must anticipate and adapt to change. The absence of planning for demographic and social changes is one reason for some of the present difficulties encountered by schools. During the 1970s, school systems learned that it costs much more to react to changes than to anticipate them. During the latter half of the 1980s, demographic and social trends will continue to bear heavily on the education system. Of these trends, four observable phenomena provide important background to the context and future directions of public school business management. They involve changing demographic trends, the interaction of technology and education, the pressures for accountability, quality, and access, and the expanding role of the schools.

Changing Demographic Trends

Declining enrollments is the first demographic trend that bears importantly on the function of public schools. Following the baby boom of the 1950s and 1960s, enrollments began to drop steadily. The transition from growth to decline has been painful for many public schools because falling enrollments have often meant higher costs, program cutbacks, staff reductions, school closures, and eroded community support. Problems connected with enrollment loss have been many and diverse, reflecting conditions both internal and external to the schools. Throughout the 1980s, many school districts, especially urban districts, will continue to experience declining enrollment. The school population of the metropolitan centers will increasingly contain a high percentage of minorities, a high dropout rate, and a high percentage of special needs students. The challenge of meeting the needs of this population will be compounded by the erosion of the tax base resulting from the flight of many businesses and the more affluent families to the suburbs, and by the reduction in state aid resulting from a reduced student enrollment.

While many districts will be experiencing a decline, nationally the number of children in elementary schools is expected to begin increasing by the mid-1980s. The National Center for Education Statistics (1982b) projects a 9 percent increase in K-8 enrollments from 1980-81 to 1990-91. By 1990, there should be approximately as many children ages 5 to 13 as there were in 1960. However, the pattern of enrollment decline and recovery will vary greatly from locality to locality, principally because of differential migration. Declines are projected for the Great Lakes and New England regions, and continuing the trend of the 1970s, increases are projected for the South and the West. These enrollment increases will result in an increasing demand for teachers, facilities, and support services (and the tax dollars to finance them) by the mid-1980s. An increase in the number of elementary/secondary students also portends greater competition for financial support between elementary/secondary education and higher education.

While the overall population of the United States will continue to increase through the end of the century, the largest population increases will not be among school-age children, but in the over-65 population (see Table 1-1). Over 6,000 people a day reach the age of 65; there are now over 25,000,000 people in that pool, a population equal to that of the twenty-five smallest states. The growing trend toward an older population will create competition for resources between the schools and other social service programs. This shift in the age distribution of the population signals not only an increase in the demand for selective social programs and fire and police protec-

Table 1-1. Population of the United States: Age Cohorts, 1970-2000.

	0-17	18-24	25-64	65 and Older
1970	69,644,081	23,697,340	89,805,003	20,065,502
1985	58,502,000	27,853,000	115,429,000	27,305,000
2000	65,414,000	24,653,000	134,826,000	31,822,000

Source: U.S. Department of Commerce, Bureau of the Census, *Statistical Abstract of the United States, 1980*, p. 29, Table 53; U.S. Department of Commerce, Bureau of the Census, *Projections of the Population of the United States: 1977 to 2000*, Table 8, Series 11. Washington, D.C.: U.S. Government Printing Office.

tion services, but also a shift in the balance of political power in the direction of a population with no direct stake in eduation and who are often the "No" voters in local bond or mileage elections (Kirst and Garms 1980).

The growing population in the next decade will not only reflect a shift in age distribution, but a shift in racial composition as well, especially among the school-age population. Between 1980 and 1990, the number of minority children and youth is projected to increase by 4.9 percent while the proportion of white children will decline by 9 percent. The percentage of Hispanics in both the younger and older age groups is expected to grow more rapidly than either black or white populations (Reisler 1981). Traditionally, minority populations place greater demands on the schools in terms of support programs such as compensatory, bilingual, and special education. While necessary and desirable, these higher cost programs will place additional strain on an already depleted educational budget. Concommittently, a greater representation of minorities in the overall population often results in greater demands for the social support and service programs that compete with general education for the public dollar.

Another demographic and social trend with implications for education programming and management is the steadily increasing number of single-parent families and married working women with children (see Table 1-2). These changes in the family structure are likely to have significant implications for education. For example, there will be an increasing demand by the working parents that schools

Table 1-2. Trends in Single-Parent Families and Married Working Women with Children.

	Labor Force Participation Rate, Married Working Women with Children	Persons under 18 Living With Single Parents as Percent of Persons under 18
1960	39.0%	n.a.
1975	52.3%	17.0%
1979	59.1%	19.2%

Source: U.S. Department of Commerce, Bureau of the Census, *Statistical Abstract of the United States, 1980*, p. 403, Table 671, and p. 52, Table 75. Washington, D.C.: U.S. Government Printing Office.

provide facilities to care for their children from early morning to late afternoon. In addition, schools will be required to fill the void in family life caused by working parents and will need "to help the students cope with personal problems of loneliness, inner conflict, and the need for interpersonal and intercultural understanding, and purpose" (Hoyle and McMurrin 1982).

Interaction of Technology and Education

Society's demand for educated workers is increasing. The continued revolution in telecommunications, computerization, and other new technologies has put a premium on workers with complex technological knowledge and skills. At the same time, the rapid obsolescence of technology means that the competence of many of these technical workers and managers will never be completely current with technological strides. Training and retraining will be needed as never before and a sound general education on which to base this retraining will assume new importance.

The advancing technological revolution, specifically as it relates to computers, has enormous implications for school management and education. In fact, *U.S. News and World Report* (1983) predicts that the very key to the expansion of education in the next fifty years is the computer. The schools have been placed in the position of not only adapting to and adopting computerization, but of having the major responsibility of preparing the manpower needed by a computerized society. U.S. Department of Labor statistics show that three out of the top five fastest growing jobs during the 1980s are in the computer industry, and three-fourths of today's kindergarten students will one day be employed in occupations requiring computer literacy.

Computers affect education in many ways. The computer can be used as a medium through which students working either alone or in groups at a computer terminal learn curricula content. Alfred Bork, a leading computer education advocate, predicts that by the year 2000 the major way of learning in almost all subjects, at all levels, will be through the interactive use of the computer (Barger 1982). Computers can be used to manage instruction by keeping track of student progress and prescribing individualized assignments for all students from the handicapped to the gifted and by keeping all classroom records. Computers can also be the object of instruction where computer literacy/computer science is the goal.

The labor-intensive nature of education has often been the subject of criticism. Typically, over three-fourths of a school district budget goes to personnel costs. The increased use of computers will help in lessening the labor-intensive nature of education. However, although some funds will be freed in the process, it may well be that new systems and new methods will be needed to finance the capital-intensive educational technology.

The introduction of computers into education is changing the concept of what it means to be well educated. Naisbett (1982) predicts that to be really successful in the future one will have to be trilingual: fluent in English, Spanish, and the computer. An increasing number of educators share in a concern that as competence with computers becomes equated with access to information, existing differences in equality of educational opportunity will be exacerbated. Poorer districts will have fewer computers on a per pupil basis and less software; thus, their students will be deprived with respect to computer education.

As home computer terminals, two-way interactive phone-video consoles, and laser and satellite communications become economically within the reach of many citizens, there will be increasing demands for more coordinated/cooperative relations among public schools, colleges, libraries, museums, private firms, and the home. With the constraints of schooling within a certain physical facility removed and given the expanded involvement of community resources and the home in the learning process, education (learning), as contrasted with schooling, will be enhanced by the learning network made possible by technology. Lest they loose a larger and larger share of the market to nonschool vendors of educational services, a major challenge to school managers will be to develop new organization strategies to deliver education services. Pogrow (1983) and Tucker (1983) provide detailed suggestions for incorporating technology into the education delivery system.

Accountability, Quality, and Access

Education is once again front-page news. In the recent past, reports sponsored by a variety of organizations recommending improvements in elementary and secondary education have received considerable attention (e.g., in 1983, National Commission on Excellence, *A Nation at Risk*; Education Commission of the States, *Action for Excellence*; John Goodlad, *A Place Called School*; The Carnegie Foundation, *The Condition of Teaching*). While each report has a slightly different orientation, they all focus on ways to make schools better and urge the American people to take a deeper interest in their schools. The various reports cite an alleged disintegration in the quality of American education and express concern over the ability of schools to prepare a workforce for the technological society and economy that lie ahead. Some reports call for revisions in teacher training or changes in curriculum; enhanced utilization of technological developments; increasing graduation requirements and competency testing for students and teachers; or merit pay for teachers, improved methods for dismissing incompetent teachers, higher teachers' salaries, long school days and school years, and more homework. To implement these recommendations would require significant alterations in the way schools are organized and in the way services are delivered.

Many of the recommendations of these recent reports have been made in numerous other indictments of the schools published over the last several decades. Levine (1983) suggests that reform proposals do not seem to have a lasting effect on the public schools because of their focus on external measures and control of education rather than on the school itself. She also asserts that the reports contain a serious flaw in their focus on inputs and outputs, rather than on what happens in between. This strategy for improvement is flawed because it creates an illusion that improvements can be made by fiat. The reports, according to Levine, aim too heavily at what ought to be the outcomes of schooling, with little attention paid to the realities that facilitate or obstruct reform.

Nonetheless, for the school manager the flood of advice on ways to improve the quality of schools represents and will continue to represent a real form of accountability. The public expects a response to the wide variety of issues concerned with academic quality. Comments from consumers (parents and students) and dissatisfied taxpayers focus on curriculum standards, access and equity, competency testing, and the quality of teacher performance. Curriculum standards are viewed by many to be inappropriately low. This has allegedly resulted in a decline in academic test scores for American students in international comparisons; rampant functional illiteracy among adults and older teens; lower average standardized achievement results than twenty-five years ago; a steady decline in Scholastic Aptitude Test scores; increased remedial education needs in post-secondary institutions, business, and the military; and a reduction in *higher-order* intellectual skills. Naisbett (1982) includes many of these phenomena in the concept of *education mismatch*, a term descriptive of the fact that the generation graduating from high school today is the first generation in American history to graduate less skilled than its parents. School personnel are to a great extent being blamed for a "nation being at risk" by virtue of the conditions of schooling. The future will understandably introduce renewed efforts to find ways to hold school personnel accountable for student outcomes and sound financial management.

While the United States is advocating "Action for Excellence," the drive for access to quality education by minorities, the poor, handicapped, women, and other subgroups of society has not abated. These continued "equity" demands can be expected to create real tension between those who value access and equity and those who advocate more stringent standards. In this environment, the challenge for school managers is to provide the leadership necessary to create school policies and environments that will overcome mediocrity as well as the barriers to education that poverty, ignorance, and inequality create.

Improving the quality of the existing and future line of teachers is one of the most essential ingredients to improved academic quality. Recent national reports have not only underscored this point but have shown that not enough of the finest and brightest students are attracted by the teaching profession, that teacher preparation and staff development programs need substantial improvement, that the professional working life of teachers is on the whole unacceptable, and that, if given the chance to start over, fewer than one in five current teachers would pursue a teaching career. In addition, a serious shortage of teachers exists in key fields such as mathematics, science, foreign language, and special education, with a more widespread shortage likely in the future. Inadequate pay for teachers is a key part of the problem as is the fact that the women's movement has resulted in the introduction of other professions, such as law and medicine, to those who once provided the majority of the teacher supply. However, the problem surrounding the quality of the teaching force are more complex than can be accounted for by either of these phenomena. With an aging teaching force (more teachers over the age of 40 than under age 30), the call for new, entering teachers is great and the profession's development has been seriously underfunded. While most school districts spend 8 to 10 percent of their budgets to maintain physical capital (buildings and equipment), investment in staff development is less than 1 percent.

Fox (1983), reporting on a major national conference of teacher educators, provides a listing of twenty challenges for teacher training and staff development that emphasize the need for school professionals to establish closer ties to teacher educators and researchers in constructing environments that support the work of teachers. The *Wilson Quarterly* has devoted an entire issue (Braestrup 1984) to summarizing the body of relevant new research on teaching. Looking to the future, the authors of this four-part report see a rare opportunity to upgrade teaching in the nation's schools. If, indeed, the quality of the instruction program (output) is primarily dependent on the quality of the instruction staff (input), school districts must recognize the importance of upgrading the *human capital* of the school—the professional educators.

The Diverse Role of Schools

During this century public schools have become the leading social institution in our nation in terms of enrollments and the most comprehensive in terms of public demands and program variety. There are no social mechanisms that do as many things as well as the public schools. The accomplishments of the public school system reflect a tradition of decentralization, pluralism, and diversity. They have come to be the very symbol of the diverse and heterogeneous character of our society. Traditionally, the goals of education (and of the schools) have reflected the values held by the individual or the group. For example, to some, education is the transmission of a cultural heritage; to others, it is the initiation of the young into worthwhile ways of thinking and doing; and to yet others, it is a fostering of the individual's growth. Many of the basic conflicts and controversies in schools arise from the tension between these three goals. As

Ravitch (1983) concludes in her assessment of the potential for education reform, while the reform steps are easily identified, real difficulty arises because of an inability to agree on goals.

The present demands for reform of public education reflect skepticism about school quality, uncertainty about the present and the future, and confusion over society's changed expectations for the schools. But there is no consensus on the specific directions public schools should take to meet the challenges of the future. Many people are dissatisfied with the traditional role performed by schools, and other people claim that the schools are failing to respond to the emerging needs of the 1980s. Some authorities counter with charges that the public's expectation for the schools is both unrealistic and fails to recognize the extent to which society's problems beset the schools. Thus, confusion exists as to what the schools should do and how they should do it.

The pluralism and diversity that characterize public perceptions of the role of schools has several implications for school management. Educators, parents, and students must work in concert with the larger community to define reasonable expectations for the schools. At the same time, school management must be able to mediate among diverse factions to produce a constructive consensus on education's role. And, in the process, the school system should clearly delineate that which it can accomplish alone, that which it can accomplish only by cooperation with nonschool organizations, and that which it cannot accomplish at all. Above all, school management must exhibit a commitment to excellence in public education for all children of all abilities as the American ideal of a just society.

GOVERNANCE AND FINANCING

The national school system has, to a large extent, evolved from a tradition of decentralization of organization, finance, and service delivery from the federal and state level to the local school district. As a result, the schools are characterized by differing missions and objectives, fragmentation by governmental level (local, state, federal) interests, frequent conflicts among parents, school boards, teachers, and administrators, and confusion over who is accountable. This following section describes some of the changing school governance and finance variables and the demands that are being made on school management.

Governance

In the late 1960s and early 1970s, governance of the public schools underwent a dramatic transformation. Prior to this, the school boards association, the teachers' association, and the state department of education cooperated on school issues, and acting in concert with sympathetic lawmakers, were the main source of state policy initiatives. Beginning in the mid-1970s, this consensual pattern was supplemented by educational policies that were initiated and implemented in a setting that was pluralistic, politicized, and competitive (Campbell and Mazzoni 1976). Educators are currently fragmented into contending factions. Political leaders formulate and decide education policy at the state and federal levels, and teacher organizations have become a recognized political force. Educational issues are, as a result, resolved in the mainstream of general government, rather than being insulated from partisan forces.

Over the last two decades there has also been a gradual shift in where the authority to establish the mission, purpose, and direction for local school systems is vested. This shift of authority has not been obvious because, in a formal sense, no change has occurred. Each state still has the authority and responsibility to provide educational opportunities for all of its citizens. This responsibility, in turn, continues to be delegated to local school boards or school committees. It is the *informal* structure of authority that has changed and continues to change. This structure determines who, in reality, exercises the power to influence, or set the direction for, the local schools.

Another shift in authority has taken power away from the local school district. Kirst and Garms (1980) forecast that the 1980s will bring a decline in influence to school boards, superintendents, and central administrations with a corresponding gain in influence for the federal and state governments, the courts, interstate organizations, private business, teacher and administration collective bargaining, and community-based interest groups. Although one can point to the formal erosion of local school district power because of an increase in the influence of federal and state governments and the rise of teacher associations and unions, the growth in program demands made by local constituencies is the biggest reason for the loss in the local school district's authority to change policy or direction. Greater participation by various consumer publics has led schools to initiate new programs such as computer literacy, career preparation, handicapped and gifted education, and many, many more.

Until the 1950s, there was considerable deference to the authority of the educational professional, manager, and teacher. The major decisions concerning who was hired to administer and teach, what programs would be offered, and what the educational philosophy and procedures would be were left to these professionals. During the 1960s and 1970s, along with society's general questioning of all forms of authority (family, church, and government), came the questioning of the authority of educational institutions. Ironically, it was probably the greater access to and effectiveness of the public schools that led to a better educated, more aware, and more critically thinking public who became the harsh critic of the schools.

Recent education changes embrace a much wider variety of issues and concerns than was the case in the past when there was limited public participation in the decisionmaking process. The line between participation and governance has increasingly blurred. Levine (1983: 5) explains one of the reasons for this trend:

> Political debate about education is often deplored but it is a sign of recognizing the political nature of education: in the context of the United States, it is the realization that different individuals and different levels of government have different interests, much as is the case for different interest groups. And today, as in the past, a persistent danger is the tyranny of the majority.

For a variety of reasons it appears there will continue to be a general demand by parents for greater involvement in planning, implementing, and evaluating all school services. Unfortunately, too often lack of information about rights and responsibilities inhibit parent participation in educational decisionmaking. The availability of information on the structure, financing, and decisionmaking process and the ways parents can organize stimulates participation; withholding this information keeps people powerless (Davies 1979a). Although some of the more threatened educators may view this as a desirable alternative, the educational *professional* must recognize that only through participation in the process of school governance can citizens learn to respect the work of teachers. Questions will likely continue concerning: Who owns the schools? Who should influence the mission, purpose, and goals of schools? And what forms of participation are appropriate for educator and citizen? The implications of these changes in governance imply that school managers must recognize and accept the political nature of the schools; develop new modes of flexible public participation and decisionmaking; observe the intent as well as the letter of the law regarding open meetings; provide information about the schools and train all citizens in using this information as part of a systematic education program; and become fully involved in any activities outside the district office and local school boundaries that provide direction for education policy.

Financing

Because education commands a substantial share of public sector resources, it is the legitimate object of political debate. The many reform reports will certainly stimulate much debate on the ways to finance educational excellence with limited new resources. The education system's ability to attract significant additional resources to finance change is, at best, problematic. As school enrollments decline as a percent of total population, and as the politically powerful demands of the aged mount, as does concern about other high social priorities (energy, crime control, rebuilding archaic cities and disintegrating transportation systems), can education's share of the GNP keep pace? The extent to which education maintains its relative position in governmental finance in the future, or meets the increasing demands being placed on it by state and federal mandates to implement programs for special needs populations, will without doubt depend on how successfully education can compete with other social programs for state and local tax revenues.

The trend to reduce federal aid to education that began in the early 1980s is projected to continue into the second half of the decade, if not for philosophical reasons, then because of the already large federal deficits. The diminished involvement of the federal government will place increased demands on state and local taxes for school support. Consequently, it will understandably be state and local governmental tax policies, in at least the near future, that will determine the fiscal support for innovation and school reform.

Table 1-3. Revenue Receipts of Public Elementary and Secondary Schools, by Source, 1942-1979.

School Year Ending	Percentage Distribution			
	Total	Federal	State	Local
1942	100.0	1.4	31.5	67.1
1946	100.0	1.4	34.7	63.8
1950	100.0	2.9	39.8	57.3
1954	100.0	4.5	37.4	58.1
1958	100.0	4.0	39.4	56.6
1962	100.0	4.3	38.7	56.9
1966	100.0	7.9	39.1	53.0
1970	100.0	8.0	39.9	52.1
1974	100.0	8.5	41.7	49.8
1978	100.0	9.8	45.7	44.5
1980	100.0	9.8	46.8	43.4

Source: National Center for Education Statistics, *Digest of Education Statistics, 1977-78, 1981, 1982.* Washington, D.C.: U.S. Government Printing Office.

In terms of fiscal responsibility for the public schools, states have increasingly assumed more of the costs since the early 1970s. By 1980, state sources contributed almost half of all public school revenues (see Table 1-3). State-collected taxes on wealth, income, and consumption will provide the primary service of school support in the future. The shift away from locally collected revenues will mean a reduced reliance on the property tax for the support of the public schools, and will thus bring more equity to the tax structure supporting education. At the same time, the broadening of the base of allocation brought about by the increased reliance on state revenues should bring more equity to the allocation dimension.

After two decades of rapid and large increases, expenditures for education appear to have peaked in the late 1970s (see Table 1-4). Total expenditures for public schools increased by over 100 percent from 1969-70 to 1980-81 ($40.7 billion to $99.8 billion). During the same period, enrollments declined. In constant dollars, the expenditures increase over the twelve-year period was $2.1 billion, or an average yearly increase of slightly over 2.5 percent. However, in 1981, expenditures actually represented a 9 percent decline in constant dollars from 1980 levels. What does this leveling off of total

Table 1-4. Public Elementary and Secondary School Expenditures, 1959-60 to 1980-81.

	In Billions of Dollars				
	1959-60	1969-70	1977-78	1978-80	1980-81
Total Expenditures					
Current $	$15.6	$40.7	$80.8	$96.0	$99.8
Constant $	38.5	78.3	93.2	87.7	80.4

Source: National Center for Education Statistics, *Digest of Education Statistics 1980, 1982.* Washington, D.C.: U.S. Government Printing Office.

spending for the public schools, accompanied by a greater reliance on state revenues and a diminishing of federal and local revenues, mean for the long-term fiscal support of education? Can the schools meet the demands for academic reform and improve their vital missions of social integration and human development in a climate of scarce resources? Will adaptation of traditional school management and pedagogy to the cost-effective technologies rapidly becoming available provide sufficient efficiencies to make up for stable or declining revenues? Will our revenue and allocation systems permit funding for both access and excellence?

Kelly (1982) has argued that the five major sources of influence on school financing for the balance of the 1980s will be fiscal federalism, equity demands, productivity issues, technological substitutions, and public opinion. Federalism (intergovernmental relationships between local, state, and national levels), according to Kelly, absorbs political conflict over tax and spending policies at each level, each year and is as resilient as ever. Further, he predicts that during the 1980s equity issues will be more closely linked to issues of quality and school effectiveness than was the case in the 1970s. To be more productive, schools will be expected to be more results-oriented. Teachers, principals, and students must be expected to work harder and to meet higher standards of performance. Kelly also maintains that although the technological revolution in communications will cause education to get cheaper—while expenditures rise—schools will persist. And, finally, parents and nonparents will continue to believe in and support the schools.

The school financing trends summarized here have the following implications for school district management:

- The per pupil costs of schooling, even with emphasis on productivity and use of technology, will continue to increase.
- Schools will continue to play a key role in shaping the distribution of scarce resources in our society.

SCHOOL ORGANIZATION AND MANAGEMENT

As school systems engage in major program and service reforms, changes in organization and management are essential. Despite the many issues and concerns being voiced by the private sector, the educationally disadvantaged, the linguistically different, and the resurgent middle class, values and interest (which are deeply imbedded in the present system of managing the schools) have changed very little. School systems continue to organize themselves in a hierarchical manner patterned after the military, the church, and big business. As a result of centralization (concentration of power and authority in one central location) and the merging together of school districts, there has been a significant decrease in the number of administrative units. Between 1950 and 1978, reorganization reduced the number of school districts in the United States from 84,000 to 16,000. As the number of school districts decreased so did the number of decisions made at the school building and community levels. Accompanying this centralization were policies that left more and more decisions to the professional manager: the superintendent and his or her staff. School boards tended to allow their superintendents and their central office administrators to dominate policymaking and implementation. The major benefit espoused by the centralization movement was more efficient operation of the schools. The costs have placed schools at a greater distance from the public, and school boards are dominated by educational professionals rather than the lay public. Reaction to these trends has been a grassroots effort aimed at putting the public back into the public schools and a concern by school managers and school boards for an improvement in the organizational structure and the management performance of the schools.

Peters and Waterman, in their book *In Search of Excellence* (1982) describe eight basic attributes that characterize the excellent, innovative companies they studied. The distinctive features are as follows:

1. *A bias for action*, for getting on with it.
2. *Close to the customer.* These companies learn from the people they serve.
3. *Autonomy and entrepreneurship.* The innovative companies foster many leaders and many innovators throughout the organization.
4. *Productivity through people.* The excellent companies treat the rank and file as the root source of quality and productivity gain. They do not foster we/they labor attitudes.
5. *Hands-on, value drive.* The basic philosophy of an organization has far more to do with its achievements than do technological or economic resources, organizational structure, innovation and timing.
6. *Stick to the knitting.* The odds for excellent performance seem to strongly favor those companies that stay reasonably closer to businesses they know.
7. *Simple form, lean staff.* The underlying structural forms and systems in excellent companies are elegantly simple. Top-level staffs are lean.
8. *Simultaneous loose-tight properties.* The excellent companies are both centralized and decentralized. Autonomy has been pushed to the production level while a few core values are very centralized.

Further, Peters and Waterman (p. 13) show that:

The excellent companies were, above all, brilliant on the basics. Tools didn't substitute for thinking. Intellect didn't overpower wisdom. Analysis didn't impede action. Rather, these companies worked hard to keep things simple in a complex world. They persisted. They insisted on top quality. They fawned on their customers. They listened to their employees and treated them like adults. They allowed their innovative product and service "champions" long tethers. They allowed some chaos in return for quick action and regular experimentation.

What can school systems and school managers learn from the practices of the best-run private sector companies? Can selective implementation of these ideas contribute to a reshaping and reform of the management of our schools? Can schools provide effective yet efficient support services to their instructional enterprise? Goodlad (1983) in his in-depth study concludes that schooling, as a human service provided by individuals, requires a precise understanding on the part of teachers of what their purposes are. He describes teachers' roles as complex, often requiring subjective judgment and continuous decisionmaking. Goodlad concludes that little in their environment supports teachers in this role. The conclusions reached by Peters and Waterman (1982) appear to be consistent with the generalizations made by Goodlad about the schools. School business managers need to study the applicability of effective management and education principles to schools and to provide leadership in their application. School business managers must recognize the need to manage people, not budgets, buildings, and buses. Their concern must focus on outcomes of learning and teaching, the products of the schools. Systemic changes in the organization of school support services, including decentralization/school site management, cooperative relationships with the private sector, and the expanded use of collective bargaining to improve conditions of work, must accompany changes in school programs and services. Each of these areas is a part of the general environment of the public schools and each bears on the role and activity of the school business manager.

Decentralization/School Site Management/ Community Control

Concurrent with the strong centralizing tendencies in society (e.g., television, computer data banks, instantaneous video communication), a renewed demand for decentralization has arisen. As school systems grew larger and authority became centralized, parental choice in education appeared to be limited by rigid school district boundaries, inflexible attendance areas, and district and individual school policies that made choices among different education delivery systems the exception and choices among specific teachers a thing of the past. Rising demands for tuition tax concessions (credits and deductions) and for vouchers reflect a growing dissatisfaction with this lack of choice within the publicly regulated school system. Other evidence of the dissatisfaction associated with centralization is the increasing number of people who believe that only a greater trust, inventiveness, and involvement at the grassroots level can address the numerous education challenges today. At the same time that the clientele of the schools are seeking decentralization, individual schools and teachers are seeking more autonomy. In addition, parents, teachers, and citizens without children in the schools are demanding more participation for themselves and greater accountability by the school personnel.

Davies (1979b) provides an excellent summary of the evolution of grassroots activity through three stages: community control, decentralization, and school-based management. Community control is a relatively new form of school governance. The movement toward community control grew in the 1960s through the efforts of low-income and minority parents who were dissatisfied with the slow pace of school desegregation and the inadequate services centralized education bureaucracies were providing to their neighborhood schools. The basis of community control is that parents should have a major responsibility in determining who teaches and what is taught in schools. Community control is generally conceived of as a school or cluster of schools in a public school district that is autonomous or self-governing in major policymaking areas such as budget, personnel, and curriculum. Policymaking authority becomes the responsibility of local community school boards of education.

School systems opposed the concept of community control because it challenged fifty years of consolidation and centralization. However, one response to parent demands for community control was school district decentralization. While community control sought to break up large school districts into much smaller ones with their own elected school boards, school district decentralization called for keeping one central board while giving lower levels of the bureaucracy more discretion. For school decentralization to be effective there must be real change in the ways decisions regarding budget, staff, and programs are made. Consequently, in operational terms, whether school district decentralization leads to more access for parents and citizens depends on who has discretion, at what level, whether parent advisory councils are used, and whether the system creates a new layer of administrators.

School-based or school site management is an extension of the decentralization idea to the school building level. Davies (1979a: 10) describes the school-based management concept as having three components:

1. *Financial.* The financial aspect of school-based management involves school site budgeting—lump sum allocations to individual schools based on district-wide rule.
2. *Administrative.* In addition to lump sum allocations, the school principal and the teaching staff have the authority to make decisions about budget, personnel, and curriculum.
3. *Participation.* Decentralization of authority to the school principal is shared between principals and community representatives through school site councils.

Garms, Guthrie, and Pierce (1978) assert that school site management will increase the responsiveness and effectiveness of local schools, solve many of the problems inherent in centralized budgeting and management, and ensure more understandable and effective public schools.

Decentralization, community control, and school-based management lead to power sharing and system reform and thus have significant implications for school business officials. Important implications for delivery of support services include such diverse aspects as: decentralization of negotiations and administration of union contracts; the complexities involved in budgeting, auditing, and financial control in a decentralized system; purchasing and supply-management decentralization; the management of support personnel, facilities, and equipment in a decentralized setting; and provision of support staff to building principals.

Collective Bargaining

Within the public school sector it appears that the continuing effort of parents and citizens to exercise more control over the schools is colliding with the struggle of teachers and other school employees to improve their collective economic, political, and social conditions, and to control the conditions of their work. Since 1959, when Wisconsin passed the first law granting public employees, including educators, bargaining rights, the collective bargaining movement has gained acceptance through legislation or practice in most states. Teacher organizations and organizations comprising noncertified school employees are growing. Bargaining now takes place in most states, with or without statutory collective bargaining rights. Tensions between the public sector movement and the school employees movement may well be inevitable. However, it is essential for changes to be made in the traditional decisionmaking model. It is also important for innovative but realistic thinking about the critical issues at stake. Unless some new approach is tried, the forces for employees' rights, parents' and citizens' rights, and public agency policymaking and management prerogatives will continue to clash, thus preventing the needed consensus on school governance among educators and the public from taking place in the decades ahead.

A fundamental need exists for decisionmakers at all levels to seek better policies and practices for school governance. Modifications in collective bargaining policies and practices would be a partial answer to the problem. However, a more thorough response requires moving beyond current restraints imposed by bureaucratic styles of management and employer/employee relations to more profound changes: assigning significant aspects of educational decisionmaking to the individual school and communities they serve, and continuous development of collegial, collaborative forms of communication and power sharing among teachers, administrators, parents, students, and the public (Davies 1979b). Under these conditions, the conventional bilateral collective bargaining mode will be much less useful to all parties than other mechanisms through which the interested parties can exchange resources, both tangible and intangible (Sarason et al. 1977).

The issue of collective bargaining is of critical importance to school business management for several reasons. First, the school business official often is charged with the responsibility of negotiating contracts with noncertified school employees, or at least has the responsibility for administering the negotiated agreement. Second, the school business official frequently is a part of the management negotiating team that bargains with teachers and other certified personnel. Finally, since the salaries and benefits for employees make up such a large portion of the district operating budget, negotiated contracts with employee organizations set the tone for the entire school budget.

The status quo of adversarial negotiations does not serve the best interests of any of the stakeholders. School boards have lost their credibility; teacher unions, despite new-found power, are vulnerable to voter and taxpayer backlash; superintendents feel helpless as their relationships with the board, teachers, and other administrators become more ambiguous; school principals are uncertain of their identity as management or labor; parents and citizens feel left out; politicians face various dissatisfied constituencies and interest groups; and students must assume that someone else represents their interests. Each group is vulnerable and uneasy. Such is the current environment in which the school business official must operate.

Relationship with the Private Sector

The national education reform reports issued during the past year have invited businesses and business people to assume a greater role in improving schools. The recommendations urge business leaders to become more active, not only in supporting the schools financially, but also in developing curricula and programs and in sharing nonfinancial resources.

Boyer (1983) has suggested that business can provide volunteer tutorial programs, enrichment opportunities, cash awards for outstanding teachers, grants for outstanding principals, training facilities, and help in upgrading equipment. *Action for Excellence* (Task Force for Economic Growth 1983) recommends that leaders outside education take specific steps to marshall resources, communicate skills, and create partnerships with education involving team teaching and joint courses of study. Technical experts from business and government should work cooperatively with educators and professional societies to promote curriculum evaluation and development for mathematics, science, and technology according to the *Educating Americans for the 21st Century* report (National Science Board 1983). In addition, this report urges the private sector to explore ways to extend teachers' employment year while providing supplementary income and a revitalizing experience. Top executives in the computer, communication, and information retrieval and transfer industries are asked to develop plans that, in a good, economical, and quick way, enable school systems to use their technology.

Partnership and collaboration are becoming such popular terms in education circles that they are in danger of becoming meaningless. It is important, therefore, to combine the emphasis on collaboration with an emphasis on a specific outcome, for example, student learning or teacher performance. Collaboration or partnership can become merely a way for educators and business leaders to meet endlessly, leading, perhaps, to better mutual understanding, but not necessarily better student performance. For purposes of improving the productivity of school systems, school managers must make certain that collaboration is directed toward a specific goal.

Schools and business communities have a long history of cooperation on an ad hoc basis. There are many prototypical programs in existence that reflect successful school and business collaboration (McNett 1982). Recently, however, new forms of direct involvement of business with education have emerged. Rather than cooperating with the schools in creating actual curriculums and programs, business has directed energy and resources at the policy level. The California Business Roundtable (CBRT) has become a crucial new actor in state education politics. Based on a consultant study to provide specific directions for state policy changes, CBRT implemented an action plan that resulted in $800 million in new school funds for 1983 and included eighty substantive reforms (Kirst 1983). In 1983, the Minnesota Business Partnership hired the same consulting firm, and a comprehensive study of education outcomes in Minnesota is underway.

A more comprehensive framework for business community involvement with schools is contained within a proposed research agenda for the Committee on Economic Development or CED (Levine 1983). This framework provides a much more complete model for systematic research, analysis, and action by the business community. The proposed agenda is organized into three broad areas containing multiple elements.

The first area is *education and public policy* and includes: (1) identifying output measures, standards, and testing; (2) improving teacher quality; (3) curriculum—hidden and visible; (4) governance, organization, and management of schools; (5) quantitative changes for increasing output, for example, specialized schools, length of school day and school year, and class size; (6) financing reform and the reform of financing; and (7) the federal role in education.

The second area contained in the CED research and action agenda highlights *the business perspective on quality education* and points to: (1) assessing the cost of failure; (2) identifying the purposes of education; (3) specifying the education requirements for economic growth; and (4) clarifying the role of the schools and the work ethic. The third and final area addresses the *corporate roles in school improvement* and includes: (1) social responsibility and enlightened self-interest, retrospective and prospective; (2) barriers and incentives to collaboration with schools; and (3) models for business involvement with the public schools.

It appears that the business community has recognized that they have a direct stake in the improvement of public education and that their role need not be limited to philanthropy. The private sector is seeking to expand its role in setting new policy directions for the schools. Whether these efforts will result in new partnerships and new forms of collaboration or whether the result will be a conflict between business, labor, and the schools will depend on the extent to which: (1) the schools adapt to the more aggressive activity of the business community; (2) the schools are willing to make tradeoffs and adapt to changes that will sustain business interest over the long term; (3) the traditional public education coalition of support groups (parents, teachers, special interest) develop cooperative relationships with the business community; and (4) educational leaders at all levels, including school business management, develop adequate strategies to utilize the expertise and influence of the business community fully.

SUMMARY AND FUTURE DIRECTIONS

The preceding sections suggest that as the public schools respond to demands for educational reform, variations of current practices with respect to school business management will be necessary. The nature and process of providing support services to the instructional program of schools will change because the external and internal environments of the schools are changing. If school systems are to meet the fundamental challenges of the future, leadership from all sectors and levels of the education community will be essential. As all school systems struggle with change, the design and management of the support services essential for high quality teaching and learning will present a formidable challenge. While these conditions may arouse little enthusiasm among school business managers, the opportunities will indeed be great.

In summary, the social and political environment of education has changed and will continue to change. The shifting age distribution of the population, differential migration patterns, the changing composition of the family unit, increased minority and special populations in the schools, and competition between the various education systems will be among the important factors shaping the emerging context in which schools will operate. Each of these variables is beyond the direct control of the schools, yet they provide both dilemmas and opportunities for school business managers. Innovations in technology will create new systemic and programmatic challenges for the schools. Education in the broadest sense has never been "placebound." Access to new communication vehicles will permit schooling to take place everywhere and anywhere. How will the school systems manage and finance these new opportunities? Continued tensions are likely to persist as advocates of equity, access, and excellence search for a common ground on which to decide what should be the outcomes of schooling. Educators, parents, and students will need to work with the larger community to define a reasonable role for schools, accepting the fact that in a pluralistic and diverse nation consensus will always be tentative.

The governance and financing of public schools will be characterized by decentralization and scarcity. As the line between governance and participation increasingly blurs, public interest in education decisionmaking will remain high. The political and public nature of the schools will provide both opportunities and dilemmas for school management. Financing excellence and equity in the face of limited resource availability will place new demands on fiscal and programmatic planning in the schools. With little chance of improved revenues from the federal level, the public schools will face difficult competition from other social programs for the available state and local taxes.

School management and school boards will be pressured to reform and reshape the management. The work environment of teachers and the supportive services to the instruction mission of the schools will necessarily be high priority for action. The application of contemporary management and organization theory may help guide the needed changes. But the fundamental challenge will be to energize the crucial component of the system—the school. The transfer of power to building principals, teachers, parents, and the community will require new policies and procedures for managing human and material resources. Stewardship of public resources in the decentralized setting will significantly change school business operating systems.

As business leaders and the private sector both assume a greater role in improving our schools, school business managers will need to help evaluate new partnerships and collaboration models. Expanded coalitions involving the private sector, education professionals, parents, and the general public should be directed toward specific outcomes of the schools and include strategies to utilize fully all available internal and external resources.

Finally, it is clear that public school reforms will be both programmatic and systemic. Resource limitations will cause increased attention to be directed at school outcomes and school productivity. The effective and efficient management of school support services will increase in importance, and the school business administrator will be expected to provide committed and knowledgeable leadership in reforming our schools.

REFERENCES

Barger, Robert N. 1982. "The Computer as a Humanizing Influence in Education." *Technological Horizons in Education Journal* 9, no. 4 (May): 95–96, 105.

Boyer, Ernest L. 1983. *High School: A Carnegie Foundation Report on Secondary Education in America.* New York: Harper & Row, Publishers, Inc.

Braestrup, Peter, ed. 1984. "Teaching in American—A Special Report." *The Wilson Quarterly* 8, no. 1 (January): 46–105.

Campbell, Ronald F., and Tim L. Mazzoni, Jr. 1976. *State Policy Making for the Public Schools.* Berkeley, California: McCutchan Publishing Corporation.

Davies, Don. 1979a. "Public Schools: Knowing the Territory." In *Education For All People: A Grassroots Primer*, edited by Jane de Groot, pp. 5–16. Boston: Institute for Responsive Education.

Davies, Don. 1979b. "Introduction." In *Opening the Door: Citizen Roles in Educational Collective Bargaining*, edited by J. Hamer, C. Cheng, and M. Barron, pp. 9–32. Boston. Institute for Responsive Education.

"Education? By Computer, Naturally." 1983. *U.S. News and World Report* 94, no. 8 (May 9): AS.

Education Commission of the States. 1981. "Collective Bargaining Strikes and Arbitration." *Issuegram*, no. 3 (June). Denver, Colorado: Education Commission of the States.

Fox, G. Thomas, Jr. 1983. *Challenging How Teachers Are Educated: A Source for Dialogue and Action.* Washington, D.C.: ERIC Clearinghouse on Teacher Education and the American Association of Colleges for Teacher Education.

Garms, Walter I.; James W. Guthrie; and Lawrence C. Pierce. 1978. *School Finance: The Economics and Politics of Public Education.* Englewood Cliffs, New Jersey: Prentice-Hall, Inc.

Goodlad, John I. 1983. *A Place Called School: Prospects for the Future.* St. Louis, Missouri: McGraw-Hill Book Company.

Hoyle, John R., and Lee R. McMurrin. 1982. "Preparing Leaders To Anticipate and Manage the Future: Part II, Critical Challenges for Leaders who Anticipate and Manage the Future." Columbus, Ohio: University Council for Educational Administration.

Kelly, James A. 1982. "Making Things Happen." An address presented at the 1982 meeting of the National School Finance Reform Network, Wayzata, Minnesota, September 12.

Kirst, Michael W. 1983. "The California Business Roundtable: Their Strategy and Impact on State Education Policy." Paper prepared for the Committee on Economic Development, New York.

Kirst, Michael W., and Walter I. Garms. 1980. "The Political Environment of School Finance Policy in the 1980s." In *School Finance Policies and Practices. The 1980s: A Decade of Conflict*, edited by James W. Guthrie, pp. 47-75. Cambridge, Massachusetts: Ballinger Publishing Company.

Levine, Marsha. 1983. "School Reform: A Role for the American Business Community." A background paper prepared for the Committee for Economic Development. Washington, D.C.: American Enterprise Institute.

McNett, Ian E. 1982. *Let's Not Reinvent the Wheel: Profiles of School/Business Collaboration.* Washington, D.C.: The Institute for Educational Leadership.

Naisbett, John. 1982. *Megatrends.* New York: Warner Books.

National Center for Education Statistics. 1970. *Digest of Education Statistics 1970.* Washington, D.C.: U.S. Government Printing Office.

National Center for Education Statistics. 1977-78. *Digest of Education Statistics 1977-78.* Washington, D.C.: U.S. Government Printing Office.

National Center for Education Statistics. 1980. *Digest of Education Statistics 1980.* Washington, D.C.: U.S. Government Printing Office.

National Center for Education Statistics. 1981. *Digest of Education Statistics 1981.* Washington, D.C.: U.S. Government Printing Office.

National Center for Education Statistics. 1982a. *Digest of Education Statistics 1982.* Washington, D.C.: U.S. Government Printing Office.

National Center for Education Statistics. 1982b. *Projections of Education Statistics to 1990-91, Volume I: Analytical Report.* Washington, D.C.: U.S. Government Printing Office.

National Center for Education Statistics. 1983. *Digest of Education Statistics 1983.* Washington, D.C.: U.S. Government Printing Office.

National Science Board Commission on Precollege Education in Mathematics, Science, and Technology. 1983. *Educating Americans for the 21st Century.* Washington, D.C.: National Science Foundation.

Peters, Thomas J., and Robert H. Waterman, Jr. 1982. *In Search of Excellence: Lessons from America's Best Run Companies.* New York: Harper & Row, Publishers, Inc.

Pogrow, Stanley. 1983. "Linking Technology Use to School Improvement: Implications for Research Policy and Practice." In *School Finance and School Improvement Linkages for the 1980s,* edited by Allen Odden and L. Dean Webb, pp. 127-142. Cambridge, Mass.: Ballinger Publishing Company.

Ravitch, Diane. 1983. "On Thinking About the Future." *Phi Delta Kappan* 64, no. 5 (January): 317-20.

Reisler, Raymond F. 1981. "An Education Agenda for the Eighties." *Phi Delta Kappan* 62, no. 6 (February): 413-14, 435.

Sarason, Seymour B.; Charles F. Carroll; Kenneth Maton; Saul Cohen; and Elizabeth Larentz. 1977. *Human Services and Resource Networks.* San Francisco: Jossey-Bass Publishers.

Task Force for Economic Growth. 1983. *Action for Excellence: A Comprehensive Plan to Improve Our Nation's Schools.* Denver, Colorado: Education Commission of the States.

Tucker, Marc S. 1983. "Computers in the Schools: The Federal Role." Paper presented at Special Interest Group on Computer Uses in Education of the Association for Computing Machinery, Washington, D.C., September 3.

U.S. Department of Commerce, Bureau of the Census. 1977. *Projections of the Population of the United States: 1977-2000,* Table 8, Series 11. Washington, D.C.: U.S. Government Printing Office.

U.S. Department of Commerce, Bureau of the Census. 1980. *Statistical Abstract of the United States, 1980.* Washington, D.C.: U.S. Government Printing Office.

2 ACCOUNTING, INTERNAL CONTROL, AND AUDITING

Suzette Pope and Stan Tikkanen

Financial reporting in an era of change and limited resources presents many challenges to the school district financial administrator. Such challenges are not insurmountable, however, if one understands that the goal of financial reporting is to communicate the financial position and results of operations of the district to a wide-range readership with diverse informational needs. The purposes of this chapter are to focus on contemporary financial accounting and reporting trends in public education and to discuss related issues. Topics addressed include accounting, external and internal reporting, cash management, single audits, internal controls, current issues, and current trends.

Communicating financial results is not a new concept. Traditionally, accounting tasks were oriented to control; i.e., the monies had to be accounted for to assure the school district's patrons that tax dollars were being spent in the proper amounts and for the proper purposes. A control orientation served its purposes in the past, but pressures to address new public demands for accountability have changed the focus of financial reporting.

ACCOUNTING

Accounting may be defined as the composite activities of analyzing, recording, summarizing, and interpreting the financial transactions of any economic enterprise. Governmental accounting comprises these same activities for the organized legislative, executive, and judicial machinery of the state which by law governs and provides certain public services for citizens (Municipal Finance Officers Association 1968). Governmental accounting is multifaceted and complex because there is more than one level of government in operation. With governmental revenue frequently limited and often less than expenditure demands, prudent budgetary planning and control are essential to efficient utilization of available resources in providing required public services, whether it be rapid transit, water, and sewer service or public schools. Properly classified and accurate financial data are the cornerstone of required budget preparation.

Accounting and School Management

Accounting is a significant tool of management; it provides essential financial information to legislative and governing bodies. The Municipal Finance Officers Association (1968) identified four principal groups outside of the governmental organization that have a concerted interest and make decisions based upon information provided by the governmental accounting system. These are identified as:

1. General public—taxpayers, individual citizens, political groups.
2. Investors—investment bankers, and bond rating services.
3. Other governments because of complex inter-governmental fiscal relationship (grants-in-aid, shared resource).
4. Educational and research organizations, statistical reporting agencies.

School administrators are now operating in a new environment which places great importance on communicating with the public, school boards, and employees. The financial manager is placed in a role of leadership in addressing meaningful financial reporting. Regardless of the school district environment, the accounting function serves several varied purposes. Among the most important are:

1. Maintaining an accurate record of significant details in the business transactions of the school system.

2. Providing a basis and medium for planning and decisionmaking by both policymaking and administrative bodies at local, state, and federal levels.
3. Providing a control system to assure the appropriate use of resources in the educational enterprise.
4. Expediting the process of setting priorities; establishing, analyzing, and selecting alternatives in the budgeting process.
5. Providing a medium for reporting the financial condition of the school system to the patrons of the schools district as well as other groups and agencies at the local, state, and federal levels. This is done for purposes of planning and policymaking, accountability, control, and comparative study.
6. Providing basic input information to calculate and extend school district budgets, tax levies, and state and federal subventions or transfer payments. (Candoli et al. 1976.)

Accounting Concepts and Principles

To satisfy the many "publics" with comparable information, governmental accounting must utilize the same well known accounting concepts, principles, and practices applicable to private business enterprises. These include: (a) double-entry system of accounts; (b) consistency; (c) objectivity; (d) costs; (e) full disclosure; (f) materiality; and (g) conservatism.

Generally speaking there is uniformity in terms and account titles used in commercial and governmental accounting. However, although these similarities are recognized, there are significant differences which have led to the establishment of accounting principles and concepts applicable only to governmental entities. Perhaps the single most recognized difference is the profit motive of the private sector. Governmental agencies, on the other hand, exist primarily to provide selected activities and services, such as policy, fire and safety, health service, and public schools, on a nonprofit basis. In those governmental units which are user charge oriented, such as parking garages, utilities, and tollways, accounting methods will be modified. Specific areas in which governmental accounting and reporting differs from that generally used by commercial enterprises include: (a) the reporting format; (b) the reporting entity; (c) the focus on expenditures rather than on expense recognition; (d) the treatment of long-lived assets and depreciation; and, (e) the role of the budget (Drebin 1979).

Recognizing that the government environment differs markedly from that of business enterprises, and that the information needs to be met by governmental accounting systems and reports differ accordingly, the authoritative bodies responsible for developing, revising, and promulgating standards and principles for the accounting discipline developed a set of basic principles applicable to governmental accounting and reporting (Municipal Finance Officers Association 1979). These principles are specific fundamental tenets which, on the basis of reason, demonstrated performance, and general acceptance by public administrators, accountants, auditors, and others concerned with public financial operations, are generally recognized as essential to effective management control and financial reporting. These guiding principles may be summarized as follows:

1. *Accounting and reporting capabilities.*
   A governmental accounting system must be capable of producing reports in conformity with generally accepted accounting principles, and legal requirements if the two are significantly different.
2. *Fund accounting systems.*
   A governmental accounting system must be organized on the basis of funds.
3. *Types of funds.*
   A governmental unit should establish and maintain the least number of funds possible.
4. *Accounting for fixed assets and long-term liabilities.*
   Fixed assets and long-term liabilities not related to a specific fund should be accounted for in the General Fixed Assets and General Long-Term Debt Account Groups, respectively.
5. *Valuation of fixed assets.*
   With certain minor exceptions, fixed assets should be recorded only in specified types of funds.
6. *Accrual basis in governmental accounting.*
   The accrual basis of accounting should be used in certain specified types of funds and the modified accrual basis in others.

7. *Budgeting, budgetary control, and budgetary reporting.*
   Every governmental unit should adopt annual operating budgets and certain of those budgets should be reported in the financial statements.
8. *Transfer, revenue, expenditure, and expense account classification of revenues, expenditures, and expenses into certain specified categories.*
9. *Common terminology and classifications.*
   A governmental accounting system should consistently utilize terminology and classifications common to the funds maintained.
10. *Interim and annual financial reports.*
    Interim financial reports (format and content unspecified) and and annual financial reports (with format and content specified) should be issued by every governmental unit.

School Accounting Tasks

A specific area of governmental accounting is that of public school systems. The Association of School Business Officials of the United States and Canada (ASBO), School Accounting Research Committee has identified five work/task clusters which formulate the working definition of school accounting. The five work/task clusters of the School Accounting Committee are briefly described as follows:

Cash Management — planning for the management of temporarily idle school funds, preparing a cash investment program, monitoring invested funds, reporting investment activities to the school board, and continuous appraising of the investment program.

Capital Fund Management — determining fiscal needs for the building program of the school district, short and long range planning for financial capital improvements, determining methods of financing capital needs, preparing the capital fund budget, making debt service payments, and accounting for school bond payments and debt service revenues and expenditures.

Financial Planning and Budgeting — preparing the educational budget, the reconciliation of available resources and expected revenues with the fiscal needs of the school or school district, the development and operation of a fiscal control system to monitor and verify school expenditures, and continuous appraisal of the adequacy of the educational budget.

Fiscal Accounting and Financial Reporting—establishing procedures for classifying fund and receipt accounts, managing the fiscal accounting systems as well as budgetary controls and current operations reports, preparing financial reports and submitting them to the local school board and state board, coordinating and monitoring fiscal accounts, and continually appraising the accounting system.

Fiscal Audits and Reports—developing a plan for the continuous internal audit of fiscal records to assure regularity and accuracy of those records, pre-audits to prevent unauthorized or illegal expenditures, the systematic investigation, verification and critical review of financial operations by an independent auditor, regular reports of fiscal effectiveness to the chief school officer and school board, and the continuous appraisal of the fiscal operations of the school district.

Cost Allocation

Another accounting procedure which is evolving as a result of diminishing resources is that of cost allocation. In an attempt to provide the maximum amount of resources to the educational programs, expenditure allocations are being made to activities and programs which receive categorical or other funding. Traditionally, these programs would have only been charged for direct cost of salaries, supplies, and equipment. Cost allocations for administrative overhead, custodial services, utilities, among others, expand the actual costs reported for these programs. Project managers are therefore faced with the problem of maintaining the current level of service within the revenue entitlement or instituting a fee structure to supplement the deficit. The cost allocation procedure does provide a financial disclosure of the true cost of providing a given service.

FINANCIAL REPORTING

The key concept contained in the design of a reporting system is multiple reporting. In order to be considered efficient, the reporting system must be derived from a single set of accounting records. The report merely summarizes transactions captured as part of the accounting process. If the report includes data from outside of the accounting system the result is skepticism of the financial report. Anticipation of the data needs will enable the accounting structure to yield the maximum benefit and eliminate the need for special studies.

Financial accounting and reporting of resources utilization are basic to the use of public monies. Accounting and reporting systems have evolved to meet the needs of governing bodies. In the initial stages of development, the accounting systems were characterized by cash basis accounting and simplistic account structures.

Cash basis accounting and reporting were developed in response to statutes and served well at a time when cash basis reporting reflected the manner in which state and local governmental units operated. Because of the impractical recognition of receipts and disbursements, cash basis accounting provides little or no value in assessing the financial position of an entity. For this reason generally accepted accounting principles (GAAP) do not permit the use of the cash basis of accounting. In order for a school district's financial statements to be in compliance with GAAP, the governmental fund types (general, special revenue, debt service, expendable trust, and capital projects) must use the modified accrual basis of accounting. Enterprise, internal service, pension trust, and other nonexpendable trust funds must use the accrual basis of accounting.

Utilizing GAAP-based accounting and reporting procedures in an era of declining resources is a means of establishing a formalized method of communication between the district and community. Meaningful and relevant financial statements do provide the means of demonstrating accountability. The public, school board and administration will only have a clear understanding of pending financial problems or impact of declining fiscal resources if GAAP-based financial records are maintained.

A milestone in the evolution of governmental financial reporting was achieved by the National Council on Governmental Accounting (NCGA) with the March 1979 issuance of its *Governmental Accounting and Financial Principles* (Statement 1). The most significant aspect of Statement 1 concerns financial reporting. Prior to the issuance of Statement 1, critics of school district financial statements suggested they contained so much information that readers were unable to obtain an understanding of the overall financial position and results of operation of the district. The high level of detail was, however, required by certain readers of the financial statements, e.g., securities analysts and higher levels of government.

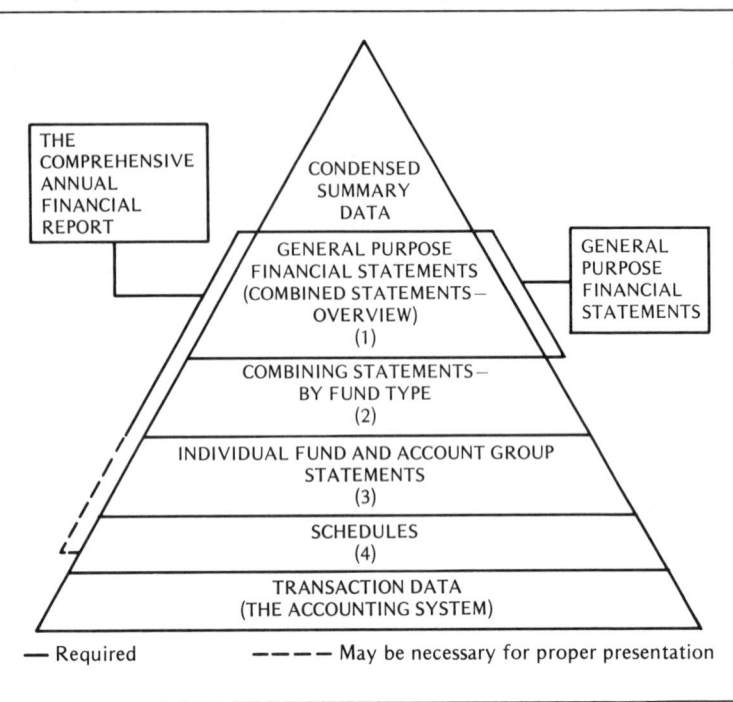

Figure 2-1. The Financial Reporting "Pyramid."

```
                          /\
                         /  \
                        /    \
        ┌─────────────┐/      \
        │ THE         /        \
        │ COMPREHENSIVE  CONDENSED \
        │ ANNUAL      /  SUMMARY   \
        │ FINANCIAL  /    DATA      \
        │ REPORT    /                \
        └──────────/──────────────────\
                  / GENERAL PURPOSE    \   ┌──────────┐
                 /  FINANCIAL STATEMENTS\  │ GENERAL  │
                /   (COMBINED STATEMENTS-\ │ PURPOSE  │
               /      OVERVIEW)           \│ FINANCIAL│
              /          (1)               │ STATEMENTS│
             /──────────────────────────────\─────────┘
            /     COMBINING STATEMENTS—      \
           /         BY FUND TYPE             \
          /              (2)                   \
         /──────────────────────────────────────\
        /   INDIVIDUAL FUND AND ACCOUNT GROUP    \
       /              STATEMENTS                  \
      /                  (3)                       \
     /──────────────────────────────────────────────\
    /                 SCHEDULES                      \
   /                    (4)                           \
  /────────────────────────────────────────────────────\
 /              TRANSACTION DATA                        \
/           (THE ACCOUNTING SYSTEM)                      \
──────────────────────────────────────────────────────────
```

—— Required   - - - - May be necessary for proper presentation

Source: Municipal Finance Officers Association, 1979.

In recognition of varying needs of readers of financial statements, the NCGA developed the financial reporting "pyramid" (Figure 2-1).

Statement 1 suggests that there are basically two types of financial reports for governments; a comprehensive annual financial report (CAFR) and the general purpose financial statements (GPFS), with the primary difference between the two being the level of detail included in the reports. The GPFS is composed of the following:

- Combined balance sheet—all fund types and account groups.
- Combined statement of revenues, expenditures, and changes in fund balances—all governmental fund types. (These are the general, special revenue, debt service, capital projects, special assessments, and expendable trust funds.)
- Combined statement of revenues, expenditures, and changes in fund balances (budget and actual)—general and special revenue fund types.

- Combined statement of revenues, expenses and changes in retained earnings (or equity)—all proprietary fund types. (These are the enterprise, internal service—formerly the intragovernmental service—and nonexpendable and pension trust funds.)
- Notes to the financial statements.

The CAFR contains the GPFS plus: (a) the Director of Finance's transmittal letter; (b) combining financial statements for each fund type, i.e., columnar presentations of the individual funds in the fund type; (c) individual fund financial statements, if necessary, in order to present budgetary data, prior year comparative data, or other data considered useful and informative to the readers, e.g., detail of expenditures or expenses that cannot be presented in the GPFS or combining statements; (d) schedules, if necessary, in order to demonstrate legal compliance or to present other information that is considered useful, e.g., combined data that encompasses more than one fund or details of data summarized in the financial statements; and (e) statistical tables.

Governmental units are encouraged to publish the CAFR which translates to an official annual report. Such reports must use the same uniform format and sections, as follows:

1. Introduction.
2. Financial.
    a. Auditor's Report.
    b. GPFS (combined statements—overview).
    c. Combining, Individual Fund, and Account Group Statements and Schedules.
3. Statistical Tables.
    a. Essential schedules.

The Municipal Finance Officers Association encouraged the use of the CAFR for a long while, believing that governmental agencies have a special responsibility to fully and fairly disclose their financial affairs. In fact, the CAFR has been a requirement to quality for the Certificate of Conformance issued by MFOA.

Implementation of Statement 1 reporting principles has been received with mixed emotion in educational circles. Supporters of the pyramid concept suggest the reporting format provides information to meet varied needs. With a little understanding of the format, desired information can be found in summary form in some level of detail. This format permits an easier method to explain transactions in the various school funds.

Opposition to the pyramid reporting concept has focused basically on the volume of the report. Generally, it is argued that the benefits of the additional statements and schedules do not justify the cost of preparing the report. An additional emerging factor in school district financial reporting is the organizationwide audit or single audit. A single audit is a comprehensive financial and compliance audit of the school district which is conducted by one audit firm or audit organization to achieve both the objectives of a general audit and of all federal-program audit needs. The single audit is discussed in the next section.

AUDITING

Auditing is the process of examining documents, records, systems of internal control, accounting and financial procedures, and other evidence for one or more of the following purposes:

1. To ascertain whether the statements prepared from the accounts present fairly the financial position and results of financial operations.
2. To determine the propriety, legality, and mathematical accuracy of a governmental unit's financial transactions.
3. To ascertain whether all financial transactions have been properly recorded.
4. To ascertain stewardship of public officials (Municipal Finance Officers Association 1968).

Auditing as Accountability

Factors that have focused attention on the audit process are: (a) recognition that the scarcity of resources makes it imperative to understand the financial status of the school district precisely; (b) preparation for decisionmaking; and (c) demand for reliable financial information by investors and by federal agencies that provide asistance to state and local governments.

The fact that periodic audits are required by law is only one of the reasons why local governments would want them. There are many others:

- An audit conducted with an understanding of and a sensitivity to government and the way it functions helps pinpoint the key information on which certain decisions should be based and contributes to the information being presented in a manner that facilitates decisionmaking.
- A well-designed and executed audit can uncover deficiencies in the accounting system, and provide suggestions for improving the efficiency and effectiveness of that system.
- An audit provides elected officials and management with the opportunity to establish close working relationships with individuals who specialize in governmental financial management and accounting and who are familiar with the latest developments in the field.
- Qualified auditors can assist local governments and securities underwriters in presenting information used in marketing securities.
- An auditor can assure federal granting agencies about compliance with administrative program requirements.

Auditing Process and Standards

The auditing process may be described as follows:

1. *Preaudit*—an examination of financial transactions prior to completion.
2. *Postaudit*—when transactions are completed, or at various stages.
3. *Internal*—those examinations performed by an auditor who is an employee of the governmental agency.
4. *External*—audits performed by an auditor who is independent of the agency.
5. *General*—audits which embrace all financial operations and records of a government unit.
6. *Special*—audits which are restricted to a specific segment such as school lunch, after-school care, or federal programs.

Nowhere are standards more important than in auditing. Auditing standards are measures of the quality of the work performed. The standards as developed and promulgated by the American Institute of Certified Public Accountants, through its committee on Auditing Procedures, are as follows (Municipal Finance Officers Association 1968):

General Standards

1. Examination performed by a person having adequate technical training and proficiency as an auditor.
2. Independence in mental attitude.
3. Due professional care.

Standards of Field Work

1. Work adequately planned.
2. Study and evaluation of internal control as a basis of reliance.
3. Competent evidential matter as a basis of opinion.

Standards of Reporting

1. Report shall state whether statements are presented according to GAAP.
2. Consistency between reporting periods.
3. Disclosures.
4. Opinion regarding statements.

Auditing procedures are not to be construed as the same as auditing standards. Auditing procedures are the actual operations to be performed by an auditor in any audit engagement. For example, in audit tests, when evidence exists that the system of internal control is effective, the auditor may properly conclude that the accounting records and supporting data have a higher degree of dependability and limit the testing accordingly. Conversely, when points of weakness are detected, the auditor extends the scope of testing to a degree that he professionally deemed necessary. Another factor to consider in the planning of tests is the materiality of an item to be tested, and any relative risk of the existence of irregularities.

The Internal Audit Function

The primary reason for the existence of an internal audit function within a school system should be the enhancement of the system of internal controls. State legislatures mandate that every school district shall be responsible for keeping adequate records and accounts of all financial transactions in the manner prescribed by the commissioner in the state manual. Thus, it behooves administrative officials to ascertain that accounting controls are organized so as to provide reasonable assurance that school property (assets) is safeguarded from unauthorized use or disposition and that financial records are reliable for the purpose of guiding effective decisionmaking.

Many school systems have chosen to rely upon state legislative auditors or an outside independent CPA for the total audit function. Although this may seem to be a simple solution, it may be shortsighted. Many areas of the school system need review in terms of efficiency, productivity, compliance with Board policy, optimum use of personnel, and proper utilization of resources allocated. Too often, auditing is viewed as having the sole purpose of detecting fraud and overlooks the positive aspects.

While it is not necessarily advisable to turn over all school district auditing responsibilities to those outside the district, by the same token it would not be advisable for all auditing to be performed internally. The primary function of the external audit is to examine the financial statements of the school system for the purpose of determining if such statements are fairly presented and in conformity with established standards. This opinion will add credibility to the district's financial statements in the minds of the public, other governmental agencies and creditors.

The Internal Operations Audit

In the late 1960s, the public sector began to seriously challenge and question the usefulness of financial statements which generally were not issued for several months after the close of the fiscal period. This led to a movement by many corporate boards to engage outside consultants to come in and perform an auditing function by auditing the present operations and analyzing future projected operations. The major complaint with previous financial statements was that they were mostly historical data and provided no information for making decisions relative to the future of the company. This development was the forerunner of the trend toward operational audits since the consultants could specialize and address such issues as management competency, resource utilization, and production efficiency. Although this concept originated in only very large corporations over time it has been perceived by some to make the operations audit a regular audit task. In fact, operational audits are the focus of many internal audit departments. Results can lead to improvement in methodology, increased productivity, reduction in staff, and recognition of problems otherwise not identified. This ultimately is less expensive and more effective than having external auditors or consultants coming in to evaluate the school system.

The internal auditor's function essentially begins where financial statement auditing ends. Instead of auditing numbers and expressing opinions on financial statements, the internal operations auditor independently and neutrally takes a hard look at the system's operating procedures. The auditor will check the accuracy of basic data and reporting deviations, examine operational efficiency, and ensure adherence to board policy and various procedures. The major purpose of the internal audit is to safeguard board assets.

Another function is to help overcome resistance to change. Generally, the audit can serve as an early warning system that change is needed by producing data and recommendations concerning potential crisis situations. The auditor should make a preliminary survey of the organizational structure and operating procedures of each division. Manuals, memos, and reports should be reviewed to determine if auditing is necessary. The areas selected for indepth study are those with greatest potential for improving, for increasing productivity, or economizing in the use of resources. As a staff person, the auditor should be perceived as an advisor, not an autocrat or someone in quest of an administrator's position. Neutrality and confidentiality are necessary for the auditor to function effectively for the system.

Audit Costs

It seems appropriate to consider the costs of auditing. There has been concern in the last few years over the increasing number and costs of audits. Some of the factors which have led to this concern can be summarized as follows:

1. Numerous audits may be performed in a governmental agency, reflecting different levels (i.e. local, cognizant agency, state, federal).
2. Duplication of effort for same or similar purpose.
3. Excessive interruption of staff in the business office and related program offices where applicable.
4. Strain on physical facilities when two or more audits are ongoing at the same time.
5. Excessive costs to governmental agency in duplicating the same data for different audit teams.
6. Inordinate amount of staff time required for exit conferences and required responses to audit exceptions and/or questioned costs.

Although the cost of audits was an allowable cost in numerous federally funded projects, other levels of audits, such as consortium, cognizant agency, internal audit of the agency, state and board appointed independent CPA's, have entailed considerable costs. Because billions of dollars have flowed each year from the federal, state, and local governments into a plethora of special grant programs, entitlements, and various assistance programs audits have been required for each one. The specificity of the audit requirement beyond the normal accounting operation caused considerable effort to collect data, generally creating redundancy and increased costs. To insure that grant funds were effectively used to meet the intent or need, the specific audit was required to test whether or not funds had been properly utilized. There has never been a question but that the audits were inordinately complex, and caused many problems.

Federal Audit Emphases

President Carter, in his first year in office, called upon the heads of departments and agencies to improve their audit systems, particularly as they relate to grant programs. He urged them to upgrade audit planning and to use their audit plans as a basis for making greater efforts to improve interagency cooperation on audits, to increase federal coordination with state and local auditors, and to increase reliance on audits made by others. To address this issue, which impacted on nearly all governmental agencies, especially public schools receiving many types of federal direct aid, Congress requested a study of grant audits. Results of this study were published in November (Arthur Anderson and Co. 1982), and the conclusions were alarming:

1. The present system was not an effective method for auditing grants.
2. Many grants were not even audited.
3. Audits reflected varying types of accountability.
4. Some grant recipients were audited but without coordination.
5. Excessive audit requirements were not properly interpreted.
6. Numerous different federal guides have been developed.
7. Auditing of grant programs was deficient in that there was no effective system for achieving audit coverage of all grant programs.
8. There was no effective coordination among federal agencies.
9. Inconsistent federal laws and regulations needed to be corrected.
10. There was inefficient use and apparent shortage of audit resources.

The study also offered several recommendations to provide remediation and strengthen the government's ability to monitor all the grant programs. The salient points are as follows:

1. A system should be developed for coordinated financial and compliance audits on a grant recipient basis rather than a grant-by-grant basis.
2. Audits should be acceptable to all funding agencies which will rely on them and only do what additional audit work is necessary.
3. The federal government should develop a standard audit guide and eliminate inconsistent audit requirements which hamper coordination.
4. Maximum reliance should be placed on nonfederal auditors to perform the audits. Federal auditors should have the right to do

additional work as needed and judge the quality of outstanding audits.
5. Audit oversight should be assigned to cognizant federal agencies.
6. Federal agencies should not pay for audits that do not follow federal audit guidelines.

Meanwhile, the U.S. Office of Management and Budget (OMB) had been wrestling with, among other things, the issues addressed not only in this study but the sharply critical audits which have been made on such federally funded grants as Head Start and CETA. In October 1979, after two years of study and consultation, the OMB revised the audit rules in Circular A-102, "Uniform Requirements for Grants to State and Local Governments." The revised rules built on the Carter study report and made it clear that recipients of federal aid are responsible for a basic audit of all programs they carry out. The new rules state that audits of federally assisted programs should build upon audit work already done by state and local government auditors and public accountants at the recipient level. This approach has been called the "single audit concept," because it represents a departure from grant-by-grant audits and moves toward audits of recipient organizations as a whole.

The revised audit requirements call for (a) independent single audits of state and local governments at least every two years; (b) a standardized fiscal and compliance audit guide to replace the almost 100 individual program guides presently in use; (c) designation of a single cognizant federal agency to provide coordinated oversight for all federal programs affecting a particular state or local government recipient; and (d) a standardized federal "compliance supplement" summarizing the major program compliance audit requirements related to federally assisted programs.

Single Audit Concept

The evolvement of the single audit concept is one of the most significant developments to come out of Washington. Following and closely related was the massive consolidation of numerous categorical grants into a new grouping and renamed block grants. The Omnibus Reconciliation Act of 1981 established the first group of nine major block grants in programs monitored by the U.S. Department of Education, Health and Human Services, and Housing and Urban Development. These grant programs do require a financial and compliance audit. OMB has advised that the single audit will fulfill the necessary requirements.

Now that the monstrosity of the multi-audits has been resolved, what does the single audit accomplish and what can be construed as advantageous? The Arthur Anderson report (1982) suggested the following advantages:

- Allows more purposeful use of funds.
- Ensures a coordinated approach.
- Facilitates a coordinated response to audit findings.
- Eliminates redundant audits.
- Can be cost effective.

In addition, the single audit approach to auditing federal programs represents an opportunity to demonstrate savings to school districts. Because the financial aid compliance audit is carried out in such a manner, it avoids duplication among audit organizations and eliminates duplicate procedures. Savings result because of the expansion of the reporting requirements which permit all audit demands to be met with a single audit. Efficiency in audit coverage is provided since compliance features are incorporated with the normal audit program and a report on the compliance audit is added to the report on the financial statements and report on internal control. In addition to the labor savings, a portion of the audit fee can be recovered through the indirect cost rate.

Internal Control

The term "internal control" has broad implications in the world of financial transactions. Internal control comprises the plan of organization and all of the coordinate methods and measures adopted within a business to safeguard its assets, check the accountability and reliability of its accounting data, promote operations efficiency, and encourage adherence to prescribed managerial changes. The concept developed to provide assurance that the work of employees was subdivided to provide some measure of security. The MFOA (1968) defines internal control as a plan or organization under which employees' duties are so arranged and records and procedures so designed as to make it possible to exercise effective accounting control over assets, liabilities, revenue, and expenditures. Under such a system, work of employees is subdivided so that no single employee performs a complete cycle of operations. For example, an employee who handles cash cannot post the accounts receivable records. Procedures must be clearly laid out and require proper authorization by designated officials for all actions to be taken. This division of responsibility is justified by the increased operational efficiency which results from the specialization of labor, and the decreasing probability of any type of fraud. It assuredly increases accuracy as every form and document must be checked or verified by another person.

Moore and Stettler (1963) contend that establishing effective internal control is a major factor in the successful operation of any business, and that public schools must be operated in the most businesslike manner. They note that management has always had concern for the accuracy of accounting records and the prevention and detection of fraud. Years ago, the thrust of such protection was in hiring an auditor who would verify the accuracy of records, and account for cash. As the country prospered and businesses grew, the paper flow increased, the amount of records which must be audited increased, and the auditors' fee grew larger. With the increasing number of workers, it was possible to practice the division of workers and develop specialization of clerical labor. This evolved into automatic checking for accuracy and fraud, and has become an important part of the basic accounting function (Moore and Stettler 1963). As such, the need for outside auditors is decreasing and decreasing costs.

The auditors must maintain independence, but they can reduce the total time involved in checking records if the company or school system keeps good records. Controls need to be similar, or even standard, so that auditors moving from one firm or school to another would have no real difficulty in determining what the true issue is.

A simple but latent control is the requirement for proofing and dollar controls. Some examples of this would be: (a) balancing subsidiary accounts to control accounts; (b) columnar addition and cross footing; (c) prenumbered forms; and (d) reports to higher levels. The frequency for these procedures will depend upon the type of transaction, and the asset involved. When sets of figures must be reconciled, any variance will surface, and require explanation and resolution.

Safeguarding of assets refers only to protection against loss arising from errors or irregularities in processing transactions and in handling related assets. Internal control should be a primary objective in establishing the organizational framework which includes all the people associated in carrying out the purposes, goals and objectives of the school system, whether a part of the financial and accounting function or not. If the organizational plan has not been developed with this objective in mind, no amount of auditing could, nor should be, expected to cure such a deficiency. Even so, there can be failures in actual operations because of a variety of possible factors.

Public school systems are very dynamic in that changes are constantly occurring both within and without the organization. The educational program and related means of financing are frequently changed by legislative and administrative actions at higher levels, either state or federal government. Personnel turnover has accelerated during the last decade. Those employees who understand *why* and *how* are often replaced for political expediency. Replacements may or may not have the level of ability or training to provide the stability and controls. Human frailty and lack of dedication can cause short cuts to occur and while they may not initially cause failure or deficiencies, they may permit failure to occur without expected warning signs (Kuhn 1981).

CASH MANAGEMENT

In the last decade, effective cash management has taken a new place in the priorities of the school business official. Cash management involves the dual functions of cash forecasting and cash investment strategies. As pointed out by Drebin (1979), the most efficient management practices for these two functions are often hindered by local and statutory constraints under which state and local governments must operate. The treasurer or finance director generally has the primary duty to estimate cash inflows and outflows as accurately as possible.

Among the cash management strategies is maximizing the relationship with local banks. Until the last few years, before legislation was enacted to provide more flexibility in the prudent investment of funds, the local banks had little incentive to be very competitive. School funds were most often placed in certificates of deposit (CDs).

Now, many smaller school districts can utilize the State Board of Education Investment Pool where the pooling concept allows a high yield regardless of the amount available.

Also, until very recently, temporarily available funds from federally funded projects could not be invested to local advantage. Any interest earnings had to be returned to the state education agency for remitting to the U.S. Treasury. Federal regulations now permit these funds to be invested and earnings retained by the local education agency.

As resources become more limited, the proper managing of cash requires detail preparation of the anticipated revenues and planned expenditures to project cash needs on a weekly and monthly basis. Based on the previous twelve months' expenditures and revenues, a reliable cash flow chart can be developed and summarized by day, week or month. Projections can be made for day-to-day, or month-to-month expenditures. The essential expenditures to be considered in developing the cash forecast include: (a) salaries (payroll net); (b) payroll deductions; (c) fringe benefits (board share of FICA and retirement); (d) special centers, such as exceptional child, or vocational/technical, (e) utility payments, all types; (f) debt service; (g) purchased services, (h) insurance premiums, all coverages; and (i) other—equipment and vehicles.

The above is merely a suggested list which encompasses the most important categories. Total expenditure items may be charted to reflect different objects.

A revenue summary can be developed to reflect major categories of revenue such as: (a) federal direct aid anticipated; (b) federal grants through state; (c) state foundation program; (d) state categorical or transitional program; (e) local property taxes; and, (f) local miscellaneous receipts. The projected revenue and expenditure will be based upon the current budget. With the prior year's actual data as a guide, a school district can more effectively manage resources, regardless of fund source.

A major problem for school districts which have 30-50 percent of the operating budget coming from local property taxes, is the timing of annual collections. In Florida, for instance, real property taxes are due November 1 and become delinquent April 1. When interest rates began to spiral upward, the small discount incentive (4 percent—November, 3 percent—December) for prompt payment lost much of its appeal. Consequently, heavy tax revenue came in late December through February, well beyond the mid-point of the fiscal year. The academic year generally begins anywhere from mid-August to Labor Day week which means full staffing and full payrolls. Although state funds are released monthly, because tax revenues are not yet available, many school districts experience a negative cash flow in the third to fifth months of the July 1–June 30 fiscal year. This condition leads to the short term borrowing provided by state statutes for the specific purpose of meeting immediate and necessary expenses and maintaining the public instruction of the particular district during that current year. This function requires considerable legal preparation and computation of amounts needed.

The current trend in short term borrowing is to seek the most favorable interest rate on a competitive basis to provide the loan in its entirety fairly early in the year, or at least prior to the first period of anticipated deficit. However, a controversial technique has been utilized to manage this money to great economic advantage to school districts.

Since the loan amount is intended to meet maturing obligations of both accounts payable and employee payrolls for several periods, it is prudent to invest the funds on a basis of maturity schedules as deemed adequate for each estimated expenditure outlay. Naturally, the finance officer will seek to maximize the return by investing funds in the highest yielding and safest security available. The objective is to earn more interest than will be paid on the total loan, thereby effectively managing the resources newly available. The cause for concern in use of this technique arose because the tax-exempt interest rate negotiated was always lower than taxable interest rates, and when funds were invested, a material gain resulted. The Internal Revenue Code of 1954, as amended, addressed this issue. Section 1.103-13, published in June 1979 and known as the Final Arbitrage Regulation, provided guidelines for those in quest of this technique. In April 1983, new legislation was enacted which greatly impacted this procedure by clarifying the rules.

STUDENT ACTIVITY FUND MANAGEMENT

During the last decade, school board members have become increasingly aware of the fiscal significance in the student activity funds which are generally handled at the school site level. Of growing concern to not only board members, but parents and citizens as well, is the proper accountability of these monies. In some senior high schools in large urban centers, thousands of dollars flow through these internal funds with only minimal internal controls. And, although these funds belong to the students who either pay required fees or generate the funds through various fund raising activities, except for such trust fund accounts as the United Way or the Red Cross which are subsequently remitted to those agencies, all funds become board responsibility and should be accurately accounted for by board approved procedures. Thus, it is imperative that funds should be used for the purpose identified and in a timely manner so that students generating funds will also benefit from their use.

This goal may not be realized for a variety of reasons. In some schools the year end balance can reach $40,000 to $50,000. A major problem encountered is the lack of financial expertise or understanding on the part of the principal, assistant principal or treasurer normally responsible for the record keeping, of the available investments which might earn a much greater interest income for their particular school. The most common errors in internal audits of activity accounts are the excessive cash balance, and the poor investments, such as savings accounts paying 5.85 percent. During 1981-82 when interest rates soared to 18 percent many schools had $5,000 or $10,000 safely tucked away in a certificate of deposit at 6 percent. When challenged about this type of audit deficiency, most principals quickly defended their position by indicating that they needed money available for current bills.

A look at one school district practice, however, shows brighter promise. In Dade County, Florida Public Schools, the concept of a pool investment program was on the drawing board for several years, but planners moved with caution. Principals generally opposed the idea, and felt threatened with a further loss of authority and responsibility. There was also great concern that once the student activity funds were placed in the general fund investment pool, it would be possible, in the event a revenue short fall occurred in state funding, to lose a portion of, if not all, the transferred funds. Another major concern was the accessibility of funds and fairness of interest distribution. These issues were addressed by the superintendent in meetings with the principals, by the ad hoc committee finalizing the proposal, a revised procedures manual on Internal Funds and finally the acquisition of a money-max system to handle the detailed investment accounting and distribution.

The pooling concept was implemented in July 1983 with eight Dade County junior and senior high schools participating on a voluntary basis, and investing a total of $161,000. At the end of six months, the pool was comprised of forty-nine schools with an average daily portfolio balance of $1,366,290. The earned interest yield for December was 9.8 percent.

This program places the responsibility for best cash management of available funds with a central office administrator whose primary task is the investment program. The following summarizes the procedures in place:

1. Initial investment of $5,000 for senior high and adult, $3,000 for junior high, and $1,000 for elementary.
2. Interest will be wired quarterly to the schools' checking account.
3. No service fees are charged.
4. Additional investment may be made in multiples of $1,000.
5. Withdrawals may be made in multiples of $1,000 on Thursday or Friday.
6. Status reports are prepared on monthly basis.
7. Written instructions to the schools' bank regarding persons authorized to make transfers.

A pooling investment program similar to that of Dade County has been operated by the Greenville, South Carolina School District for several years (McLawhorn 1983). As audit reports continue to be critical of poor fiscal management at the school site, more principals will likely turn to this type of service to aid them in overcoming audit deficiencies as well as relieve them of a specific task for which they may feel unsuited.

CURRENT ACCOUNTING AND REPORTING ISSUES

Among current issues impacting on public school accounting and reporting are the following: (a) accountability for consortiums; (b) change in coupon bonds; (c) recognition certificates, (d) productivity accounting, and (e) accounting and financial reporting for joint ventures of governmental units. The impact of each of these trends is described in the following sections.

Consortiums

The condition of limited resources has been favorable to the development of consortiums where several smaller school districts join forces to engage in such activities as self-insurance. Each school system experiences considerable savings compared to their risk management costs if insurance is purchased under the conventional method. Such consortiums must institute and agree on some accounting activities. Arrangements might include designating a host district that is responsible for preparing all necessary financial reports and processing all transactions or some division of accounting and reporting responsibilities. By whatever arrangement, some accountability for consortiums must be required.

Change in Coupon Bonds

Effective July 1, 1983, the municipal securities market moved to the mandatory registered-form security for compliance with federally dictated change (Hough 1983). The impact is that every long-term, tax exempt security issued from that date will be a matter of current record. Federal law provides the force to enforce this regulation. Governmental officials will need to become familiar with the responsibilities of issuer officials and others trading registered securities. A guide has been prepared and released by MFOA.

Recognition Certificates

The Certificate of Excellence in Financial Reporting in School Systems sponsored by ASBO, and the Certificate of Conformance sponsored by MFOA are designed to accomplish the following:

1. Encourage school systems to adopt and use generally accepted accounting principles;

2. Encourage school systems to adopt sound budgetary and financial reporting procedures; and
3. Contribute to the enhancement of credibility of financial management of school systems by recognizing excellence in school financial reporting.

The receipt of an award reflects that the school system has met the highest standards of excellence in reporting and has complied with the Government Accounting and Auditing Principles. The recognition programs offer an antidote to the maligned image of school business management instilled by several well-publicized fiscal crises during the last decade.

Productivity Accounting

Nationwide, worker productivity has been declining for several years, with a resulting increase in labor costs. This has a negative impact on resources, and more than ever, managers are concerned about improving the productivity and effectiveness of their agency. One proposed approach to the problem is what is termed "productivity accounting." According to Oatman (1979) the principles and techniques of productivity accounting should improve an organization's performance. Productivity accounting is similar to cost accounting—it is a method of allocating the costs of providing program services to cost centers to provide a basis for internal financial analysis. Productivity accounting information can also be used to establish product standards.

Financial Reporting for Joint Ventures

Joint ventures of governmental units present unique problems. There are many types of joint ventures with varied types of relationships to support them. The primary issue related to accounting and financial reporting is in the consistency between governmental agencies. Some joint ventures produce reports using principles set forth in NCGA S-1. Some produce reports to meet the provisions of contracts and agreements, and still others do not prepare public financial reports.

What does the future look like in the accounting discipline as it may impact public school systems? According to Gary Harmer, Vice-Chairman of NCGA, the salient developments during the past year include:

1. Rejection of recommendations of local and state government organizations regarding GASB by the Financial Accounting Foundation (FAF).
2. The prospect of a Governmental Accounting Standards Board being created under the oversight of the FAF appeared very dim.
3. Possible reconstitution of the NCGA into a GASB with a foundation for oversight modeled after the final report of the GASB Organization Committee (Harmer 1983).

Site Based Management

Trends and issues presented in the preceding sections have addressed general accounting and reporting concepts and principles which are external to school organizations. Also of concern is the influence these financial trends have on internal reporting needs of the school district. A current trend in internal reporting which must be addressed by the financial administrator is that of site based management. This concept of placing the planning and operational decisions at the school level rather than the district level requires an accounting structure and cost allocation system to support the site based management team's need for planning, controlling and measuring. Such a system must contain clearly defined accounting and reporting parameters for control that insure student's needs are being met within fund allocation. Establishment of control procedures for site based decisionmaking redefines the traditional role of the central administrator by decentralizing fiscal management.

The financial administrator, under this concept, becomes a facilitator to be utilized by principals, teachers, parents, and students to further enhance educational concepts unique to a particular schools' service area. The financial administrator must be involved with ongoing dialogue between the board, central office, school, and community to foster this relationship. Pushing authority to the grassroots level involves more people in the educational process which in turn places increased demands on the internal financial reporting system to provide timely and meaningful information to more diverse groups of decisionmakers. Financial reports and analysis must be presented in a format and language commonly understood by people who traditionally have had little or no involvement with the financial management system.

SUMMARY

In summary, the scarcity of financial resources present a substantial challenge to the school financial administrator. As demonstrated in this chapter, this challenge will manifest itself in a number of ways— accurate financial information, presentation in a format that is understandable, and efficiencies in accounting and reporting.

Accounting and reporting functions cannot be divorced from the budgeting function. They are all integral elements in the financial arena. Accounting and reporting functions are flexible and must be structured to accommodate budgeting. Methods of approaching educational budgeting as discussed in the next chapter must be supported by the districts' internal and external reporting system. The challenge for the financial administration is to align the accounting and reporting process with legal requirements and generally accepted accounting principles (GAAP) while structuring the financial system to accommodate local, state, and federal financial reporting requirements.

REFERENCES

Anderson, Arthur and Company. 1982. *Auditing of Grants—The Single Audit Concept.* Washington, D.C. (April).

Candoli, Carl, Walter Hack, John Ray, and Dewey Stollar. 1976. *School Business Administration: A Planning Approach.* Boston: Allyn and Bacon, Inc.

Drebin, Allan R. 1979. "Governmental Versus Commercial Accounting: The Issues." *Governmental Finance* 8 (November): 3–8.

Harmer, W. Gary. 1983. "NCGA Meeting Summary." *School Business Affairs* 49, no. 10 (October): 56.

Hough, Wesley C. 1983. *Municipal Bond Registration Requirements.* Washington, D.C.: Governmental Finance Research Center.

Kuhn, Robert A. 1981. "The Internal Audit." *School Business Affairs* 47, no. 2 (February): 13, 31.

McLawhorn, Charles W. 1983. "Pool Investment Programs." Paper presented at the 69th Annual Conference of the Association of School Business Officials of the United States and Canada. Chicago (October).

Moore, Francis E. and Howard F. Stettler. 1963. *Accounting Systems for Management Control.* Homewood, Ill.: R. D. Irwin Publishing Company.

Municipal Finance Officers Association (MFOA). 1968. *Governmental Accounting, Auditing and Finance Reporting Principles.* Chicago: MFOA.

Municipal Finance Officers Association (MFOA). 1979. *Governmental Accounting, Auditing and Finance Reporting Principles.* Chicago: MFOA.

Oatman, Donald W. 1979. "It's Time for Productivity Accounting in Government." *Governmental Finance* 8 (3): 9-14.

Office of Management and Budget. 1979. *OMB Circular A-102.* Washington, D.C.: U.S. Government Printing Office.

3 BUDGETING

Charles H. Sederberg

INTRODUCTION

Scarcity of resources, increased state share of school revenue, accountability for educational outcomes, and development of Program Planning Budgeting Systems (PPBS) and Zero-Based Budgeting (ZBB) have focused increased attention on budgeting for elementary/secondary education. The thrust of these forces has been to expand the role of budgeting from a business operation akin to financial accounting and reporting to a broader planning, management, and policy-making tool. The changes are taking place along an uneven and uncharted course with reversions to previous conditions.

Unlike accounting or industrial relations, budgeting has not become a discipline. Its knowledge base is scattered through the literature of management, public administration, accounting, political science, and other fields. Financial statements from a random sample of districts would be similar in format and permit interdistrict comparisons; the same comparability would be less likely among adopted budgets from the same districts. Courses focused on budgeting for elementary/secondary education are rarely part of school administrator training programs. Workshops and professional articles tend to emphasize particular approaches such as PPBS or more recently ZBB.

This chapter examines definitions, presents opposing orientations, and discusses three current issues in an effort to place budgeting for elementary/secondary education in a broader perspective. The definitions distinguish between budgets as compiled sets of allocative decisions and the process by which the decisions are made. Overviews of opposing orientations, rationality, and political process indicate sources and the nature of tensions in deciding who gets what. Three contemporary issues selected for discussion are (1) conceptualizing a district budgeting approach, (1) centralization versus decentralization, and (3) political involvement. Discussion is focused on the state-local portion of the framework because of the primacy of the state-local educational policy continuum and the lesser financial role played by the federal government.

DEFINITIONS

For a working definition, it is useful to distinguish between budgets and the allocative decisionmaking or budgeting process. *A public sector budget is a set of data that records proposed or adopted allocative decisions in terms of goals to be accomplished (program plan), resources available (revenue plan), and anticipated services and materials to be acquired (expenditure plan) during a specified period of time (fiscal period).* School districts actually adopt several budgets. Under governmental fund accounting each fund is an independent accounting entity and should have a separate budget. Annual budgets for funds, such as general, food service, or transportation, that do not make capital outlay expenditures are called *operating budgets.* Elementary/secondary districts also adopt *capital budgets* containing revenue and expenditure plans for acquisition or improvement of equipment, buildings, or land in a multiyear time frame. While it may or may not be formally adopted, the *cash flow budget* is a management tool for analyzing the timing of anticipated receipts and disbursements. Cash budgets (1) project the adequacy of future cash balances to pay anticipated obligations, (2) identify opportunities for short-term investment of idle cash, and (3) indicate needs for short-term borrowing.

In contrast to the systematic structure of budget documents, *public sector budgeting is the process by which actors (elected officials, appointed officials, technical staff, and lobbyists) representing constituencies (geographic populations, coalitions, interest groups, and governmental agencies) identify, define, and prioritize social needs and preferences (education, welfare, public safety, transportation, etc.) and decide how much resources will be appropriated from the total economy, how those resources will be collected (income, sales, property, and other taxes) and how those resources will be allocated to programs addressing the identified social needs and preferences.* The meaning of this definition is enhanced by the concepts of *separation of powers* and the *budget cycle.* Separation of powers refers to the constitutional distribution of authority among executive, legislative, and judicial branches. Its historical roots are associated with the emergence of the English parliament and the wresting of unilateral taxing power from the king (Lee and Johnson 1977: 5). Application of separation of powers to public budgeting in the United States is characterized by the following principles: (1) the *executive branch prepares* the budget; (2) the *legislative branch approves* it; and (3) the *executive branch implements* the approved budget. The principle of separation of powers is readily apparent at federal and state levels, but a subtle difference occurs in elementary/secondary districts. While administrators prepare budgets for board approval, separation of powers does not exist because administrators are executive employees of the board. Separation of powers may become a significant and dramatic factor in federal and state government if executive and legislative branches are controlled by opposing parties and appropriations for elementary/secondary education become political issues.

Constitutional, statutory, and procedural requirements and guidelines define the mechanics of the budgeting process. Responding to these requirements and guidelines for successive fiscal periods results in the *preparation, adoption, implementation,* and *audit phases* of the *budget cycle.* Budget cycle phases can be distinguished by both timing and primary activities involved. The *preparation phase* consists primarily of scanning, planning, and analyzing activities. Scanning provides an overview of the organizational environment: demographic trends, recurring obligations, financial condition, economic activity, etc. It results in a view of realistic possibilities and limitations. Planning activities include goal setting, developing alternative strategies, revenue forecasting, and expenditure estimation. Analyzing activities compare estimated revenue and expenditure associated with program alternatives to project future financial conditions. In the event of a projected excess of expenditure over revenue, officials are confronted with program change, revenue increase, or expenditure reduction decisions. The preparation phase ends when the elected chief executive presents a budget message to the legislative branch or the superintendent brings preliminary budgets to the board.

The *adoption phase* is dominated by influencing and deciding activities. Influencing consists of attempts to affect budgeting decisions without exercise of formal authority. While frequently not identified as part of the budgeting process, influencing occurs in all phases but may become intense during budget adoption. An example would be a teacher bargaining unit voting a strike authorization to influence board and administration into adopting a higher salary schedule. An example at the state level would be a threatened lawsuit by education organizations and the Civil Liberties Union to persuade legislators to vote against tuition expense deductions for parents with children in nonpublic elementary and secondary schools. Deciding activity is essentially making choices among competing preferences. School districts struggle with decision issues like salaries versus course offerings and class size, closing a school building, and access to educational opportunity versus fees for services. At the state level, elementary/secondary education competes with other public services. Phrases like "hard-ball politics" and "pressure-cooker climate" have been used to describe situations in which the governor's office, legislative factions, and interest group lobbyists press for competing allocative decisions as conference committee or floor votes are cast in the shadow of adjournment. At state and federal levels, budget adoption is complete when tax and appropriation bills have passed in the legislative branch and signed into law by the executive branch. At the school district level, the adoption phase is complete when reasonably valid estimates of revenue and expenditure are accepted by board resolution. At times, districts face budget adoption deadlines without reliable estimates of revenue from a major source or with master work agreements still under negotiation. If deadlines are statutory and cannot be delayed, districts may comply by adopting partial or tentative budgets to be amended when reliable data are available. Adoption of partial or tentative budgets may be necessary to facilitate purchasing operations, but should not contain estimates of future salary expenditure that limit the board's position at the bargaining table.

Budget *implementation* is a function of the executive branch in federal and state government and of administrative employees in school districts. Implementation phase tasks are carried out by the

Office of Management and Budget (OMB) in the federal government, by departments of finance in state governments, and by superintendents and business officials in school districts. Implementation activities include establishing systems of allotments and encumbrances to control expenditure for designated program services, monitoring revenue receipts, cash-flow management, and updating projected fund balance forecasts. Projected fund balances are important management information because state constitutions and statutes typically prohibit deficit spending. During fiscal crises legislatures may be called into special session to reduce expenditure, increase revenue, authorize shifting revenue and expenditure from or to other fiscal years, or all of the above. Under conditions of fiscal uncertainty school districts should review adopted budgets at intervals during the year. District capacity to amend budgets is limited once personnel and other contractual obligations have been incurred. Some deviation of actual revenue and expenditure from budget estimates is expected, but big "surprises" at year's end are an indictment of budget management during the implementation phase. The implementation phase for operating budgets ends with the close of the fiscal year.

Auditing, the final phase in the budget cycle, consists primarily of using summarized accounting data for evaluation and reporting. Summarized accounting data presented in statements of revenue and expenditure and the fund equity section of balance sheets are compared with budgeted amounts. Differences indicate the degree of success in keeping the state or school district on the fiscal course charted a year or more earlier. Other dimensions of the audit phase are compliance with (1) statutory authority in use of resources, (2) generally accepted accounting principles, and (3) governmental fund accounting. Reporting is a matter of communicating summarized financial and evaluation data to the board and the public.

Timing of the budgeting process results in cycle overlap. At a particular point in time, federal, state, and local governments may be implementing the current year's budgets, preparing or adopting budgets for subsequent years, and auditing activities of the previous fiscal period.

BUDGETING ORIENTATIONS

Attempts to explain or predict the budgeting process give meaning and relevance to problems and issues that arise in practice. Two opposing budgeting orientations, rationality and political process, provide a useful perspective.

The rational budgeting orientation assumes that people will collectively identify needs, formulate alternative strategies to meet the needs, and allocate sufficient resources toward implementation of the strategy that promises a satisfactory level of benefit for a minimum investment. Zero-Based Budgeting (ZBB) and Planning Programming Budgeting Systems (PPBS) are two well-known rational budgeting approaches. Because of the widespread attention it received in education, PPBS will be used to illustrate the rational orientation.

In 1967, President Lyndon Johnson directed the U.S. Office of Education to follow the example of the Department of Defense in implementing PPBS. It was later considered for adoption in several states and many local districts. The appeal of PPBS was its attempt to link resource inputs with educational outcomes at a time of growing pressure for educational accountability. The nature of rational budgeting theory as reflected in PPBS is indicated in Figure 3-1 from Knezevich (1973: 4). Federal, state, or local educational governments employing this approach would (1) specify goals and objectives, (2) generate alternative educational strategies to accomplish the goals and objectives, (3) translate educational strategies into alternative operational plans, (4) analyze alternative operational plans and rank them in terms of cost effectiveness, (5) decide on an optimum course of action, (6) evaluate program outcomes, and (7) recycle the process-making adjustments on the basis of evaluation feedback.

The political process budgeting orientation assumes that allocative decisions are functions of influence and power as well as need. The nature of political process orientation is illustrated by Wildavsky's (1975: Chapter 1) comparative budget theory summarized in Figure 3-2. Wildavsky postulates two constants: scarcity (never enough resources to meet everyone's expectations) and complexity (individuals in multiple social organizations have many, competing needs). These constants constrain allocative decisionmaking; scarcity results in formation of advocate and guardian roles. Advocate roles are taken by representatives of interest groups seeking the same level or, preferably, more resources for the goals or services their organizations provide. In the guardian role, legislators and school boards cannot allocate more resources than can be made available; pieces of the

BUDGETING 65

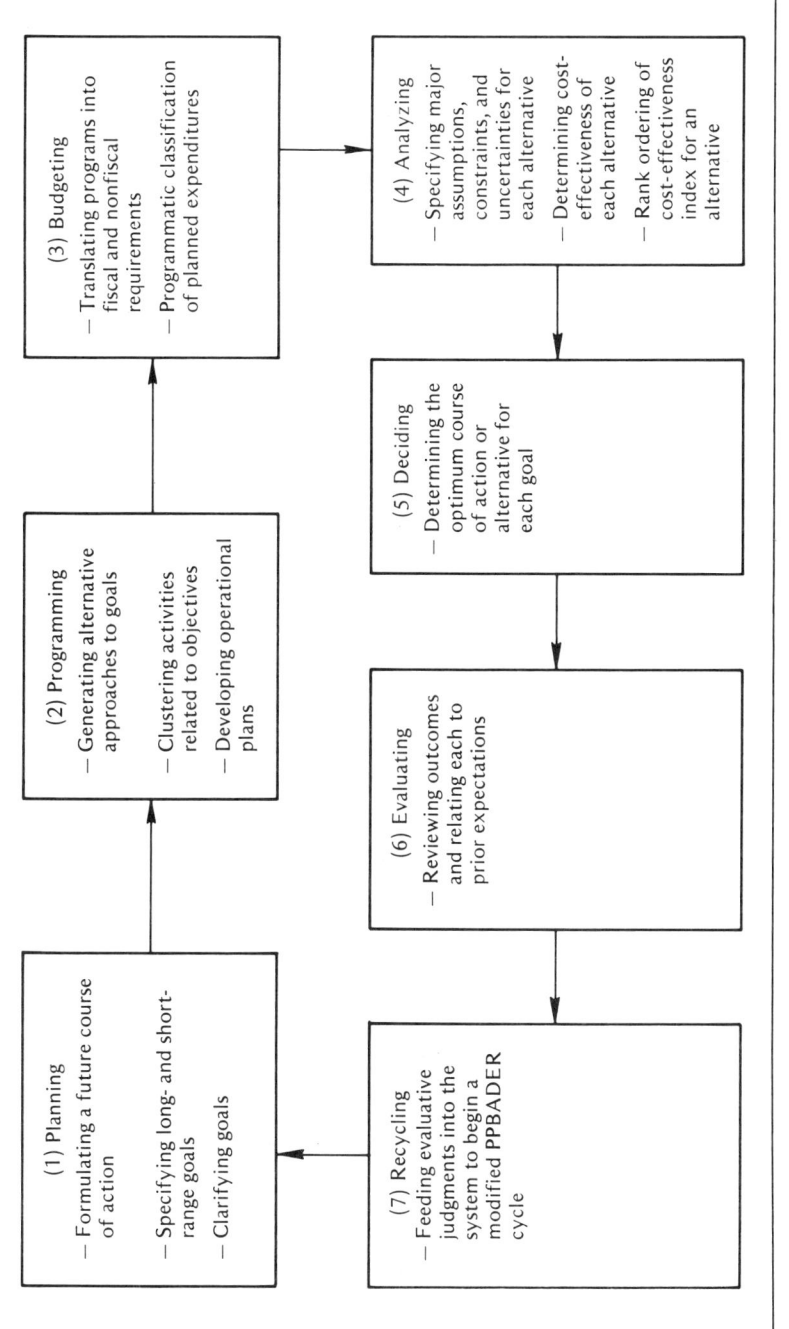

Figure 3-1. The PPBADERS (PPBS) Cycle of Activities.

```
(1) Planning                 (2) Programming              (3) Budgeting               (4) Analyzing
— Formulating a future      — Generating alternative     — Translating programs      — Specifying major
  course of action             approaches to goals          into fiscal and             assumptions,
— Specifying long- and      — Clustering activities         nonfiscal requirements      constraints, and
  short-range goals            related to objectives     — Programmatic                 uncertainties for
— Clarifying goals          — Developing operational       classification of            each alternative
                               plans                        planned expenditures     — Determining cost-
                                                                                        effectiveness of
                                                                                        each alternative
                                                                                     — Rank ordering of
                                                                                        cost-effectiveness
                                                                                        index for an
                                                                                        alternative

(7) Recycling               (6) Evaluating                                           (5) Deciding
— Feeding evaluative        — Reviewing outcomes                                     — Determining the
  judgments into the           and relating each to                                     optimum course
  system to begin a            prior expectations                                       of action or
  modified PPBADER                                                                      alternative for
  cycle                                                                                 each goal
```

Source: Knezevich, Stephen J., 1973 *Program Budgeting*. Berkeley, California: McCutchan Publishing Corporation, p. 4.

Figure 3-2. Wildavsky's Political Process Orientation.

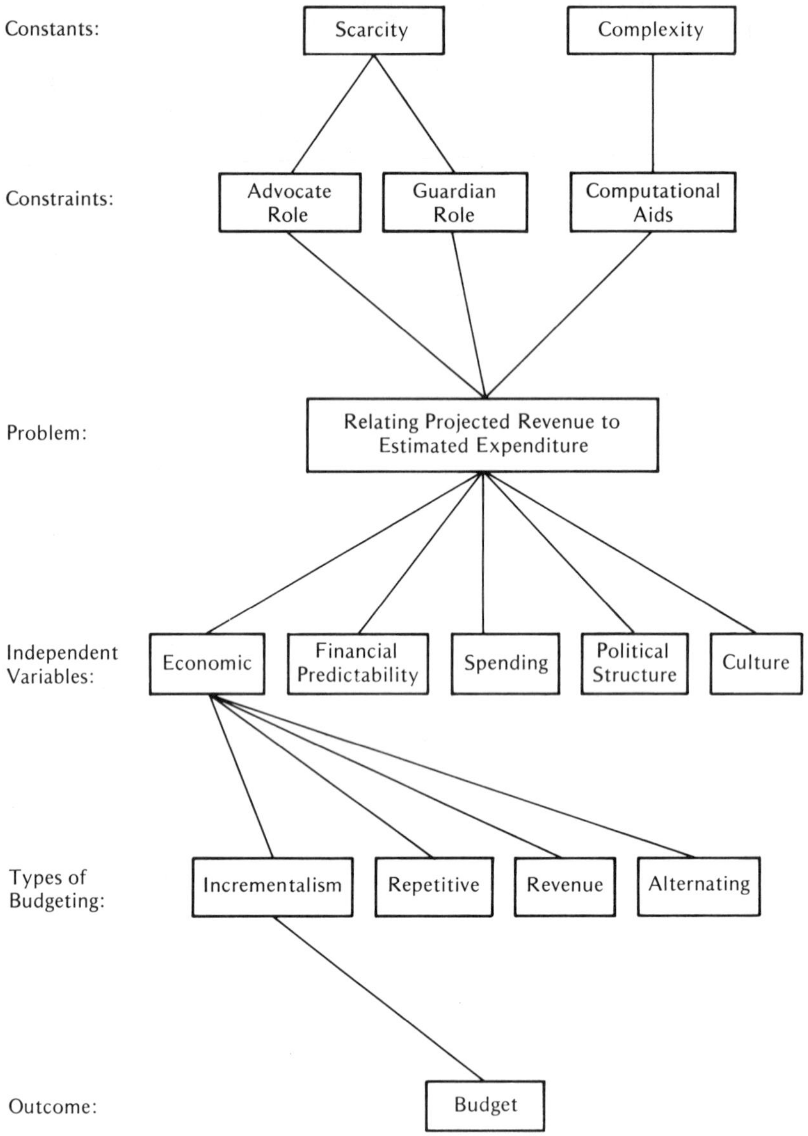

Constants:	Scarcity	Complexity
Constraints:	Advocate Role — Guardian Role	Computational Aids
Problem:	Relating Projected Revenue to Estimated Expenditure	
Independent Variables:	Economic — Financial Predictability — Spending — Political Structure — Culture	
Types of Budgeting:	Incrementalism — Repetitive — Revenue — Alternating	
Outcome:	Budget	

Source: Author's adaptation.

budget are cut from a finite fiscal pie. Of these roles Wildavsky (1975: 8) writes:

> Guardians and advocates play in a mixed motive game. Though they conflict, they must also cooperate. Both require trust. Each role implies its opposite; guardianship expects advocacy to provide a choice among items to cut, and advocacy needs guardianship to supply at least tacit limits within which to maneuver. Resources, after all, cannot be allocated without either proposals for spending or boundaries within which to fit them. The classic strategies participants use to improve their position—asking for more than they expect to get and making percentage cuts across the board—depend on keeping within accepted limits so that budgets have meaning.

Complexity leads to heuristic aids for calculation that simplify budgetary decisionmaking. For example, budgeting for something as vague as "a uniform system of public schools" or "equal access to educational opportunity" can only be accomplished by means of proxy formulas expressed in terms of percent reimbursements, dollar allowances per pupil, adjusted assessed valuation mill rates, etc. that are tangible and understood by policymakers.

Within these constraints the budgeting problem remains one of maintaining a balance between anticipated revenue and expenditure. As indicated in Figure 3-2, Wildavsky identified wealth, revenue predictability, spending size, political structure, and culture as interactive independent variables that ultimately determine budgeting outcomes. Interactive effects can be briefly illustrated using wealth and revenue predictability. Governments with access to high wealth and with high revenue predictability would be expected to engage in incremental budgeting. Low wealth and high revenue predictability are associated with revenue budgeting; public services become a function of tax collections regardless of need. Low wealth combined with low predictability tend to produce alternations between incremental and repetitive budgeting.

Budgeting for elementary/secondary education in the United States has been shaped by circumstances of high wealth (with variation among states and among districts within states), high revenue predictability, participatory/representative government, and a democratic culture. Under these circumstances budgeting has been largely incremental. In describing incrementalism Wildavsky (1975: 5-6) writes:

> Budgets are almost never actively reviewed as a whole, in the sense of considering at one time the value of all existing programs compared to all possible

alternatives. Instead, this year's budget is based on last year's budget, with special attention given to a narrow range of increases or decreases. The greatest part of any budget is a product of previous decisions. Long-range commitments have been made. There are mandatory programs whose expenses must be met.... Incremental calculations, then, proceed from an existing base. By "base" I refer to commonly held expectations among participants in budgeting that programs will be carried out at close to the going level of expenditures. The base of a budget, therefore, refers to accepted parts of programs that will not normally be subjected to intensive scrutiny. By encapsulating the past in the present through the base, budgeters limit future disputes. Since many organizational units compete for funds, there is a tendency for the central authority to include all of them in benefits or deprivations to be distributed. Budgeters often refer to expectations regarding their *fair share* of increases and decreases. The widespread sharing of deeply held expectations concerning the organization's base and its fair share of funds provides a powerful (although informal) means of coordination and stability in budgetary systems.

In summary, differences between the two orientations provide a useful perspective in which to examine issues. There is a natural tension between rationality and political process in the governance/management of elementary/secondary education. Organizational expectations of management tend to support rational approaches: stated objectives, alternative strategies, decisionmaking, control, and accountability. On the other hand, making allocative decisions by counting votes of school board members or legislators is the essence of political process.

DISTRICT BUDGETING APPROACHES

The subject of the following section may be framed by the question, *"What budgeting approach can districts use to facilitate recognition of local preferences, operation within state and federal requirements, and meeting their own management needs?"* There are many diverse local preferences in public education. A band mothers' organization wants instrumental music in the elementary grades. Parents aspiring to college educations for their children want electives in mathematics, physical science, foreign language, and computer science. The teacher bargaining unit wants higher salaries, more planning time, and increased medical coverage. A "Blue Line Club" of parents and community boosters wants a hockey program capable of putting a team into the state tournament. Many local preferences vie for inclusion in district budgets.

State constitutions mandate legislative establishment and support of public schools. School finance reform during the 1970s increased state funding to compensate for differences in property wealth among school districts. Both state and federal governments have enacted an increasing number of policies affecting elementary/secondary education. For example, state statutes determine amounts of aid, limit district taxing authority, mandate programs and services, require public employee bargaining, and set minimums for length of school year and hours of instruction in specific subject areas. Federal laws (with implementing state statutes and regulations) require education for children with handicaps, racial desegregation, and observance of civil rights. Implementation of state and (to a lesser extent) federal requirements is a major function of school district budgeting.

District budgets are important management tools for planning and control. Districts need to know what programs and services they will offer during the next school year. Program planning clarifies organizational objectives and identifies instructional, pupil personnel, cocurricular, transportation, and other services necessary to accomplish them. Districts need to know what financial resources will be available to support future services. Revenue planning estimates receipts from local, state, and federal sources applicable to the next school year. Districts need to know the costs of future programs and services they want to provide. Expenditure planning estimates salary, supply, equipment, and other costs associated with future services. Expenditure planning is an integral part of work agreement negotiations because personnel costs may constitute up to 80 percent of operating budgets. Districts need to know the relationship between estimated expenditure and projected revenue to make appropriate decisions concerning program, expenditure, revenue, and district financial condition. When acceptable relationships exist among projected program services, revenue, and expenditure, budgets are adopted. Adopted budget amounts are entered into one accounting system as bases for expenditure control and monitoring revenue receipts. Program plans guide staffing, purchasing, and other management operations.

The "one best budgeting approach" for all districts may not exist. Publicity and bandwagon effects surrounding innovative approaches often promise more benefits than they deliver. The following approaches, used or available to districts, are summarized to place the issue in a perspective of available alternatives.

Fiscal Control Budgeting

Fiscal control budgeting is an outgrowth of financial accounting. As the title suggests, its primary concerns are protection of assets and expenditure control. Use of this approach is indicated by fund-function-object budget documents in which allocations for similar expenditure objects, for example, teachers' salaries, textbooks, or fuel, are aggregated to district-wide categories to facilitate control. The approach focuses on revenue and expenditure planning, tending to isolate financial management from educational programs and services. Budget revenue and expenditure data are used primarily for comparison of source and object totals from previous years. Local program preferences and concerns about educational outcomes are shunted to community relations or curriculum and instruction subsystems. Extensive supplementary analysis is necessary to determine comparative costs of current educational programs, particular instructional or support services within programs, and proposed alternatives. In this approach, budgeting is a business management function akin to accounting and financial reporting. Certainly, protection of assets and expenditure control are essential in district management, but the approach de-emphasizes important linkages between resource inputs and educational services or learning outcomes. The approach is simple and has been widely used.

Performance Budgeting

The performance budgeting approach became widely recognized as a budgetary reform during the 1930s. It is an outgrowth of managerial cost accounting with a primary focus on efficient use of resources in organizational subunits. Use of the approach in district budgets is indicated by aggregation of object expenditures to programmatic cost centers such as board of education, building administration, kindergarten, and mathematics. Estimated object expenditures for salaries, employee benefits, supplies, purchased services, and equipment are aggregated to yield estimated program total expenditure.

Program or "cost-center" totals are aggregated to series or function totals (e.g., administration, operation of plant, etc.), which are then spread to the appropriate accounting funds. In supplementary analysis, program totals can be interacted with selected unit data to yield classroom, student, contact hour, or other appropriate unit costs.

The performance budgeting approach lends itself to generating a great deal of information—sometimes more than can be meaningfully used for district management purposes. For example, suppose the teaching of English was identified as a high-cost program due to teacher seniority and training. State-mandated instruction in English, continuing contract laws, and district class size policy would limit district ability to increase unit-cost efficiency, at least in the short run. The performance budgeting approach is sometimes referred to as "program-oriented budgeting" or "program budgeting" (not to be confused with PPBS) because of its program cost-center structure. While program total and unit-cost data are useful and informative, the approach does not link resource inputs to educational outcomes. Use of this approach is becoming widespread with support from multidimension transaction codes and computerized financial management systems.

Program Budgeting—PPBS

In the PPBS approach, budgeting is an integral part of a larger decisionmaking system. As indicated in a preceding section, PPBS received considerable attention from policymakers during the late 1960s and early 1970s. The approach is an outgrowth of systems analysis—a discipline that emerged from the combination of operations research, cybernetics, systems theory, and computer science. Its primary concern is cost effectiveness or maximum realization of organizational goals and objectives for the amount of resources invested. Steps for implementation of the PPBS approach were presented in Figure 3-1.

Use of this approach was dropped by the federal government and its use has never been fully implemented (sustained use) in any state or local district. Problems encountered by the PPBS approach are instructive for policymakers and managers in elementary/secondary education. First, it requires consensus on a prioritized set of goals and objectives. Beyond the basic and symbolic 3R's, consensus on a broad range of goals and objectives is nearly impossible among diverse subpopulations with multiple expectations for public schools. Statements of goals and objectives draw divisive attention to such issues as phonics, traditional versus modern math, sex education, values clarification, and bilingual education. Secondly, many desirable educational outcomes do not lend themselves to quantitative measurement. Scores on civics tests do not measure citizenship, sight counts do not measure racial tolerance, and the number of plays or novels read does not measure appreciation. Thirdly, emphasis on effective and efficient realization of measurable learning outcomes (e.g., reading and mathematics) suggests alternative "people-machine" systems that might replace the traditional grade-level, subject-matter classroom delivery system. The educational establishment will not bring political muscle to bear in support of an approach perceived as a possible threat to job security. Fourthly, implementation of the PPBS approach is administratively cumbersome. It requires extensive time commitment, special budgeting expertise, and additional administrative expense. In spite of the low probability of districts choosing a PPBS approach, its emphasis on planning, multiyear time frames, and educational outcomes represent an important contribution to school administration. PPBS may be the ultimate expression of rationality in budgeting, but it found few takers in an arena where allocative decisions are ultimately made by counting votes.

Zero-Based Budgeting—ZBB

ZBB, like PPBS, is a rational budgeting approach. It differs from PPBS in that (1) it is more a decisionmaking process than a complete resource allocation system and (2) it works bottom-up from basic organizational activities as opposed to top-down from organizational goals and objectives. Developed in industry and adapted for use in the public sector, ZBB emphasizes identification, ranking, and choosing alternatives (Pyhrr 1973). Basic steps in ZBB involve developing and ranking "decision packages," and Pyhrr (p. 12) defines a decision package as a discrete activity, function, or operation. In preparing each decision package, managers at the base of the organizational structure (1) identify a basic activity or function, (2) state its purposes, goals, or objectives, (3) predict the consequence of nonperformance, (4) indicate measure of performance, (5) specify alternative courses of action, and (6) estimate costs and benefits. Ranking decision packages is a technique by which limited resources can be located. Packages are ranked at the organizational level at which they are prepared and ranked again at successively higher organizational levels in consolidation with other packaged. The purpose of ranking is to prioritize decision packages in order of importance or benefit to the organization. Cutoff levels may be set at each consolidation level to focus management attention on borderline decision packages. Once ranked in order of priority, decision packages can be selected, in order, until an acceptable level of cumulative expenditure is reached.

Several variations are possible in application of ZBB to elementary and secondary education. At the district level, a logical approach would be to designate each class or service as an activity with decision packages prepared by department chairs or building principals, depending on the size of the school. Decision packages would be ranked at the initiating and successive consolidated review levels. Cutoff levels expressed as a percent of current year expenditures might be used if budget reductions were anticipated. There is little doubt that ZBB could generate information about costs and administrative preferences for programs and services. More important questions relate to applicability of the assumptions underlying the approach, for example:

1. Why prepare decision packages for English, mathematics, social studies, special education, and other mandated services?
2. Can authority of public school principals, superintendents, and elected board members to select or reject decision packages be equated with that of executives in private industry where profit is the primary decision criterion?
3. Does a low priority ranking mean that an educational service is nonessential?

There has been limited use of ZBB in budgeting for elementary/secondary education. Like PPBS, it requires a substantial time commitment, special expertise, and additional administrative cost. While its emphasis on program justification is a strong "antidote" for incrementalism, the title "zero-base" may involve a degree of overstatement in the context of elementary/secondary education. Mandated programs, continuing contracts, graduation requirements, and large investments in plant and equipment to support a particular curriculum are not characteristics of an organizational environment in which goals and activities can be readily or realistically turned back to "zero" on short notice.

Local Planning and Budgeting Model

In the future, school administrators may hear more about a new acronym, LPBM—Local Planning and Budgeting Model. The Institute for Research on Educational Finance and Governance at Stanford University is developing a budgeting approach for districts based on a resource-cost model (Brackett, Chambers, and Parrish 1983, Project Report No. 83–A21). Billed as a rational approach, LPBM will be a planning and budgeting approach that integrates adequacy-equity-efficiency considerations into a resource-cost-base rationale. The Resource-Cost Model (RCM), which has been used in special education and in state finance formula development, is described by Brackett, Chambers, and Parrish (p. 41) as follows:

> Essentially, the RCM is an "ingredients" approach to costing out educational programs. This requires the *listing* of a uniform set of educational programs, the *determination* of specific resources that are appropriate for each of these programs, and the *costing out* of these resources to determine program costs. On the basis of these standardized cost data and the number of pupils enrolled in each educational program, overall costs of education can be determined and broken down by the categories desired.

The LPBM approach would operate in four stages: (1) Program Category Committees would develop initial lists of programs and resource configurations; (2) a representative from each program category committee would make up a Program Review Panel that would evaluate and standardize programs; (3) board, parent, student, and other community representatives would be added to the review panel to form an RCM Committee that would make recommendations to the district board; and (4) the Board of Education would make final decisions concerning allocations of resources. Equity, adequacy, and efficiency issues are addressed as the program list and levels of resources are developed. Each stage provides opportunity for evaluation, negotiation, and tradeoffs. Stages two, three, and four are supported by an RCM computer program to translate educational options quickly into financial terms, thus allowing revenue expenditure comparisons. More data and experience are needed, however, before evaluation of the approach can take place.

In summary, the "one best approach" probably does not exist, but accountability and scarcity of resources will make conceptualizing a district budgeting approach a persistent issue. Perhaps the most prudent course for districts to follow, though, is to retain present budgeting procedures, carefully examine alternative approaches, identify concepts or procedures that might improve planning, decisionmaking, and control, and then adapt the promising concepts and practices for incorporation into the present approach.

CENTRALIZED VERSUS DECENTRALIZED BUDGETING

Decentralization is the delegation of authority or functions to subordinate organizational units. The issue of centralized versus decentralized budgeting can be framed by the question, *"Who should be involved and at what organizational level in making budgetary decisions to maximize educational benefits from available resources?"* The phrase "decentralized budgeting" is misleading because budgeting is not a singular management action, but a cluster of related activities. The issue will be addressed here by decoupling the budgeting cluster in order to explore the feasibility and implications of centralizing or decentralizing selected budget activities. In Table 3-1, program, expenditure, and revenue planning alternatives are placed along centralization/decentralization continuums in the context of a state-local system.

The state-prescribed curriculum at the extreme left of the educational program planning continuum is highly centralized. A relatively small number of education agency personnel, state board members, and legislators on education committees would participate in policy decisions. Input might be obtained from interest groups, advisory committees, and public hearings, but basic curriculum content, methods, and standards would be established at great organizational distance from students and communities to be served. At the other end of the continuum, site management (Garms, Guthrie, and Pierce 1978: 278-293) calls for decentralizing educational program plan-

Table 3-1. Centralization/Decentralization Continuums for Programs, Expenditure, and Revenue Planning Activities.

Centralization

Program Planning
- State prescribed curriculum
- State mandates + State minimums + District discretion
- State mandates + State minimums + District discretion + Professional curriculum committee
- State mandates + State minimums + District discretion + Professional curriculum committee + Parent advisory committees
- Site management (Parent advisory committee, teachers, and principal cooperatively plan program)

Expenditure Planning
- Statewide salary schedule
  State standard expenditure allowance
- District sets salary schedule
  District sets standard supply allowances
- District negotiates salaries
  Supply expenditure based on departmental and building requests

Modified Site Management
- Teachers work under district contract
  District allocates supply allowance to schools

Site Management
- District board allocates lump sum to schools

Revenue Planning
- Full state funding
- Partial state funding + Mandatory district tax levy
- Partial state funding + District discretionary tax authority
- Partial state funding + Limited district discretionary tax authority + Unlimited district tax authority with voter approval
- Partial state funding + Unlimited district tax authority with voter approval
- Full local funding with voter approval

Decentralization

ning to those closest to the teaching/learning situation. Participation in program planning decisions would be extended to a committee of teachers, parent representatives, and the principal in each school building. In contrast to fifty state educational programs, site management has the potential for locally planned educational programs in neighborhoods and communities surrounding approximately 85,000 schoolhouses across the United States.

Many degrees of decentralization and participation are possible along the program planning continuum. Short of a prescribed curriculum, state educational government might (1) mandate instruction in subjects such as health, state history, and special education for students with handicaps, (2) prescribe minimum hours of instruction in broad areas such as language arts, mathematics, or vocational education, and (3) grant district boards discretionary power to offer other programs they deem appropriate. Discretionary board powers decentralize and broaden participation in educational program planning from the state to the district level. Further decentralization and participation become matters of district policy. Conceivably, a board, with executive assistance, might choose to exercise discretionary program powers without the formal involvement of teachers or parents.

The mandates/minimums/discretion/advisory committee alternative near the center of the continuum is more typical of program planning practices in United States schools today. While the district board remains the official decisionmaking body, its authority over program planning is shaped and limited by statutes, court decisions, and political forces. Public employee bargaining laws have given teachers a stronger voice in program planning as they negotiate conditions of employment. Courts participate indirectly through decisions on educational opportunity for minorities, students with handicaps, and constitutional rights of all students. Sex education, "secular humanism," and competency in basic skills have become politicized program issues in some districts. Advisory committees have been established as forums in which diverse preferences can be expressed, tradeoffs or consensus established, and recommendations prepared for the board.

Program and expenditure planning are closely related. Relative degrees of decentralization and participation in expenditure planning are presented as alternatives along the second continuum in Table 3-1. Highly centralized expenditure planning might be characterized by adoption of a statewide textbook and state purchasing of supplies and equipment. With a high degree of centralization, the base of participation in decisions is narrowed. At the other end of the decentralization continuum is site management. Under a "pure" site management scheme the district board would allocate lump sums of resources to schools on a formula basis. The same committee of teachers, parent representatives, and the building principal that planned the educational program would formulate an expenditure plan. Expenditures would include salaries and employee benefits for teachers and aides selected for employment by the local school committee.

Between the extremes of state expenditure planning and site management, several degrees of decentralization and participation are possible. The second alternative from the left, highly centralized district expenditure planning, may no longer exist in practice. Under this alternative the district board might unilaterally adopt salary schedules and set standard costs for supplies, books, and other similar items. Participation in expenditure planning decisions under this alternative would be extended from the state level to board members and central office administrators in all districts.

With public employee bargaining laws has come broader participation in expenditure planning. The third alternative from the left is perhaps typical of current practice. A portion of district authority to set pay schedules is decentralized or shared with recognized bargaining units. Participation is extended through employee votes on negotiated master work agreements. Supply and equipment budget sections are based on departmental and building level requests.

The modified site management alternative is a compromise between prevailing contemporary practice and "pure" site management. It is currently used on a trial basis in elementary schools that received site management pilot grants from a private foundation. The modified alternative is of interest because it excludes salaries and fringe benefits from site expenditure planning. Personnel work under terms and conditions of district master work agreements, but a local parent advisory board cooperates with teachers and the principal in program and expenditure planning for supplies, field trips, and equipment.

Degrees of decentralization and participation in revenue planning are presented along the bottom continuum in Table 3-1. Full state funding on the left is a highly centralized alternative with a relatively narrow base of direct participants. At the other end of the continuum is full local funding requiring voter approval. Under this latter alternative support of elementary/secondary education would be decentralized to approximately 16,000 district finance systems across the United States and participation extended to all eligible voters. Options between the two ends of the continuum are functions of the size of the state share, the discretionary taxing power of district boards, and the approval required. Revenue from partial state funding and mandatory levels of local funding (i.e., property tax) are essentially other versions of full state funding. In both cases total revenue is planned at the state level; only the mix from state and locally collected tax sources is different. Revenue planning becomes decentralized and participation broader as district boards are given discretionary levy authority. In response to a severe fiscal crisis, one state (Minnesota) moved toward more decentralized revenue planning. The foundation aid formula adopted for Fiscal Year 1985 is billed as empowering districts to determine their own revenue needs beyond a basic weighted-pupil unit allowance supported primarily by state-collected income and sales taxes and a mandatory power-equalized county-collected property tax. The mechanism for decentralized revenue planning consists of five discretionary level tiers, above the basic allowance, that are power-equalized at progressively declining rates, from full power equalization in the first tier to none in the fifth.

Revenue planning is further decentralized and participation broadened when district boards are given unlimited tax authority subject to voter approval. In fiscally dependent districts, participation in revenue planning is broadened by local charter requirements that district budgets be submitted to city councils or boards of taxation for approval.

In summary, centralization/decentralization of budgeting activities is a state-local educational, policy continuum issue. State establishment of district boards to govern and manage schools is, in itself, a decentralized implementation of state constitutional mandates for public education. Participation (local control) exists within the framework of powers and duties delegated to district boards. Boards may in turn delegate authority or seek advice from administrators or committees, but responsibility cannot be delegated. Matters of program mandates, minimum instructional hours, licensure, collective bargaining, state aids, and local taxing authority are policy matters established and changed through state political processes. Because of the state-local partnership, involvement in budgeting and other issues requires participation at both state and local levels.

Centralization and decentralization of budgeting decisions are desirable or undesirable only in terms of educational purposes or goals. Budgeting activities and particular issues need to be dealt with separately rather than by broad generalizations about decentralization. For example, without centralized state mandates for special education, thousands of students with handicaps would be denied access to educational opportunity. On the other hand, decentralized program planning may be an effective strategy to increase teaching effectiveness and community acceptance of schools in unique neighborhoods and communities. The major issue in centralization versus decentralization of expenditure planning is local versus regional versus state collective bargaining. Decentralizing expenditure planning for supplies, equipment, and purchased services to the user level involves a tradeoff between additional time and effort versus appropriate and effective use of resources. Centralization versus decentralization of revenue planning is essentially a school finance equity issue.

POLITICAL INVOLVEMENT

This issue may be framed by the question, *"To what extent should educators become involved in partisan political activities to influence budgeting for elementary education?"* The issue arises out of a difference between the nature of the budgeting process and the traditionally nonpartisan political image projected in elementary/secondary education. On the nature of the budgeting process, Wildavsky (1975: 5) writes:

> Little can be done without money, and what will be tried is imbedded in the budget. If one asks "who gets what the government has to give?" then the answers for a specific moment in time are recorded in the budget. If politics is regarded as conflict over whose preferences are to prevail in the determination of policy, then the budget records the outcome of this struggle. Let us, then conceive of budgets as *attempts to allocate financial resourc through political processes to serve differing human purposes* (italics by Wildavsky).

The background of the nonpartisan political image is discussed by Wirt and Kirst (1982), who point out that, at the turn of the century, public schools were involved in a spoils system in which teaching positions and other contracts were awarded as political favors. Abuse was facilitated by highly decentralized local control in which board members were elected by wards. For example, in 1905, Philadelphia had forty-three elected school boards totaling 559 members (Wirt and Kirst 1982: 3). The reform leading to a nonpolitical image is described (pp. 3-4) as follows:

> Reformers contended that board members elected by wards advanced their own special interests at the expense of the school district as a whole. What was needed to counter the atomization, they believed, was election at large. A good school system was good for everyone, not just one segment of the community. Professional expertise rested on the assumption that scientific ways to administer schools did exist and were independent of the values of any particular group. This unitary community idea would help protect schools from local processes.... The primary prerequisite for better management was thought to be centralization of power in a chief executive who would have considerable delegated authority from the school board. Only under such a system could someone make large scale improvements and be held accountable.... The watch words of reform became centralization, expertise, professionalism, *non-political control* and efficiency.

Advantages claimed for maintaining the nonpartisan posture, as summarized by one school superintendent and quoted in Wirt and Kirst (1982: 5), included the following:

1. The higher social status and salary generally accorded school people by the public is better maintained and somewhat dependent upon a situation in which the schools are seen as unique rather than as a mere extension of the same local government that provides dog catchers and sanitation departments.

2. In maintaining a tighter control over the public school system, the image of "unique function" allows greater leverage by the professional school administrator than an image acknowledging that schools are "ripe for the picking" by demagogues and professional politicians.

3. The "unique function" image also provides the schools with a stronger competitive position for tax funds whenever voters are allowed to express a choice of priorities among government agencies.

The nonpartisan political posture served elementary/secondary education well during the post–World War II baby boom. In some communities, over 60 percent of all households had children receiving direct benefits from the schools. Candidates for political office were keenly aware of a consensus on the need for educational programs and plant facilities to serve the baby-boom generation. Educators could assume a nonpartisan political posture because office-seekers of all persuasions carefully avoided positions or voting records placing them in opposition to educational services desired by a large proportion of their constituents.

Conditions during the 1980s have changed. The wave of demand for elementary/secondary services swelled by the baby boom has been followed by a decline in enrollment. Communities where 60 percent or more of the households had children in school twenty years ago may now have school-age children in less than 20 percent of the households. In many states, district schools are being closed, converted to community centers, or rented. An aging population and other demographic changes have increased the demand for different social services, for example, medical care, housing for elderly, public safety, or environmental protection. The importance of elementary/secondary education has not changed, but its position relative to welfare, transportation, and corrections in state and federal budget priorities has changed. Forces driving these changes have been gradual, but cumulative. Sensing these changes, some candidates for political office have campaigned for and supported more local control of education (shifting support from state to locally collected taxes), greater choice of educational service providers (vouchers), and a shift in responsibility from government to individuals (tuition tax credits). Dropping achievement scores, charges of financial inefficiency, poor discipline, and so on, are offered as reasons justifying less support instead of constructively addressing problems in elementary/secondary education.

Universal public education is essential for participatory government, and quality education, as well as equal access to opportunity, is important in an increasingly competitive world market. School board members, administrators, and teachers can knowledgeably state the case for free public elementary/secondary education and have long served as resource persons to local legislative delegations and legislative committees on school finance and related policy matters. With smaller numbers of households receiving direct benefits from the schools comes a need for increased assertiveness in alerting policymakers to the resources needed to maintain elementary/secondary education.

Indications of changing political involvement highlight this issue. Most large urban districts now have full- or part-time lobbyists with titles like "Legislative Liaison." Groups of districts with similar circumstances have formed voluntary associations to analyze legislative proposals and to lobby for member district interests. Educational interest groups such as associations of school boards, superintendents, business officials, principals, and teachers have adopted legislative platforms and monitored legislative activity. The most significant of these efforts has been the recent increased political activity of teacher/employee groups. Teacher organizations have a dual interest in the budgeting process: gaining and maintaining power in district expenditure planning through collective bargaining, and advocating allocation of state resources to elementary/secondary education. Political activities of teacher organizations have included candidate screening, endorsements, campaign contributions, and volunteer work. Evidence of effectiveness include public employee bargaining laws, changes in licensing procedures, and higher appropriations for elementary/secondary education in several states. Organized teachers have thus become a significant political force. Other education interest associations, school boards, and administrators are debating whether or not to follow the teachers' example in increased partisan political activity.

Coalition building is another facet of political involvement. When elementary/secondary education served communities where up to 60 percent or more of households supported educational opportunity for their children, there was little need to build other coalitions for school support. Elementary/secondary education now needs to develop relationships with business, labor, municipal government, and other social services. These alliances are not made to diffuse responsibility for instruction but to coalesce support for allocating public resources to elementary/secondary education. In return, elementary/secondary education may need to pay closer attention to training and manpower needs of business and industry and to the development of cooperative working relationships with other social agencies.

In summary, budgetary decisionmaking in participatory government is essentially a political process. Demographically driven changes in demand for educational services require that resource needs and benefits of elementary/secondary education be assertively presented to policymakers. The traditional nonpartisan political image needs to be reconsidered; educators are not above participation in the democratic political systems it educates citizens to support.

SUMMARY

Scarcity of resources, increased state shares of school revenue, accountability for educational outcomes, and development of rational budgeting approaches (PPBS, ZBB, LPBM) have focused increased attention on budgeting for elementary/secondary education. The direction of these forces has been to expand the role of budgeting from a principal component of school business management to a broader planning, management, and policymaking tool. It is important to distinguish between school district budgets (operating, capital, and cash flow) and the process by which allocative decisions are made. Two opposing orientations, rationality and political process, account for natural tensions in deciding who gets what. Organization management expectations emphasize rational concepts such as objectives, alternatives, control, and accountability. On the other hand, making budgeting decisions by counting votes is a political process. In participatory government, advocates are free to pursue their preferences through political processes whenever administrative requests are denied.

Because of state constitutional mandates for the establishment and support of public schools, state educational government is the senior partner in the federal-state-local framework. Implementation of state and (to a lesser extent) federal education policies is a major function of school district budgeting. Local preferences are incorporated into district budgets through the manner in which state and federal requirements are met, discretionary powers of district boards, and initiatives supported by local taxes.

Accommodating local preferences, operating within state and federal guidelines, and meeting local management needs make selecting the district budgeting approach an educational issue. Budgeting approaches in use or available include (1) fiscal control budgeting, (2) performance budgeting, (3) Planning Program Budgeting Systems

(PPBS), and (4) Zero-Based Budgeting (ZBB). A new approach, the Local Planning and Budgeting Model (LPBM) is now under development. Probably no "one best budgeting approach" for all districts exists. Selecting concepts and procedures from available alternative approaches has the potential for increasing the efficiency and effectiveness of approaches currently used in districts.

Opposing pressures for broader-based involvement in budgeting decisions and increased accountability for educational outcomes have led to the centralization/decentralization issue. The key to addressing this issue is recognition that (1) budgeting is not a unitary management action but a cluster of related activities, and (2) centralization or decentralization per se are neither inherently desirable or undesirable. Purposes and goals of education should determine the most appropriate levels for various policy requirements and which budgeting activities (program, expenditure, and revenue planning) should be decentralized.

Early twentieth century reforms that took schools out of a political spoils system resulted in cultivation of a nonpartisan political image in elementary/secondary education. The political nature of the budgeting process, particularly at the state level, and declining demand (enrollment) for educational services are causing educators to reconsider this nonpartisan political image. Educators are realizing they are not "above" the political process that supports elementary/secondary education.

REFERENCES

Brackett, John; Jay Chambers; and Thomas Parrish. 1983. "The Legacy of Rational Budgeting Models and a Proposal for the Future." Project Report No. 83-A21, Stanford University. Mimeo.

Garms, Walter I.; James W. Guthrie; and Lawrence C. Pierce. 1978. *School Finance—The Economics and Politics of Public Education.* Englewood Cliffs, New Jersey: Prentice-Hall, Inc.

Knezevich, Stephen J. 1973. *Program Budgeting.* Berkeley, California: McCutchan Publishing Corporation.

Lee, Robert D., Jr., and Ronald W. Johnson. 1977. *Public Budgeting Systems.* Baltimore, Maryland: University Park Press.

National Center for Education Statistics. 1983. *The Condition of Education.* Washington, D.C.: U.S. Government Printing Office.

Pyhrr, Peter A. 1973. *Zero-Base Budgeting.* New York: John Wiley and Sons.

Wildavsky, Aaron. 1975. *Budgeting a Comparative Theory of Budgetary Process.* Boston: Little, Brown and Company.

Wirt, Frederick M., and Michael W. Kirst. 1982. *The Politics of Education: Schools in Conflict.* Berkeley, California: McCutchan Publishing Corporation.

4 FISCAL MANAGEMENT— INVESTMENTS

Guilbert C. Hentschke

INTRODUCTION

Investment in public school districts is a severely constrained function when compared to fiscal management and investments in other businesses, especially in the private sector. Because it is so constrained, the opportunities for innovation are limited, and most of those few issues associated with investment by public school district officials have been under study for a number of years. Despite this history, the issues remain important today, and, almost surprisingly, important innovations are taking place.

This chapter opens with a description of investments as a management activity, contrasting the concept of investment across different types of organizations in order to delineate how limited the concept is when applied to public school organizations. The second part of the chapter summarizes the basic operations associated with public school investment practices. Even within the relatively narrow use of the term in public schools, various operations are required to support investment functions. These operations, including cash management, highlight the major variables affecting investment performance in public school districts as well as the tradeoffs facing school district fiscal managers. The variables and tradeoffs are discussed in part three of this chapter. As school district fiscal managers pursue utility, they find ways to solve investment problems and to get around constraints. The last part of this chapter describes the efforts of some school districts to improve their investment practices.

"INVESTMENT" AS A MANAGEMENT ACTIVITY

According to *Webster's Dictionary*, to invest is "to commit (money) in order to earn a financial return": an investment is "the outlay of money for income or profit, also the money invested or the property purchased." The implication here is that money committed in one period is expected to yield money in a future period. "Investment" means very different things to managers located in different sectors of our economy, and its definition is most restrictive in the public sector, including public schools. The subsequent paragraphs describe what public school investing is and what it can not be, as well as what investing means in other organizations.

Investment in the Private For-Profit Sector

Webster's definition comes close to the very reason for being of a private for-profit organization since much of the time and energy of managers in these organizations goes into committing resources for the purpose of generating financial return. Varieties of seemingly unrelated specialities are merely special cases of investment practices.

Capital budgeting involves investment in a firm's capital goods (goods that provide a stream of financial benefits for a period of more than one year). *Introduction of a new good or service* involves commitment of resources in the present with the expectation of financial return over a future period of time. *Purchasing stock in other companies* (including take-overs) is investment involving equity shares in organizations. *Placing temporary surpluses of cash into short-term (debt or equity) instruments* constitutes short-term investment. In all of the above instances, management is involved in evaluating relationships between the marginal costs and the marginal benefits of investment alternatives, be they in terms of people, programs, factories, organizations, stocks, certificates of deposit, or what have you.

Investment in the Private Nonprofit Sector

Investment is also a fundamental managerial activity in many private nonprofit organizations. Managers in this sector (e.g., headmasters, college presidents, museum directors) continually evaluate investment alternatives, estimating the relationships among the marginal costs of a new program, tuition increase, or fund drive, and the resulting marginal revenues.

From the standpoint of the investment orientation of management, working in the private nonprofit sector is little different from working in the private *for*-profit sector. The differences between investment practices in these two (private) sectors and the public sector, however, are much more pronounced.

Investment in the Public Sector

Investment practice in the public sector is much more restricted by law than in the private sectors. Generally, "investment" in the public sector (including public schools) means only the practice of generating income by investing idle cash in a limited set of relatively short-term, low-risk debt instruments. As a consequence, public sector organizations generate only small fractions of their operating revenues from investments. (School districts usually generate between 1 and 5 percent of their operating revenues from investments of idle cash.) This stands in sharp contrast to most private organizations which generate up to 100 percent of their operating revenues from investing. School administrators and other public sector managers operate under different rules from their counterparts in private organizations, and we need to understand not only how these rules differ, but why.

Contrasting "Rights" among the Three Sectors

Managers have certain rights associated with the economic sector in which their organization is located, and what a manager does (how he "behaves") is determined to a large extent by the rights of the manager. The most fundamental of these rights deals with equity treatment, claims on tax revenues, bearing of tax costs, access to markets, and pricing of services.

Equity Treatment. Most schooling organizations have a positive market value. This value is embodied not only in the land and buildings, but the whole operating enterprise, including the value of the "human capital" of those who work there. It therefore has an equity. In the private for-profit sector, individuals (including employees) can own and transfer shares of the organization's equity. Although there is a variety of organizational forms within the private for-profit sector (e.g., single proprietorships, partnerships, corporations), all share the characteristic of permitting individual ownership. Individuals can appropriate or distribute to themselves positive cash flows (profits) and can suffer economic loss during periods of negative cash flows.

Private nonprofit organizations differ from private for-profit ones in that the ownership of the organization cannot be held and traded by individuals. A nonprofit organization is barred from distributing its net earnings, if any, to individuals who exercise control over it, such as members, officers, directors, or trustees. This does not mean that a nonprofit organization is barred from earning a profit. Many nonprofits, including schools, consistently show an annual accounting surplus. Thus, over time, some nonprofit organizations can get "richer" and other nonprofits fold.

Public schools and other nonprofit schools prohibit distribution of equity to individuals. Unlike nonprofit schools, public schools are agencies of state legislative bodies legally charged with the responsibility for providing public schooling and have elected to fulfill that charge in large measure by operating schools through local school districts. New revenues cannot be distributed to individuals, and it is difficult for net revenues to be plowed back into the organization without cost. Most often, any operating surplus in one operating period is merely used to reduce revenue-generating requirements in the subsequent period.[1]

Claims on Tax Revenues. For-profit educational organizations have no direct or continuing claim on general appropriations from public legislative bodies. (Proprietary schools have, however, benefitted from publicly funded training programs, especially those where the aid "follows" the pupil.) Public schools, of course, do have access to tax revenues—local, state, and federal. Although private nonprofit schools do not have the same broad claim on tax revenues, managers of these schools have indirect claims on various categorical sources of public money.

Bearing Tax Costs. Neither public nor private nonprofit schools bear tax costs, although both are increasingly being required to pay "user fees" for municipal services. For-profit educational organizations pay both local real estate taxes and federal-state corporate income taxes. Their exposure to corporate income taxes is mitigated in small part by the right of for-profit school managers to depreciate the value of their capital assets for tax purposes.

Access to Markets for Students. School-age students are currently compelled by states to attend either a public or a private nonprofit school. For-profit schools are generally locked out of the K-12 market, and the student market for public school administrators is usually limited by geographic boundaries of the school district.

Pricing Services. Because of their access to tax revenues, public school officials are not permitted to charge students for educational programs that students are required to attend. Public schooling is a free good to its consumers. Administrators in the two private sectors raise revenues by setting prices and engaging in price discrimination (charging students differing prices for the same service) in any manner they feel best reflects their interests. For-profit schools usually must charge a price that reflects cost; in many private nonprofit schools, gift and endowment income partially offset costs, resulting in prices somewhat less than costs. (Although "free" to the consumer, public schools cost, on the average, at least as much as comparable private schools.)

Why *Public* School Managers Are So Constrained

Public school administrators operate within a very highly regulated environment for reasons directly related to the peculiar set of (public sector) rights described above: no rights to personal ownership of the organization's equity, rights to tax revenues, avoidance of tax costs, partially protected access to student markets, and inability to charge clients for schooling services. Briefly, public sector managers have rights that require greater monitoring by "sponsors." In order to understand more fully why this set of rights logically results in extensive regulation, we need to understand how the role of manager interacts with two other roles, and how this interaction differs across the three sectors.

The manager interacts with the *sponsor* and the *client*. Sponsors assume the roles of providing some of the resources necessary to finance the organization and of determining the organization's mission. Clients are those individuals receiving the final-stage services of the organization for which they may or may not pay. Managers rent their services to sponsors in exchange for carrying out the mission of the organization.

In all three sectors the sponsor faces the problem of trying to get the manager to do what the sponsor wants. This problem is so common in organizations that it has its own name: *the agency problem.* The manager runs the organization as the agent of the sponsor, and the manager is supposed to act in total accord with the sponsor's preferences. The problem arises because the preferences of any two individuals are almost never identical all of the time, and the manager will be inclined to behave in accord with the manager's own preferences, not those of the sponsor.

This general problem takes on a different character in each sector, but the greatest difference exists between the public and private sectors. In the private sector, a variety of factors operate that keep the agency problem from getting too far out of hand. In both private sectors, "poor" performance (performance not in accord with sponsor preferences) results in declining sales as clients (customers) fall away. Because this phenomenon adversely affects managers as well as sponsors, managers continually seek to be responsive to sponsors' and clients' preferences.

Furthermore, in the private nonprofit organization, the roles of sponsor and client often heavily overlap. Parents of private school children, for example, occupy both roles. Overlapping roles act as a built-in monitoring device for sponsors. Because they are also clients, sponsors automatically gain first-hand information about management performance. In the private for-profit organization managers are often sponsors. Managing partners in partnerships occupy both roles. In corporations managers are paid bonuses based on profitmaking performance and acquire stock in the company that employs them. In sole proprietorships the sponsor and manager are often the same people. The agency problem in private for-profit organizations is mitigated by residual claims rights, that is, the right of managers to claim as *owners* the residual cash flow when the organization succeeds. This, of all these factors, causes managers in the private sector to *want* to act as if they were sponsors to a greater degree than is the case in the public sector.

Self-monitoring mechanisms that exist in the private sector are not nearly as present in the public sector. In the public sector the roles (and preferences) of sponsor, manager, and client overlap much less, and sponsors appropriate lump sums of money (tax revenues) to managers to perform services that clients consume at no (or greater subsidized) cost to themselves. Hence, market forces are "stacked" in favor of public schools and do not operate with the same force as in other industries.

In a word, the agency problem is greater in the public sector, and as a consequence, sponsors must rely much more heavily on external, formal regulations that specify what the public sector manager must and must not do. The mechanisms that foster self-monitoring are less present in the public sector. In order sufficiently to improve the likelihood of public sector management compliance, their behavior must be formally monitored and sanctions (or the threat thereof) applied for noncompliance to a much greater degree than in the private sector. The net effect is that the discretionary investment behavior of the public school administrator is severely constrained relative to that of the administrator's counterparts in the private sector. In fact, in the context of public school management, the term "investment" refers only to short-term investment of idle cash. Very specific regulations (largely "prohibitions") are the feasible way for sponsors to align a manager's investment behavior with sponsor preferences.[2]

INVESTMENT IN A PUBLIC SCHOOL CONTEXT

Even *within* the narrow confines of investment of idle funds, government (largely state) laws constrain management behavior in four ways (Dembowski 1982). One, they constrain the manner in which cash may be collected. For example, they usually stipulate the dates and procedures that must be followed when school district managers collect taxes and fees. Two, they stipulate the kinds of investments school district managers may make. For instance, all public school districts are prohibited from investing in equity instruments such as stocks. Three, state regulations specify the conditions under which school districts may borrow money. Most school district managers, for example, are not permitted to borrow money solely for the purpose of placing it into investments whose yield is greater than its cost (loan interest). Finally, school district managers are often restricted in the types of financial institutions with which they can deal. Some states, for instance, prohibit the use of mutual savings banks and out of state banks (Dembowski 1982).

Investment, as practiced by public school administrators, is limited to the relatively small amounts of money that become available when receipts of cash temporarily exceed expenditures of cash.[3] As a consequence, investment practice in school districts is intimately associated with cash management. In order to help assure that sponsor preferences are carried out in school districts, school district managers are constrained by a variety of government statutes and school board policies affecting both cash management and investing practice. The principles and processes ("mechanics") of each are discussed briefly below. The most complete treatment of public school district cash management and investing practice is Dembowski (1982), which the reader should consult for a more detailed account of cash management and investment practices.

Interrelationship between Cash Management and Investment

Investing cash in public school districts is imbedded in general cash management practices. Cash management entails seeking satisfactory answers to the following questions: When are cash receipts expected? When are cash disbursements expected? How much cash will be available at any particular time? How long will a given amount of cash be available? When is borrowing required, for how much, and for how long? Investing idle cash entails seeking satisfactory answers to closely related questions. How much cash is available to invest, in what amounts, and for what duration? What investment instruments should be purchased to maximize yield? liquidity? safety? Although cash management and investment are interactive, each requires rather different kinds of information.

Information Requirements: Cash Management. In order to answer many of the cash management questions, the public school manager sets up and relies on information derived from the district's accounting system. Specific subsystems are described in the box below.

Information Requirements. Investment. While cash management information reveals the amount of cash that can be invested, it does not indicate the investment strategy—what instruments to buy and how long to hold them. Investment information derives from information about desired risk, yield, and liquidity as well as from estimations about the future performance of alternative, legally permitted investment instruments.

Uses of the Accounting System for Cash Management

Cash Accounting System
  To keep track of daily receipts and disbursements of cash; to provide cash balances by fund and account; to record average daily cash balances.

Cash Budget Reporting System
  To contrast budgeting with actual receipts and disbursements.

Investment Status and Earnings System
  To record information on investment transactions, e.g., purchase, sale, maturity and interest earned.

Earned Interest Apportionment System
  To redistribute interest to accounts and funds that contributed cash to the principal of the investment.

Reconciliation System
  To provide data necessary to undertake a monthly reconciliation between the balance in accounting records and the actual cash balances in bank accounts and other district assets.

Source: Dembowski, Frederick L. 1982. *A Handbook for School District Financial Management.* Ridge Park, Illinois: Research Corporation of the Association of School Business Officials, p. 17.

Investment Instruments

School districts are generally limited to investing in low-risk debt instruments. The most common are described briefly below:

A *Certificate of Deposit* (CD) is a time deposit issued against funds deposited in a bank for a specified period of time, usually not less than fourteen days nor more than one year. The interest rate is negotiated by the issuing bank and the investor. The minimum amount for a negotiable CD is typically $100,000.

A *Repurchase Agreement* is an investment in which government securities, usually U.S. Treasury Bills, are purchased under an agreement to resell at a later date. This instrument offers maximum security to an investor since the securities are literally owned by the investor as collateral until repayment at maturity. Maturities are generally up to sixty days.

U.S. Government Securities (Treasury Bills and Treasury Notes and Bonds) are government-guaranteed securities with maturities of one year or less. Both types of securities are relatively liquid since they are actively traded in secondary markets.

Federal Agency Securities, such as Banks for Cooperatives and the Federal National Mortgage Association, are backed by the U.S. government and are offered in varying maturities.

State and Municipal Obligations are tax-exempt securities issued by state and municipal governments to finance their operations. Bond, Tax, and Revenue Anticipation Notes are examples of state and municipal obligations with maturities of less than one year.

NOW Accounts offer the liquidity of a depository account with the interest-earning capability of a savings account.

The procedures necessary to acquire and dispose of these obligations varies with the instruments. Procedures vary in terms of the method by which funds are delivered, where the security will be held, and the bank accounts to be credited or debited as a result of the transactions.

The Investment Process

The investment process is most widely understood as a heuristic activity: simple rules of thumb are relied on for satisfactory results. Table 4-1 provides a simplified cash-flow chart and provides the basis for describing investing as a heuristic process. This cash-flow chart yields the following investing behaviors and rationale according to Dembowski (1982: 16):

> January shows a $200,000 cash surplus. This cash should be invested in interest-bearing securities, e.g., CDs or Repurchase Agreements. Since April shows a $50,000 deficit, an investment of $50,000 should be made from January to April. Another $100,000 could be invested from January to May to cover that deficit, with the remaining $50,000 surplus from January being invested until June. Because revenues equal expenditures, investing will continue until all surplus cash is invested in instruments that mature during the months when cash deficits are projected (July). In July, the school district needs $50,000 to meet expenses. However, all available revenue is used up. This deficit situation continues until October when property tax revenues arrive. To meet this deficit, the school district borrows $150,000 in anticipation of future revenues (probably with a tax anticipation note or TAN). In October, sufficient revenues arrive to allow for the repayment of the TAN, as well as to allow for the investment of an additional $50,000. At this point the investment process starts again.

The school district cash management/investment process described in this section has been widely discussed and understood for decades. Throughout those decades attempts to improve cash management and investment practices have revealed variations in the constraints faced by school districts and have led to a variety of innovative practices in relatively aggressive and sophisticated school districts and states.

MAXIMIZING INVESTMENT REVENUE SUBJECT TO CONSTRAINTS

Although the "rules of the game" in public school investing limit management discretion, sufficient latitude remains for some managers, even with identical legal constraints, to generate more investment revenue (play "better") than others. Part of the explanation

98   MANAGING LIMITED RESOURCES

Table 4-1. The Cash-Flow Pattern of a Sample District.[a]

Period	1	2	3	4	5	6	7	8	9	10	11	12	13
Month	Jan. 1	Feb. 1	Mar. 1	Apr. 1	May 1	June 1	July 1	Aug. 1	Sept. 1	Oct. 1	Nov. 1	Dec. 1	Dec. 31
Inflow	$400	$250	$400	$150	$100	$ 50	$ 50	$ 50	$150	$400	$400	$ 50	$ 0
Outflow	200	200	200	200	200	400	100	100	200	200	200	300	0
Netflow	+200	+ 50	+200	+200	-100	-350	- 50	- 50	- 50	+200	+200	-250	0

a. Revenues are received by the district on the first day of the month. Expenditures occur on the first day of the month. Beginning cash balance of the district on the first day of the year is $50,000.

Source: Dembowski, Frederick L. 1982. *A Handbook for School District Financial Management.* Ridge Park, Illinois: Research Corporation of the Association of School Business Officials, p. 11.

for this is attributable to situational factors of the school district, and part is due to the ability of the manager to minimize the sums of competing types of costs.

Situational Variables

Three school district variables play a major role in determining the proportion of all revenue a manager can generate from investing idle cash: the district's cash-flow pattern, the certainty of that pattern, and the magnitude of that pattern.

Cash-Flow Pattern. The *timing* of revenues and expenditures generates a district's cash-flow pattern and determines how much a district can invest as well as how much it must borrow. District managers seek to receive revenues as early as possible and to keep them as long as possible. Unfortunately for the district manager, most of the discretion with regard to timing does not lie with the manager. This is especially true with the relatively large revenue receipts from city, state, and federal agencies. Revenue flow, perhaps more than any other factor, determines the degree to which idle fund investment is a potentially lucrative pursuit.

Compare the highly simplified cash-flow pattern of Districts A and B in Figure 4-1, which are identical in all respects except for their revenue flow pattern. District A receives revenues for six months at the beginning of the period, whereas District B operates "in the red" for six months before it receives revenues. District A has idle cash (shaded areas) to invest for periods ranging from one to five months, whereas District B has to borrow money to pay its bills for the first five months. The revenue it receives has to be used to pay off the loan. (Technically, it may be possible for District B to invest some of its idle loan money, but net revenues are significantly smaller.) District A's cash-flow pattern is the desired one.

Degree of Uncertainty. The confidence with which the school district administrator can predict cash flow affects investment strategy and, hence, yield. The greater the uncertainty of cash flow, the larger the amounts of cash that must be set aside as hedges, both for unexpected expenditures and for expected but unreceived revenues during a period.

Figure 4-1. Cash-Flow Patterns in Two Districts.

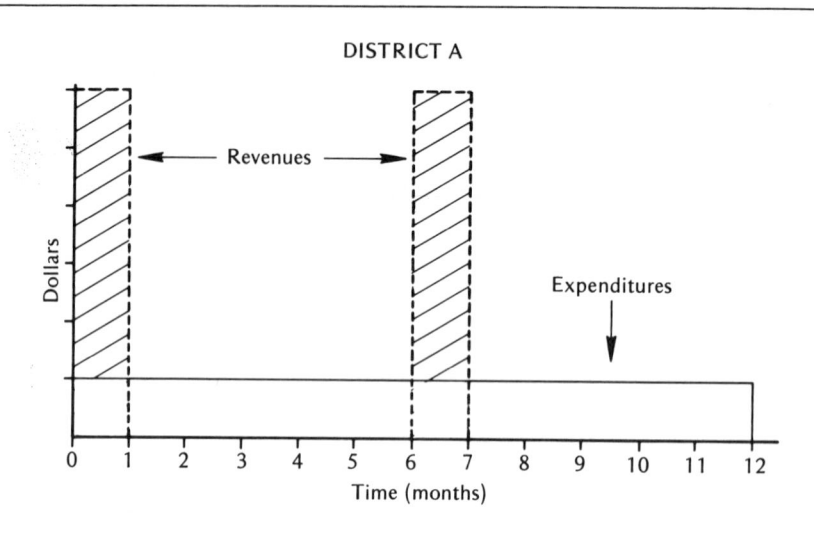

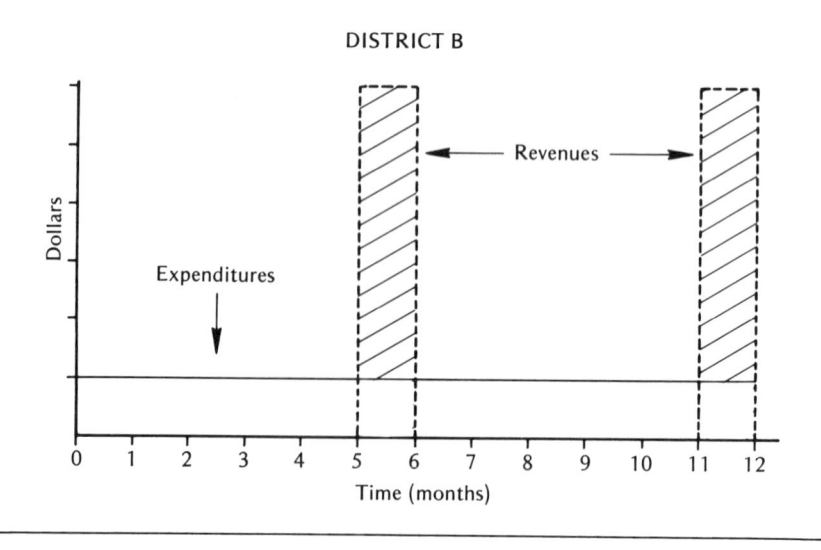

Magnitude of Idle Cash. The amount of cash available for investment, all else equal, affects yield. (See Dembowski 1980 for a review of relevant studies.) Generally, with larger blocks of cash to invest, the school district manager can secure higher rates of interest in markets for money. Larger school districts are more likely to have larger amounts of idle cash to invest and should expect larger yields.

Discretionary Variables

In one respect, situational variables are similar to the legal restrictions constraining cash management and investing discussed earlier: both are constraints around which the manager must work. It is in the area of discretionary variables where some managers outperform others. (Higher yields based on a more favorable school district situation are no reflection on managerial competence in managing or investing cash.) Despite the major constraints described above, managers do have limited discretion that enables them to secure more idle cash for slightly longer periods of time than would otherwise be the case.

To speed up intergovernmental transfers by a few days school district managers have flown couriers to pick up checks, set up wire-transfer systems, and created letter-of-credit financing methods (Comptroller General 1975) to speed the inflow of funds. To slow down the outflow of funds some district managers have resorted to paying bills only once a month (rather than continuously as they are received) and to aging accounts even more when the penalties for doing so appear to be less than the benefits of holding the money longer. Most of the advantages of slowing expenditures have been more than wiped out by districts instituting direct deposit of paychecks. This practice reduces the several days "float" available to the district when checks are issued to employees instead of directly to banks. (The direct-deposit example points up how many worthwhile objectives ultimately come into conflict. The reduced interest on payroll check "float" is part of the price of improving services to employees.)

Other tactics have included more detailed monitoring of cash flows, more frequent transactions, and bidding depository funds (MacPhail-Wilcox 1983; Allen 1981). However, most attempts to improve investment yield soon become subject to the combined laws of diminishing returns and increased compensating costs. Longer-term instruments yield higher returns, but at the expense of liquidity. More frequent and more detailed monitoring and control yield more investable cash at the expense of more expensive administration. It has even been shown that "higher quality" school business officials improve the school district's yield, but, again, higher quality probably connotes higher price (Dembowski 1982). Years of collective experience have brought many school districts to a level where major improvements in cash management/investment are not likely without a fundamental change in the field as we currently know it.

There is one exception to this rather pessimistic forecast. One discretionary variable that has been examined seriously only in the last several years may result in large increases in yields before the laws of diminishing returns and compensating costs set in. The concept is known as "pooling."

INNOVATION IN PUBLIC SCHOOL INVESTMENT PRACTICE: POOLING

Developments in public school investment can be segmented into three arbitrary (and overlapping) periods. The first, occurring as late as the early 1970s was definitional: studies identified cash management/investment as a legitimate (and desired) public school management activity These studies focused on the requisite processes, factors influencing differences in yields, and ancillary special topics such as school district/banking relationships and cash-flow charting (Meulder 1952; Anderson 1968; and Sumner 1974). These early efforts mapped the entire cash management field and treated investment practices largely heuristically.

The second wave of research and development sought to incorporate more "science" into the investing process. In these studies cash management was a "given," and various optimizing techniques were applied to the heretofore simple rules of thumb of investing as described in Table 4-1. The assumption behind these studies is that greater yields were achievable through more detailed, more sophisticated decisions about investing. Models of such investing were borrowed from managerial economics and finance fields. Examples of research and development in this vein include Maldonado and Ritter

(1971), Pogue and Bussard (1972), Dembowski (1980), and Dembowski and Schwartz (1980).

Up to this point, the implicit unit of analysis was "the existing organization," for example, the school district. By the early 1980s there remained little to pursue analytically within the bounds of a single school district, although many small school districts still had not adopted rudimentary cash management/investment practices. As school business administrators continued to seek to improve yield, several leaders pursued research and development associated with redefining the "existing organization" from one school district to a consortium or federation of school districts.

Pioneers in this type of thinking, such as Linford Moyer, have investigated the theoretical benefits (and costs) that were likely to accrue from such a redefinition,[4] and the findings can be outlined.

1. A federation would have a larger pool of investable funds and could invest in instruments of larger denominations, thereby producing a higher investment yield.

2. The scale economies of professional management are large. Professional management seeks largely the same information for fifty school districts as it would for one district. The costs per district of investing—costs associated with rate shopping, execution of purchases, evaluation of investment quality, economic and interest rate forecasts, cash-flow projection, and maturity selection—fall dramatically when funds are pooled.

3. Bookkeeping and operating procedures normally associated with multiple direct investments could be reduced.

4. The investment pooling nature of a federation enables each school district, in effect, to have a more diversified portfolio than it could obtain as an individual investor without sacrificing yield.

5. With a sufficiently large federation of school districts, no single district action would be of sufficient magnitude to affect the overall operation of the pool. This makes possible several additional benefits.
    a. School districts in the pool would not have to schedule the maturities of their investments to coincide with estimated cash-flow requirements.
    b. There need be no minimum periods of investment and no penalties upon withdrawal.

c. Each district can keep its funds invested at the higher yield available to pooled investments, thereby minimizing float.

The largely economic benefits available through pooling are achieved primarily through the design and creation of a new organization. The innovation of pooling lies in the *design* of the new organization. (The economic benefits are merely the *result* of the innovation.) The ability of the new organization to achieve the theoretical economic benefits depends on the rights and resulting incentives partitioned out to various actors. The interesting research question for the late 1980s in public school cash management will be: What organization forms are most conducive to causing investment federations (the managers) to act in accord with the preferences of member school districts (the sponsors)?

Current Experience with Pooling Federations

A few pooling federations have been in operation for several years (Pennsylvania and Michigan); others are on the verge of becoming operational (e.g., New York); and still other school districts are participating in general government pooling federations (Florida, Illinois, Wisconsin). The forms of organization vary from state to state.[5] The structure of the Pennsylvania School District Liquid Asset Fund (the Fund) is, nonetheless, illustrative of how rights get petitioned and incentives set up to maximize the investment preferences of member school districts.

The Fund was created as a common law trust (a private, nonprofit organization) under the laws of the Commonwealth of Pennsylvania in January 1982. Among its many other advantages this organizational form permits continual accounting surpluses (profits) while avoiding tax costs. All of the particulars of the Fund are published in Pennsylvania School District Liquid Asset Fund or PSDLAF (1982). Four roles have been created to manage the affairs of the Fund (in addition to the role of member districts).

Trustees. Trustees (from whose number officers are elected) have "full, exclusive, and absolute control and authority" over the business of the Fund. They oversee, review, and supervise the activities of the Investment Adviser, the Co-Administrators, and the Fund's other consultants and professional advisers. The articles of incorporation require that three of the initial seven Trustees be individuals who are business officials of member school districts; three must be board members of member districts; and one may be either a school business official or a board member of a member district. The same proportional composition of the Board of Trustees, with respect to school business officials and school board members, must be maintained in the event the number of individuals serving as Trustees is changed.

The Trustees serve without compensation, but they are reimbursed by the Fund for reasonable travel and other out-of-pocket expenses incurred in connection with their duties. The Trustees are not required to devote their entire time to the affairs of the Fund. Officers are elected annually.

Investment Adviser. The Investment Adviser provides the Fund with rented expertise in short-term fixed-income management as well as economic and credit analysis. The Fund does not (cannot) engage in trading investment instruments with or through the Investment Adviser.

The Investment Adviser is paid a fee at an annual rate equal to 0.15 percent of the first $250 million of the Fund's average daily net assets, 0.125 percent of its second $250 million, and 0.10 percent over $500 million. The fee is calculated daily and paid monthly. The agreement between the Investment Adviser and the Fund requires annual approval by the Trustees or by a majority of participating school districts. The agreement is not assignable and may be terminated without penalty on sixty days written notice at the option of either party,

Currently, the Investment Adviser is Brown Brothers Harriman and Co., the oldest and largest private bank in America. As of 1982, it managed over $2 billion for corporations and large discretionary money market pools and had total assets in excess of $775 million, $40 million of which was equity capital. The company supplies the following staff to the Fund: four short-term portfolio managers, seven fixed-income advisers, four credit analysts, four economists, and twenty research analysts (PSDLAF 1982: 5). This level of expertise is, of course, far beyond the reach of any one school district, even the largest.

Administrators. The role of the Administrator is to service all member school district accounts in the Fund; determine and allocate income of the Fund; provide written confirmation of each investment and withdrawal of funds by a member school district; provide administrative personnel, equipment, and office space to the Fund; determine the net asset value of the fund on a daily basis; and perform all related administrative services for the Fund. In addition, on a quarterly basis, Administrators provide the Trustees with a detailed evaluation of the performance of the Fund, including a comparative analysis of the Fund's investment results vis-à-vis various industry standards.

The Administrators pay the Fund's expenses for printing documents; the administrative costs of the Fund such as postage, telephone charges, and computer; the fees of the Fund's independent accountants; and the costs of appropriate insurance for the Fund and its Trustees. As in the case with the Investment Advisers, the Fund does not engage in the trading of investment instruments with or through the Administrators. Administrators are paid a combined fee at the annual rate of 0.25 percent of the first $250 million of the Fund's average daily net assets, 0.20 percent of its second $250 million, and 0.15 percent of its average daily net assets in excess of $500 million.

Currently, the Fund is co-administered by E. F. Hutton and Company, Inc., and WTS Consulting Services, Inc. As of 1982, E. F. Hutton performed similar services for over $10 billion, had 274 sales offices (9 in Pennsylvania), and possessed a total capital of over $448 million, $259 million of which was equity capital. WTS Consulting Services, Inc., has developed cash mobilization plans for the state of West Virginia, the Arizona Teachers' Retirement System, and the Permanent Fund of the state of Texas.

The co-administrators' agreement with the Fund is renewable annually by the Trustees or by a majority of member districts. The agreement is not assignable and may be terminated without penalty on sixty days written notice at the option of either party.

Custodian. The Custodian acts as safekeeping agent for the Fund's investment portfolio and serves as the depository in connection with the direct transfer investment and withdrawal mechanisms. The Custodian does not participate in the Fund's investment decisionmaking process. The Fund may invest in obligations of the Custodian and buy and sell legally permitted investments from and to it. The agreement must be renewed annually by the Trustees or by a majority of member school districts. It is revokable without penalty on sixty days written notice at the option of either party. Custodian fees are a function of the quantity and kind of transactions it is instructed to undertake.

Solving the Agency Problem

The Pennsylvania School District Liquid Asset Fund is structured with a deliberate attempt to cause the actors to *want* to maximize investment income of the member districts. The Investment Adviser and the Administrator cannot benefit from "churning" the Fund, because they are compensated on the basis of net asset value, not transaction volume. The Custodian is paid on the basis of transaction volume, but cannot benefit from "churning" because it doesn't participate in investment decisions. Other checks are built in. For example, the Administrator monitors and reports on the Fund's performance (the responsibility of the Investment Adviser).

Growing experience with pooling federations makes it possible to raise a variety of questions with some hope that they will be answered in the future. The greater expertise available from pooling is evident in the Pennsylvania example, but how much greater yield do member districts of PSDLAF (or any other pool federation) enjoy by pooling as opposed to not pooling? How does the structure embodied in PSDLAF differ from structures in other pooling federations, such as Michigan's? In what way are school district relations with local banks affected? Are states that do not have pooling federations actually losing investment income by not pooling? If so, how much?

In many respects, cash management/investment in public school districts remains a highly constrained function. However, school managers—especially school business officials and financially sophisticated school board members—are forging fundamental *organizational* innovations that will reshape the school investment field in the years ahead.

NOTES TO CHAPTER 4

1. These rules constraining school district investing apply equally to most public enterprises such as municipalities. See Haskens and Sells (1977).
2. Restrictions are not static; rather, they are continuously sought and avoided. For a recent attempt by the I.R.S. to further constrain school district investment behavior, see Everett and Fausch (1983).
3. This does not mean that public school investment practice is not worthy of serious attention and study. Although accounting for relatively small proportions of district revenue, investment income is large in absolute terms. Dembowski's survey of school districts in 1979-80 shows that in that year, reporting school districts across the United States earned nearly $1.2 billion. This figure understates what all districts earned, because many states did not report the interest earnings of their districts (Dembowski 1982).
4. Among the individuals who are most knowledgeable about the status of and trends in pooling federations are: Linford Moyer, Executive Director, Pennsylvania Association of School Business Officials, P.O. Box 355, Pottstown, Pennsylvania 19464; and Ronald G. Erickson, Executive Director, Michigan School Investment Association, 4710 W. Saginaw Highway, Lansing, Michigan 48917-2696. For additional information about the pool federation in Michigan see Enrolled Senate Bills 374 and 677 (1982): Michigan School Investment Association; Paul (1982); and Rathrock and Erickson (1982).
5. The state is the logical unit of federation, as all school districts in a state are usually subject to the same state legal constraints on district investing.

REFERENCES

Allen, G. 1981. "Increase your District's Treasury by Bidding the Depository Funds." *School Business Affairs* 47, no. 8 (July): 38.

Anderson, B. D. 1968. "A Study of the Investment of Idle Funds by Large Public School Systems." Ph.D. dissertation, University of Tennessee.

Comptroller General of the United States. 1975. *Opportunities for Savings in Interest Cost through Improved Letter-of-Credit Methods in Federal Grant Programs.* Washington, D.C.: U.S. Government Accounting Office (April).

Dembowski, Frederick L. 1980. "Alternative Methods in the Evaluation of School District Cash Management Programs." *Journal of Education Finance* 6, no. 1 (Summer): 51-57.

Dembowski, Frederick L. 1982. *A Handbook for School District Financial Management.* Ridge Park, Illinois: Research Corporation of the Association of School Business Officials.

Dembowski, Frederick L., and Lee Schwartz. 1980. "An Integer Programming Approach to School District Financial Management." *Socio-Economic Planning Sciences* 14, no. 3 (March): 147–153.

Enrolled Senate Bill No. 374, State of Michigan, 81st Legislature, Regular Session of 1982.

Enrolled Senate Bill No. 677, State of Michigan, 81st Legislature, Regular Session of 1982.

Everett, R. E., and Dale S. Fausch. 1983. "Arbitrage: I.R.S. Attempts to Further Limit School District Borrowing Power." *School Business Affairs* 49, no. 9 (August): 14, 55, 58.

Haskens and Sells. 1977. *Implementing Effective Cash Management in Local Government: A Practical Guide.* Washington, D.C.: Municipal Finance Officers Association.

MacPhail-Wilcox, Bettye. 1983. "Doing More with Less: A Preliminary Study of School District Investment." *Journal of Education Finance* 8, no. 3 (Winter): 399–408.

Maldonado, R. M., and L. S. Ritter. 1971. "Optimal Municipal Cash Management: A Case Study." *The Review of Economics and Statistics* 53, no. 4 (November): 384–388.

Meulder, W. R. 1952. "The Investment of Public School Monies." Ph.D. dissertation, University of Southern California.

Michigan School Investment Association, "Bylaws." Mimeographed.

Paul, Susan. 1982. "Schools Cash in by Learning to Invest." *Detroit Free Press* (September 23): p. C9.

Pennsylvania School District Liquid Asset Fund. 1982. "Information Statement (February 24).

Pogue, G. A., and R. N. Bussard. 1972. "A Linear Programming Model for Short-Term Financial Planning under Uncertainty." *Sloan Management Review* 13, no. 3 (Spring): 69–98.

Rathrock, Paul, and Ronald G. Erickson. 1982. "Michigan School Districts Unite for Financial Planning." *School Business Affairs* 48, no. 7 (June): 28–29.

Sumner, S. 1974. "School Business Management: The Determinants of Rates of Return on the Investment of Idle Funds in New York State." Ph.D. dissertation, Teachers College, Columbia University.

5 FINANCING PUBLIC SCHOOL FACILITIES
Current Status and Trends
Richard Salmon and William Wilkerson

INTRODUCTION AND BACKGROUND

For the past fifty years the responsibility for funding the current expenditures of public elementary and secondary schools has rested with the three levels of government. However, the fiscal relationship among these three governmental levels has changed dramatically over the past half century. Early in the twentieth century local governments provided the vast majority of public school revenues. As late as 1929-30, local governments contributed 82.7 percent of the revenue receipts, the state governments 16.9 percent, and the federal government 0.4 percent. Commencing in the 1930s, state governments gradually began assuming greater fiscal responsibility for financing the public schools. By 1978-79, the state governments had acquired primary fiscal responsibility by providing 47.1 percent of the revenue receipts. During this same period, the local governments' share fell to 43.6 percent, and the federal government contributed 9.3 percent. The trend of increasing state provision of current revenues has continued through 1982-83 as the state share rose to 50.3 percent, while the local and federal shares fell to 42.3 and 7.4 percent, respectively (Salmon and Alexander 1983).

Unlike the tripartite fiscal relationship that has evolved in most states for financing the current expenditures of the public schools, major responsibility for financing public school facilities remains with local governments. In most states, it is the local governments that provide the largest percentage of capital facilities funding, with state governments contributing a much smaller percentage of fiscal support, and the federal government almost no support at all. A recent study of state-assisted capital outlay programs indicates that twenty-nine states provide assistance for capital outlay or debt service through a variety of grants, including equalization aid, percentage-matching grants, and flat grants. Ten states provide fiscal assistance for local public school building programs through loan funds, and eight states have established state or local building authorities (Salmon and Thomas 1981). Five states have established bond banks for use by their local school districts (Camp 1983).

Throughout the 1970s and continuing into the current decade, a variety of pressures, including tax limitations, a declining pupil population, state and federal mandates, and high rates of inflation, have created fiscal difficulties for many local school districts. Particularly significant have been the effects of the property tax limitation initiatives. Although such initiatives are often discussed in relation to Proposition 13 of California and Proposition 2½ of Massachusetts, the movement to curtail use of the property tax was well established prior to either of the above initiatives. According to the Advisory Commission on Intergovernmental Relations (1982), by 1981 forty-one states had enacted or ratified some form of a taxing or spending limitation. In addition to severe fiscal constraints forced upon the current operation of public schools by property tax limitations, such limitations may have profound negative effects regarding the issuance of municipal bonds.

Fortunately, many of the initiatives that have limited the use of property taxes have excluded existing debt service requirements, and some have excluded debt service entirely. Certainly, the exclusion of debt service from constitutionally or statutorily imposed tax limitations is sound public policy, since limitations on the revenue for principal and interest on long-term debt are viewed unfavorably by the investment community. Municipal bonds sold by school districts with spending or tax limitations invariably suffer lower quality rating and corresponding yield penalties.

Faced with severe fiscal constraints and competition for resources, many school districts have been forced to channel all available funds into current expenditures and have cancelled or postponed plans for

Table 5-1. Capital Outlay and Debt Service Charges (in thousands) for Selected School Years, 1929-30 to 1982-83.

School Year	Capital Outlay	Interest Charges	Total Capital Outlay and Interest Charges	Percentage Capital Outlay and Interest Charges of Total School Expenditures
1929-30	$ 370,878	$ 92,536	$ 463,414	20.0%
1939-40	257,974	130,904	388,878	16.6
1949-50	1,014,176	100,578	1,114,754	19.1
1959-60	2,661,786	489,514	3,151,300	20.1
1969-70	4,659,072	1,170,782	5,829,654	14.4
1979-80	6,506,167	1,873,666	8,379,833	8.7
1982-83	6,794,333	2,205,824	9,000,157	7.7

Sources: National Center for Education Statistics. 1982. *Digest of Education Statistics 1982*. Washington, D.C.: U.S. Government Printing Office, p. 79.
National Education Association. 1983. *Estimates of School Statistics, 1982-83*. Washington, D.C.: NEA, p. 39.

new construction or renovation of school facilities. Displayed in Table 5-1 are the capital outlay and interest charges expended by public elementary and secondary schools for selected years from 1929-30 through 1982-83. Expenditures for capital outlay and interest charges currently are consuming a significantly smaller percentage of total public school expenditures than anytime during the past fifty-three years. As a consequence, a large backlog of unmet school building needs has been created.

Since most state governments provide only modest, if any, fiscal support for the construction of local public school facilities, there are relatively few fiscal options available to most managers of school district capital outlay and debt service programs. Among those options available to most school building program managers are those that follow.

Current Revenues

Financing school facilities through current revenues involves financing the entire cost of school construction projects from the proceeds of one or more fiscal year's local tax receipts, depending upon the construction schedule and life of the project. The use of current revenues for financing school facilities has several advantages. Financing a school building program through current revenues is a relatively simple program to administer and avoids payments of interest, costs of bond elections, and related debt service expenses. Unfortunately, financing school facilities through current revenues generally is available only to some of the large or high fiscal capacity school districts. Even some of the school districts that historically have constructed their facilities through current taxation are now prohibited from doing so because of constitutional or statutory-imposed taxing or spending limitations.

Building Reserve Funds

Some states permit their local school districts to levy and accumulate receipts from local taxes in special building reserve funds. Such funds commonly are funded through special tax levies, often requiring voter approval, and are intended to generate over a period of years sufficient funds for replacement and renovation of the school districts' facilities. Similar to the use of current revenues for financing the costs of school facilities, the use of building reserve funds avoids interest and related debt service costs. If building reserve fund investments are not restricted by state statutes or regulations, wise investment of the building reserve funds has the potential of generating significant revenues. While building reserve funds have operated successfully in some instances, overall a strong success record has not been realized (Johns et al. 1983). Often the permitted local levy does not raise sufficient revenues to fund a realistic building program, and the funds are diverted to a variety of smaller projects. Most states have authorized use of building reserve funds for their school districts, but such funds provide only a small amount of the total funds expended for construction of public school facilities.

Bonds

All bonds issued by governmental agencies are referred to as municipal bonds. These bonds, a form of legal paper issued by the borrower as evidence of debt, specify interest rates, payment periods, and security (Barr et al. 1970). Interest generated from municipal bonds is exempt from federal income taxation, and most states provide similar tax exemptions for investors that purchase municipal bonds from their state or local governmental agencies. In addition to their tax advantage for investors, municipal bonds have accumulated an admirable record for maintaining safety of principal. Even during the years of the Great Depression, less than 1 percent of municipal bonds suffered any loss of principal, and less than 2 percent failed to pay interest or principal as scheduled (New York Stock Exchange 1970).

Most school districts use one form of municipals, referred to as "general obligation" bonds, that are secured by the full-faith, credit, and generally the unlimited taxing power of the school district. Most general obligation bonds issued by school districts are serialized so that the bonds comprising the issue mature at regular intervals, usually annually or semiannually. In a few instances, states permit their school districts to issue revenue bonds through dedication of specific revenue sources, such as a percentage of a local sales tax, for retirement of the bonds. However, the financing of public elementary and secondary education facilities by any type of municipal bond other than general obligation bonds provides only an insignificant portion of the total bond receipts obtained by local school districts. Although there are exceptions,[1] most states require their school districts to gain voter approval through bond referenda prior to the sale of general obligation bonds. Some states require only a simple majority of those voting at the referenda, while other states require up to 60 percent favorable votes prior to issuance of local school bonds.

CURRENT STATUS AND ALTERNATIVES

Both the local capital construction fiscal conditions and the municipal bond market environment in which a school district competes for its capital outlay funds have changed dramatically during the past decade. The principal features of the current school construction fiscal conditions and the municipal bond market environment are discussed below. In addition, several alternatives and strategies used by managers of local school district capital outlay and debt service programs are highlighted.

Construction Costs

Displayed in Table 5-2 are average costs per square foot for constructing elementary, middle, and high schools for selected years 1975 through 1982. In 1976, the average total cost per square foot for all public elementary and secondary school facilities was $37.94. By 1982, the total cost per square foot had increased to $61.63, a total increase of 62 percent, or increases of 10 percent per annum (Abramson 1977-83). However, more recent cost data[2] for school facilities suggest that the inflationary spiral that drove up the school building costs for the past several years has ebbed. While the reduced bond interest rates and flattened construction costs may be only a window of a general long-term trend of increased interest rates and construction costs, managers of school building programs likely will be encouraged to seek voter approval for the sale of school bonds in 1984.

Bond Elections

Until the late 1960s, school districts had little difficulty in convincing their citizens to approve bond sales for construction of school facilities. However, when Table 5-3 is examined, it is apparent that school districts were experiencing more difficulty during the 1970s in gaining voter approval for bond sales. By 1975, total bond sales approved had fallen to 46.3 percent, although the lowest par value approval rate (41.4 percent) occurred earlier in 1971. More recently, the approval rate of school district bond issues has improved signifi-

Table 5-2. Costs Per Square Foot for the Construction of Public School Facilities for Selected Years, 1976-1982.

Year	Elementary School Costs/Sq. Ft.	Middle School Costs/Sq. Ft.	High School Costs/Sq. Ft.	Average Costs/ Sq. Ft.
1976	$25.69	$47.89	$40.24	$37.94
1978	47.48	52.44	50.40	50.11
1980	49.93	56.35	45.57	50.62
1982	58.38	64.16	62.35	61.63

Source: Abramson, P. 1977-1983. "Educational Construction: A Statistical Summary." *American School and University*, vol. 49, 51, 53, 55.

Table 5-3. Public Elementary and Secondary School Bond Elections Held and Approved, and Par Values Proposed and Approved: Selected Years, 1965-1983.

Year	Number of Elections Held	Approved	Percent	Par Value of Bond Issues (in millions of dollars) Proposed	Approved	Percent
1965	2,041	1,525	75%	$3,129	$2,485	79%
1967	1,625	1,082	67	3,063	2,119	69
1969	1,341	762	57	3,913	1,707	44
1971	1,086	507	47	3,337	1,381	41
1973	1,273	719	57	3,988	2,256	57
1975	929	430	46	2,552	1,174	46
1977	858	447	56	2,400	1,296	54
1982	332	204	61	2,427	1,830	75
1983	352	220	63	1,778	1,314	74

Sources: National Center for Education Statistics. 1978. *Bond Sales for Public School Purposes, 1976-77.* Washington, D.C.: U.S. Government Printing Office.
The Bond Buyer. 1984. *Credit Markets.* New York: The Bond Buyer (January 3).

cantly. In 1982, voters approved 61.4 percent of the issues proposed, and for 1983, 62.5 percent of the issues proposed were approved. With regard to par value of the school district bond elections, in 1982 and 1983, the voters approved 75.4 percent and 73.9 percent respectively. It is important to note that both the number and par value of bond referenda submitted to the voters were considerably less for 1982 and 1983 than any year during the past two decades. Further, the number of school bond issues approved in 1983 comprises approximately 30 percent of the issues approved in 1973 and less than 15 percent of those approved in 1965. Even if inflationary building costs are ignored, the par value of the issues approved in 1983 comprises approximately 58 percent of the par value approved in 1973 and only 53 percent of the par value approved in 1965.

Interest Rates

Average yields in percent for general obligation bonds rated by Moody's for selected years, 1973 through 1983, are displayed in

118   MANAGING LIMITED RESOURCES

Table 5-4. Summary of Municipal Bond Yield Averages by Moody Rating, United States, Selected Years, 1973-1983.

Average Yields in Percent
General Obligation Bonds

		Moody Rating			
Year	Average Municipal	Aaa	Aa	A	Baa
1973	5.22	4.99	5.11	5.28	5.49
1975	7.04	6.42	6.76	7.36	7.61
1977	5.64	5.20	5.39	5.86	6.12
1979	6.27	5.91	6.11	6.26	6.73
1981	11.10	10.42	10.89	11.31	11.75
1982	11.62	10.88	11.30	11.84	12.48
1983	9.42	8.75	9.16	9.60	10.16

Source. Moody's Investors Service, Inc. 1984. *Moody's Bond Record.* New York: Moody's Investors Service, Inc. (January).

Table 5-4. From 1973 through 1979, the average yield on all general obligation bonds varied only from 5.22 to 7.04. However, in 1981, the average yield rose to 11.10 and increased still higher, in 1982, to 11.62 before falling to 9.42 in 1983. According to the Bond Buyer 20 Bond Index, interest rates for municipal bonds reached an historic high of 13.44 percent in January 1982. The January 1983 rate was more than double the Bond Buyer 20 Bond Index low for 1979 of 6.08 percent, and was approximately 40 percent higher than the early January 1984 level of 9.66 percent (The Bond Buyer 1984).

Obviously, if the school district has the choice, the best decision is not to sell bonds when rates are at high levels, especially if it can be reasonably anticipated that rates will fall in the near future. However, there are occasions when it may be more prudent to issue and incur high interest rates if school construction costs are escalating rapidly and if bonds can be refunded later to take advantage of lower interest rates. However, it is always difficult to predict the bond market or the direction of interest changes with any reasonable degree of certainty. In one week in December 1981, the Bond Buyer Index gained .71 percent, which was certainly an unpredictable event. If the current trend of lower interest rates demanded by municipal bond investors endures throughout 1984, a surge of issues created by the backlog of unmet school building needs likely will enter the market.

Bond Ratings

The two major rating services are Moody's Investors Service and Standard and Poor's Corporation.[3] Both rating agencies, on the basis of fees charged the issuer, assign an investment quality rating to tax-exempt bonds. Currently, it appears that the rating agencies are probing more deeply into the financial health of the school district before the assignment of ratings than they have in the past. Consequently, many school districts have been unpleasantly surprised when their quality ratings on new bond issues are lower than those previously received.

The importance of a favorable quality rating from one of the rating agencies cannot be overemphasized. As was shown in Table 5-4, in 1973 the yield of Baa-rated bonds was 10 percent greater than the yield of Aaa-rated bonds; by 1983, the yield of the Baa-rated bonds was over 16 percent greater than the yield of Aaa-rated bonds. Substantial savings in interest costs are available to those school districts that earn the higher quality ratings. For example, in 1983 a $1,000,000 bond issue would cost the average Baa-rated school district $220,800 more in interest charges than the average Aaa-rated school district over a twenty-year maturity.

Occasionally there are circumstances unique to the school district that may cause one rating agency to provide a higher rating than the other. If this is known in advance, the financial adviser and the manager of local school district building programs should consider obtaining the rating from the rating agency likely to provide the higher quality rating. This is particularly true if a rating of A or better can be predicted from one rating agency but not from the other. As previously discussed, the increased emphasis on the importance of high quality ratings is partially the result of the shift from institutional to individual purchase of municipal bonds in recent years. Institutions traditionally have conducted their own research on quality of bonds prior to purchase, while individuals have proven more likely to rely solely upon the assigned Moody or Standard and Poor rating.

Disclosure. The near default of New York City on its municipal bonds in the early 1970s sent shock waves throughout the investment community. More recently, the Washington Public Power Supply System defaulted on $2.25 billion worth of bonds, the largest municipal bond failure in history. A necessary response by school districts preparing to issue bonds is to provide full disclosure of all material facts that might affect their ability to pay interest and redeem the bonds in a timely fashion. Underwriters and prospective bond owners need to be furnished a considerable amount of pertinent information about the issue, issuer, and characteristics of the revenue base that will provide the debt service funds. Such information ordinarily will be contained in the prospectus or official statement of the issue, and such information usually will be gathered and prepared by the financial adviser retained by the local school district. However, school officials have the obligation to check the accuracy of the information submitted so that erroneous information is not conveyed to prospective purchasers. In addition, possible liability for fraud exists if material facts are misrepresented or omitted. Good intentions by responsible school officials may not be an adequate legal defense if investors experience losses due to other than normal market risks.

After the quality rating has been received and throughout the life of the municipal bonds, the issuer has the obligation to keep the rating agency apprised of pertinent facts. Financial reports of the school district routinely should be sent to the rating agency, along with information relative to future construction projects, changes in economic conditions, disposition of closed buildings, and other relevant data.

Third-Party Insurance

Increases in interest rates invariably cause the market value of a municipal bond to fall, since the interest to be paid over the life of a bond typically is fixed at the time of issuance. Any institution or individual owning municipal bonds in the early 1980s suffered severe losses in the value of their portfolio when interest rates reached record levels. The reduction in value was less for high quality bonds than for those that were regarded as more speculative. As a consequence, investors responded by reducing holdings in fixed-rate securities and by "fleeing to quality." One technique used to move a municipal bond from a speculative to a high-grade investment was for a third party to insure timely payment of principal and interest of the bond. Two entities that have been very active in providing municipal bond insurance are American Municipal Bond Assurance Corporation (AMBAC) and Municipal Bond Insurance Association (MBIA).[4] Both organizations charge premiums based on debt service requirements over the life of the issue. Premiums may be paid by the issuers from bond proceeds or by underwriters from the spread between the prices paid to the issuers and prices obtained from re-offering the bonds. One rating company, Standard and Poor, assigns its highest quality rating, AAA, to bonds insured by AMBAC or MBIA.

Participation by third-party insurers can be anticipated to increase. Other entities now are offering similar service, and insured bonds have been very favorably received in the market. The manager of a school district building program needs to consider the possibilities for savings in interest costs and weigh them against the insurance costs. A strategy available to the issuer of bonds is to obtain a commitment from one of the insurance companies but offer the bonds both insured and uninsured, at the option of the bidders. It is then possible for the school district to select the bid when both precise costs and potential savings are known.

Shift to Individual Ownership of Municipal Bonds

The high inflation rates of the 1970s pushed many Americans into high marginal income tax rate brackets. Tax-exempt income, which always had been desirable for institutions showing profits, became more meaningful to individuals and less desirable to banks and insurance companies, which were suffering reduced profit levels and severe portfolio losses as interest rates sky-rocketed. Further, partly as a result of tax legislation of the early 1980s, the traditional spread between tax-exempt interest rates and rates on taxable interest narrowed. Thus individuals became the dominant purchasers of tax-exempt bonds. Occasionally, individuals purchased municipal bonds directly from underwriters but more often they purchased shares in municipal bond funds and unit trusts. Sponsors of the managed funds and unit trusts frequently adopted a policy that all municipal bonds purchased must be rated A or better by one of the major rating agencies. This A or better policy resulted in modest sacrifice in yield but provided quality assurance to investors. Since this policy applies to the ownership vehicles most used by individuals, the dominant entity on the demand side of municipal bond issues, securing the highest possible rating has become increasingly important to the school district desiring to issue school bonds.

The Yield Curve

As a general rule, short-term interest rates are lower than long-term rates for municipal bonds. If placed on a graph, the result is a positively sloped curve referred to as a "yield curve." The characteristics of the yield curve vary over time and, as a consequence, have implications for structuring the amortization of municipal bonds.

During certain time periods over the past few years, the interest rates available for fifteen-year bonds were substantially lower than the available rates on twenty-year bonds. At other times, the yield curve rose sharply from one to approximately twelve years and then rose at a much lower rate from the thirteenth through the twenty-fifth year. In the latter instance, the decision to amortize the bonds more slowly resulted in significantly lower annual debt service costs. On the other hand, when the yield curve is steep, the annual debt service costs will be less if the maturity schedule is shortened, since the potential savings from spreading the retirements over more years are offset by the increased interest rate penalties. Certainly, the manager of a school districts' capital outlay and debt service program should utilize the yield curve in order to determine the bid that provides the school district with the lowest debt service costs.

Short-Term Rates for Long-Term Financing

The use of short-term financing instruments, which are "rolled-over" on a periodic basis, is a strategy that, although not yet in common practice in school districts, is gaining favor with other municipal bodies. The appeal of short-term financing is that the typical yield curve may show a 5 percent rate for ninety days, while a twenty-year amortization for the same quality municipal bond would likely show a rate of 10 percent.

Frequently, the rate on short-term municipal notes is a percentage of the prime rate or some other established yield index. In order for school districts to acquire funds through short-term municipal notes, the market usually requires collateral, such as a bank letter of credit. The major hazard for the school district is that the market may dictate that permanent financing be arranged at a time inconvenient for the issuer. Nevertheless, where state laws permit, and where the size of the issue and other factors make this approach feasible, managers of school building programs should consider short-term municipal notes as an alternative to obligating the school district for high rates for twenty to thirty years.

A related alternative to the use of short-term rates is the use of variable rate instruments in which the interest rates are adjusted periodically, usually annually, throughout the life of the debt. Other sectors of the tax-exempt market bonds have effectively used variable rate instruments, and they should be considered by local school districts, particularly if the school bonds have to be issued when interest rates are extremely high.

Advance Refunding and Arbitrage Considerations

Pre-refunding, or advance refunding of municipal bonds, allows the school districts to obtain the advantage of prevailing interest rates that are lower than those incurred when the issue was marketed. Although the mechanics and the legal requirements are extremely complex, the possibilities for advance refunding should be explored whenever the prevailing interest rates are approximately 200 basis points (i.e., 8 percent compared to 10 percent) lower than those of the outstanding bonds.

Advance refunding of municipal bonds by school districts is legally permissible in many states and would be a desirable policy option for all states. The Internal Revenue Service (IRS) has promulgated a series of regulations that provide the framework for such refunding (Code of Federal Regulations). The primary intent of the IRS regulations is to deny unreasonable profits to the underwriters and to prohibit issuance of tax-exempt securities by governmental units that invest the proceeds in materially higher yield, taxable securities. However, if the IRS regulations are not followed properly, such municipal bonds might be classified as "arbitrage bonds" and the school district could lose its tax-exempt status (United States Code Service 1983).

Prior to promulgation of the IRS regulations regarding the investment of municipal bond receipts, it was not uncommon for governmental units, including school districts, either to issue more bonds than needed for a particular project or to issue them much sooner than necessary. Municipal bond issue proceeds then were invested in treasury securities or similar high-yield instruments in order to gain a rate of return much greater than the rate incurred on the bonds. As a part of the legal documentation accompanying delivery of bonds, issuers now are required to file nonarbitrage certificates that indicate that use of the bond proceeds is for legitimate governmental purposes.

Currently, yields on short-term treasury securities and bank certificates of deposit typically are lower than interest rates on long-term tax-exempt securities—thus, political arbitrage earnings are negative. However, there have been occasions in recent years when the opportunity for arbitrage profits was present. Certainly such circumstances could occur again and prudent managers of school building programs should avoid any action that may jeopardize the tax-exempt status of their school districts.

Registration of Bonds

Federal legislation now requires that all municipal bonds be issued in registered form, rather than as bearer bonds. No longer do such bonds have interest coupons attached that the owner clips and presents to a bank for payment. Current federal laws require registrars to maintain current records on ownership of each municipal bond; and a paying agent, usually a large bank, writes checks for interest and for bond redemption to owners of record. The unfortunate consequence of this legislation is that most governmental agencies, including school districts, are not equipped to serve as registrar and paying agent and must contract with a major city bank for services. In addition, there is little opportunity for "float," the time period that elapses between the due date for bond and interest payments and the date when the coupons appear for payment by the issuer. Funds for debt service requirements now must be available, with certainty, on or before the due dates for such payments.

Callable Bonds

If state laws permit, municipal bonds should have a "call" feature. The usual callable bond can be redeemed at the option of the issuer, in advance of its scheduled maturity date, by paying a premium for the early redemption. Since a call device is an advantage to the issuer rather than the owner of the bond, slightly higher interest rates will usually be incurred for callable bonds than for noncallable bonds of identical quality and length of term. If bonds are made callable any time after issuance, the interest rate penalty likely will be quite high, even if such bonds can be marketed. Therefore, a compromise solution is to provide protection for both the issuer and the holder by providing a noncallable period of time, usually eight years, during which time the holder is assured there will be no early redemption of the bonds. The school district may take advantage of declining interest rates by refinancing the bonds after the noncallable time period has elapsed. Alternatively as previously discussed, if state and federal laws permit and market conditions are appropriate, the school district may be able to pre-refund the bonds.

Need for Competent Counsel

The potential legal and financial hazards that have always been associated with acquisition of funds for capital construction, including the sale of municipal bonds, have increased dramatically in the past few years. It has always been desirable that school districts obtain adequate legal and financial advice in the acquisition of capital outlay funds. However, the complexities of the current municipal bond market, the changing rules and regulations of governmental agencies, and the multitude of other factors that affect the process now dictate that competent legal and financial advisors be utilized.

The typical local attorney does not have the expertise necessary to direct school officials through all of the legal requirements of a bond issue. Therefore, nationally recognized bond attorneys should be retained, either to act as additional legal counsel or to assume sole responsibility. Advice on timing of the issue, interest rates permitted, amortization of the bonds, and other structural details should be obtained from a financial adviser. If competent legal and financial advisers have been secured early in the planning stages of the project, then proper attention to the many details and to the current and emerging legal and financial conditions can be anticipated.

Increased Use of Lease-Purchase Programs and Other Private/Public Ventures

Some local school districts are currently using other vehicles than traditional bonding to finance capital facilities. For example, several states do not require local school districts to obtain voter approval to enter into lease-purchase arrangements, since the rent is paid from current operating funds. In some instances, the lease-purchase method is used in conjunction with private agencies and may be used to circumvent unduly restrictive debt or tax-rate limitations. As an incentive to investors to provide the funds for leased facilities or equipment, their investment return may be made tax-exempt. For investors dealing in leases in which their interest returns might be taxable, recent federal revenue legislation has provided expanded investment tax credits and depreciation allowances. Since the traditional spread between tax-exempt and taxable yields has narrowed considerably, consideration should be given to leasing from the private sector.

Another private/public cooperative venture for construction of capital facilities has been used in a few instances. As early as 1966, New York City established the New York City Educational Construction Fund for construction of combined low- and middle-income housing and educational facilities. New York City Schools now share occupancy structures with private tenants in thirteen separate locations. While dual occupancy structures may not be appealing for all school districts, public/private ventures may prove desirable for those areas experiencing severe shortage of available construction sites.

SUMMARY

The current status and trends in the local options for funding public elementary and secondary education facilities have been reviewed, including funding through current revenues, building reserve funds, and sale of municipal bonds. The record of bond sales for public schools from 1965 through 1983 indicates that school districts have experienced greater difficulty in gaining voter approval for bond issues. The pattern of municipal bond yields from 1973 through 1983 shows a steady increase in interest rates. In addition, a review of the costs per square foot for construction of public school facilities shows construction costs increasing at 10 percent per annum.

While banks, insurance companies, and other institutional investors historically have been the purchasers of the majority of tax-exempt bonds, purchases of municipal bonds by individuals, either directly or through bond funds, now make up the largest segment. As a result of this shift to the individual investor in municipal bonds, the quality rating awarded the school district bond by one of the national rating agencies is more crucial than ever before. Tax-rate and spending limitations have been imposed in most states. Defaults of principal and interest payments have made the headlines on several occasions; and municipal bonds no longer can be issued in bearer form. These and other changes and events have altered the methods and procedures that should be used by school officials in managing their capital-financing programs.

NOTES TO CHAPTER 5

1. Virginia, for example permits its school districts to avoid voter approval through use of a state building authority.
2. Informal telephone survey of selected state agency officials conducted January 1984 indicated that interest charges for municipal bonds and construction costs have declined during 1983.
3. Full titles and addresses of the rating agencies are:

   Moody's Investors Service
   99 Church Street
   New York, NY 10007

   Standard and Poor's Corporation
   25 Broadway
   New York, NY 10004

4. Full titles and addresses of the third-party insurance companies are:

   American Municipal Bond Assurance Corporation
   1 Stage Street Plaza, 17th Floor
   New York, NY 10004

   Municipal Bond Insurance Association
   34 South Broad Street, Box 788
   White Plains, NY 10602

REFERENCES

Abramson, P. 1977-1983. "Educational Construction: A Statistical Summary." *American School and University*, pp. 49-55.

Advisory Commission on Intergovernmental Relations. 1982. *Significant Features of Fiscal Federalism, 1980-81.* Washington, D.C.: U.S. Government Printing Office.

Barr, W. Monfort; K. Forbis Jordan; C. Cale Hudson; Wendell J. Peterson; and William R. Wilkerson. 1970. *Financing Public Elementary and Secondary School Facilities in the United States.* Special Study Number 7. National Educational Finance Project. Bloomington, Indiana: School of Education, Indiana University.

Camp, William E. 1983. "Public School Bonding Corporations Financing Public Elementary and Secondary School Facilities." Ph.D. dissertation, Virginia Polytechnic Institute and State University.

Johns, Roe L.; Edgar L. Morphet; and Kern Alexander. 1983. *The Economics and Financing of Education.* Englewood Cliffs, N.J.: Prentice-Hall, Inc.

Moody's Investors Service, Inc. 1984. *Moody's Bond Record.* New York: Moody's Investors Service, Inc. (January).

National Center for Education Statistics. 1978. *Bond Sales for Public School Purposes, 1976-77.* Washington, D.C.: U.S. Government Printing Office.

National Center for Education Statistics. 1982. *Digest of Education Statistics 1982.* Washington, D.C.: U.S. Government Printing Office.

National Education Association. 1983. *Estimates of School Statistics 1982-83.* Washington, D.C.: NEA.

New York Stock Exchange. 1970. *Understanding Bonds and Preferred Stocks.* New York: New York Stock Exchange, Inc.

Office of Federal Registrar. *Code of Federal Regulations*, 26 CFR 1.103 et. seq. 1983. Washington, D.C.: U.S. Government Printing Office.

"Pulling the Nuclear Plug." 1983. *Time* 123 (February 14): 7.

Salmon, Richard G., and S. Kern Alexander. 1983. *The Historical Reliance of Public Education Upon the Property Tax: Current Problems and Future Role.* Cambridge, Massachusetts: The Lincoln Institute of Land Policy.

Salmon, Richard G., and Stephen B. Thomas. 1981. "Financing Public School Facilities in the 80's." *Journal of Education Finance* 7 (Summer): 96.

United States Code Service, 26 USCS §103, §1233. 1983. Rochester, New York: The Lawyer's Cooperative Publishing Co.

6 SOURCES OF ALTERNATIVE REVENUE

Lionel R. Meno

INTRODUCTION

Public school districts across the country are becoming increasingly hard-pressed financially. On one side, districts are faced with increases in expenditures due to inflation and increasing community expectations. At the same time, the traditional sources of revenue—property tax, state aid, and federal aid—are becoming less predictable and more restricted. The most recent efforts to resolve this problem have focused on control of expenditures such as labor costs and redesign of the methods by which traditional revenue sources are delivered. For more and more school districts, however, these strategies have not been successful in balancing expenditures and revenues.

Increasingly, school districts have attempted to identify and implement nontraditional methods for financing their school districts. These alternatives have included ideas such as "adopt-a-school," alternate community school utilization, district foundations, and loaned executives, all of which are designed to increase revenues or decrease expenditures. However, the full potential impact of these new financing methods on school district budgets has not been fully assessed.

THE SEARCH FOR NEW SOURCES OF REVENUE

The primary efforts of educators across the country have been to reform the traditional tax-supported methods of school financing to increase their viability. However, due to a discouraging lack of success in this task, school districts are beginning to identify new methods of financing schools. These efforts can be grouped into three different types of activities: solicitation of goods, services, and money (donation activities), selling or leasing of services and facilities to generate revenue (enterprise activities), and pooling of functions with other organizations or agencies to reduce costs (shared or cooperative activities).

Donor Activities

Donor activities are any activities that seek to initiate the donation, either in a direct or indirect manner, of funds, services, or goods from sources outside governmental agencies.

Direct Donation of Funds. The first type of donor activity is the direct donation of funds. This can be in the form of direct district fund raising for various district activities or the organized effort to obtain corporate gifts and foundation grants. Meno (1983) describes many specific examples of school district activities that illustrate this form of revenue raising.

Several school districts have received substantial revenues through this activity. In two cases, this was the result of large single donations that were provided to the district for a specific purpose. The Beloit Public Schools (Wisconsin) received $440,000 from a local foundation to buy minicomputers as part of an experimental program in computer education. The Griffin-Spaulding County School District (Georgia) received an anonymous gift of $450,000 to establish an educational trust.

The Hartford City School District (Connecticut) is specifically organized to seek foundation and individual grants and gifts. In 1982, the district received approximately $400,000 from twenty-five different sources, with donations ranging in size from $100 to

$100,000. This year the district has intensified its efforts in this area and has received $599,965 from twenty-six sources.

Another example of donor activity is an enrichment fund that has been established by local businesses and community members in the Tucson (Arizona) Unified School District to support education programs that the district could not otherwise undertake. In Wichita, Kansas, the American Dental Association is funding a Dental Prevention Model in the Wichita City Schools. The Gates Foundation has supported a health education project in the North Glenn (Colorado) School District (Maeroff 1982).

Indirect Donations through School District Foundations. A second type of donor activity is indirect donation of funds through private nonprofit organizations created to receive donations for the district (Meno 1983). A number of school districts, including those in San Francisco, Washington, D.C., Dallas, and Oakland City, have created special foundations through which money can flow to fund various school district activities. The City of Baltimore, of which the school district is a part, has established the Baltimore City Foundations, Inc., for the purpose of attracting private financial support for various city and school district programs that would otherwise have to be eliminated.

Several school districts have established single-purpose foundations. In the case of the Millcreek Township School District (Pennsylvania), the purpose is to raise money for a new athletic facility. The foundation had the goal of raising over $500,000 in 1982–83.

The specific focus of the school district foundation in the Marshalltown Community School District (Iowa) is to raise $975,000 to match a district capital allocation of $1.2 million to construct a new high school auditorium. The Escondido County Union High School District (California) formed a foundation after the passage of Proposition 13 to support its interscholastic athletics program. The foundation has been successful in accomplishing this goal with the over $200,000 it raised last year.

Indirect Donations through Support Organizations. In addition to foundations, there are support organizations that are program-centered to raise money for specific activities. These include parent organizations within individual schools and athletic, music, band, choral, debate, and drama booster clubs (Meno 1983).

In the Durham County School District (North Carolina), the Parent Teacher Organization (PTO) raised funds through Halloween carnivals ($40,000) and balloon sales ($10,000), and in the Gloucester Township School District (New Jersey), the PTO raised money to purchase minicomputers and copy machines for the schools. Each building in the Bartlesville Public Schools (Oklahoma) is provided with a $6,000 to $12,000 discretionary fund by the parent organization. This money is used by the staff to purchase playground equipment, audio-visual equipment, and general supplies.

Booster clubs are also effective fund raisers in some districts studied. In the Appleton Area School District (Wisconsin), the music boosters raised the funds necessary to send the high school band to the Orange Bowl Parade and Europe last year. It also provided money for vocal groups to travel to Denver, Washington, D.C., and St. Louis. The Rowan County School District (North Carolina) employs a matching funds concept to encourage booster fund raising in order to improve district athletic facilities. Last year, the boosters donated $200,000 for this purpose.

Donation of Services. The third type of donor activity is the donation of services, whereby individuals acting on their own behalf or as representatives from business and industry volunteer their time to the school district. A number of school districts, such as the Upper Merion Area School District in King of Prussia, Pennsylvania, have been specifically organized to encourage volunteers to participate in the schools—thus providing the school district with a rich resource of additional services (Scott 1979). In several school districts, including Buffalo and Detroit, local business and industry have loaned top executives to review school district management practices cooperatively (Ritz 1983). The work of such an advisory committee resulted in reported savings of $8 million in the Detroit City Schools.

Donation of Goods. Some public school districts have made an organized effort to receive donations of goods from the business community. In many cases, this focuses on materials or equipment that are no longer useful to specific businesses or industries but may still be of use to schools for instructional purposes.

The Fall River Public Schools (Massachusetts) has a high level of sustained donations of usable goods. District officials actively promote such donations by involving businesses associated with a training area in the operation of the program.

On a national level, the National Association for the Exchange of Industrial Resources (NAEIR) has been formed to facilitate the donation of goods from industry to school districts (Smith 1983). The NAEIR acts as a broker between the needs of districts and the goods that national businesses wish to make available.

Enterprise Activities

The four categories of enterprise activities include leasing of services or facilities, user payments, sale of school access, and technical arrangements.

Leasing of Services. A number of school districts across the country have been successful in selling food services to private nonprofit organizations or private schools. This has enabled them to reduce the overhead associated with food service production and, therefore, the cost of food service programs to the districts. In several states, school districts can also sell transportation services to public nonprofit organizations or other governmental agencies. This can spread the fixed costs of overhead over a larger volume, thereby reducing the unit cost of production to the district. The Bartlesville Public Schools (Oklahoma), for example, sells data processing services to a small liberal arts college that does not have the funds to install their own computer operation. In the same manner, the Rialto Unified School District (California) sells attendance, accounting, and test-scoring services to three local private schools (Meno 1983).

Leasing of Facilities. With declining enrollment, a new enterprise activity has been developed—the leasing of facilities to various private and public organizations. A number of school districts, such as the Denver City Schools (Colorado), have undertaken a comprehensive plan for leasing surplus space for alternative community uses (Schomp 1980). It has been further suggested that, with declining enrollment, school districts could be converted into total community service centers. This has been partially implemented in the Evanston School District (Illinois) (Burbank 1980).

Another developing concept is the leasing of excess space in school buildings to community-based organizations, not for direct revenue but in exchange for services to be provided to the school population and neighborhood, such as family and personal counseling. This has recently been initiated in the Santa Barbara (California) School District (Council of Educational Facilities Planners 1980).

With decreasing enrollments, several districts are also leasing total school buildings to private enterprises for a profit. These include a credit union in the Southfield Public Schools (Michigan) and a dating service in the Hazelwood School District (Missouri) (Meno 1983). In a unique case, the Phoenix Union High School District (Arizona) yearly rents its playing fields and locker facilities to professional sports teams for preseason practice. After expenses, the district makes a $20,000 plus profit.

User Payment. In this activity, the user of a particular service provided by a school district is required to pay for that service. This is accomplished in the form of service charges or service fees. Generally, such charges or fees are implemented in local school districts that have the option, under state or local law, of offering that service, such as swimming instruction or driver education programs.

It is important to note that user fees are not charged for basic education services. However, several states, such as Illinois, Indiana, Iowa, and Wisconsin, allow school districts to charge an annual textbook rental fee. Further, districts in Alabama, Kansas, and North Carolina charge a fee for elective courses such as those in the advanced senior year. Other types of fees utilized by school districts include driver education, summer school, locker maintenance, towel rental, student parking, and musical instrument rental fees (Meno 1983).

Sale of School Access. The sale to entrepreneurs of access to school markets is most commonly seen in the sale of advertising space in various school publications. The Wayne Central School District (New York) sells advertising space in its parent and community calendar, which is sent to every resident of the district. The revenue from such advertising pays for the publication of the calendar.

In other school districts, concessions of various types are offered to businesses for a fee. This includes such concessions as student pictures and the operation of vending machines in school district facilities. In the Phoenix Union High School District (Arizona), for example, vendors bid on the right to take student pictures. The bids in the 1982-83 school year amounted to $19,500 for access to the district's 20,000 students.

In the Appleton Area School District (Wisconsin), sale of access to school markets was utilized as a cost-avoidance technique. Approximately ten years ago, the district's school lunch program began to lose money. Since the program was projected to lose $25,000 in the next year, the district leased food-service rights to an outside company who installed vending machines. The project has enabled the district to save $25,000 or more annually and students are still offered the availability of a lunch at school.

Technical Arrangements. These are activities in which school districts operate as private enterprises to gain financial benefit. A newly developing area, based on the present tax law, is the sale/lease-back proposition. In Indiana, district officials have taken a close look at the use of private corporate funds to finance the development of school buildings on a lease-back principle (Brames 1980). The Westerville School District (Ohio) has utilized this process to implement various energy-saving programs. In this case, the company receives a percentage of the energy savings as payment for the capital expenditure.

Shared or Cooperative Activities

Shared or cooperative activities allow local public school districts to work with other governmental agencies, private nonprofit or community-based organizations, colleges or universities, or business and industry in order to share costs.

Cooperative Activities with Higher Education. A number of high school districts are involved in cooperative programs with colleges or universities. In these programs, students are enrolled either part-time or full-time in a local college or university in lieu of certain high school courses. In the Clark County School District (Nevada), for example, vocational students from the district take coursework at the local community college free of charge. Students in the Beloit Public Schools (Wisconsin) are allowed to enroll in courses at a local college on a space-available basis without cost to the student or district. In the Appleton Area School District (Wisconsin), selected seniors may enroll in one course at a local college free of charge in exchange for the college's use of district staff.

A number of other school districts are involved in graduate student internship programs with local universities. The Thornton Township High School District (Illinois) and the Martin County School District (North Carolina) have cooperative relationships with local institutions of higher education that place psychologist interns in the school districts. These interns are given full-time duties at the school district and are supervised by school district personnel. These interns, for the most part, are able to do what a regular employee would perform, and, since the cost of their services is much less, the districts are able to save money. The Chino Unified School District (California) has a similar program for college students in computer programming who take internships in the school district.

The Peoria Public School District (Illinois) shares the personnel and facilities of an occupational center with a local institution of higher learning. This sharing of facilities and personnel significantly reduces the cost of operating the program and increases the quality of the program they are able to provide to students.

Other Governmental Agencies. By far the greatest number of shared activities between school districts and governmental agencies involved the running of local parks and recreation departments. Many of these arrangements included cooperative use and maintenance of playing fields and grounds. While most of these relationships are designed to be fiscally neutral, there are exceptions. The Sacramento City Schools (California) have worked with the Sacramento Area Parks and Recreation Department in cooperative efforts such as joint facility-maintenance programs, joint use of buses, leasing of portions of schools, and joint maintenance and operation of community park pools (Committee for Recreation/Education Cooperation of California 1981).

The Vigo County School District (Indiana) cooperates with the city in operating a nature center. The city and school district split the salary of the naturalist at the center, which is used as an instructional station for the district. In the case of the Merced City School District (California), the school district provides use of the area's fields and grounds to the parks and recreation department. The parks and recreation department then makes a yearly contribution of $15,000 to the district's capital account for improvement of fields and grounds in excess of the district's additional operational costs.

There are also other types of intergovernmental cooperative activities. The Horry County School District (South Carolina) works with the state employment service to obtain daily substitutes in place of its old practice of recruiting its own substitutes. This practice has saved the school district at least one clerical position and the payment of unemployment benefits to substitute teachers who were filing unemployment claims. The Chino Unified School District (California) shares a joint dispatch station for security patrols with the local fire department, thus significantly cutting the district's cost for security. The Hazelwood School District (Missouri) operates a cooperative drug abuse treatment and counseling service with a local hospital. In this arrangement the hospital's outreach program covers the majority of the costs, allowing the district to reduce its expenditures in this area.

Cooperation with Private Nonprofit Organizations. In most school districts, cooperation with nonprofit organizations is for a single purpose or support of a specific program. But an exception to the single-purpose cooperative is the Amador Valley Joint Union High School District (California). In this district, service clubs are working together with the school district in a modified "adopt-a-school" program. Each service club adopts a particular school and tries to help that school by providing additional resources such as equipment, supplies, and volunteers. The Memphis Rotary Club, for example, cooperates with the Memphis Public School System (Tennessee) on a variety of programs. The Sioux Falls School District (South Dakota) encourages youth-serving organizations to use the school facilities free of rent after school hours and on weekends. These organizations, working in cooperation with the school district, have developed a comprehensive master plan for meeting the recreational and after-school programming needs of youth within the community. As a consequence, the district does not have to operate any elementary or junior high after-school programs.

Cooperative Activities with Business and Industry. These activities center on areas where both the school district and the business community, or a specific component of the business community, will benefit by a cooperative program. Two school districts that have developed such cooperative vocational programs are Washington, D.C., and New York City. Washington, D.C., the city schools, General Motors, Control Data Corporation, and the advertising firm of Goldberg and Marchesano and Associates have worked together to develop special vocational and career schools. Over $1 million has been committed by these corporations for the development of an engineering high school, a computer science program, and a communications school. In New York City, the Lower Manhattan Area Program at New York City's Murry Bergtraum High School for Business Careers has developed a school program in business education with the assistance of that area's business community (Vocational Foundation, Inc. 1981).

Several school districts have become involved with business and industry in a wide range of cooperative programming. In Oakland, California, individual city schools have worked with various business and industry interests to develop a wide range of program activities including student tutoring, resource persons, cultural events, clubs, apprenticeship programs, career development, maintenance, incentive awards, and staff development (National School Resources Network 1980). New York City schools have developed a number of cooperative efforts with local business and industry that concentrate on providing students with experience in the realities of preparing for employment, finding a job, and staying employed (Institute for Educational Development 1969). Activities include work/study, job placement, career guidance, basic skill training, remedial education, and curriculum development. The Detroit Public School System has undertaken a cooperative plan to encourage the business community to become involved with the public schools (Jefferson 1979). This program includes apprenticeships, career development programs, career information, counselor intern programs, preemployment training, drafting cooperatives, industrial orientation programs, school-to-employment transition counseling, and student internship programs.

Two school districts where the school/business cooperative relationship has been formalized are located in Missouri and Pennsylvania. In the Pittsburgh area, the Alleghany Conference for Community Development was designed for the purpose of supporting the Pittsburgh Public Schools (Schergens 1982). Its efforts have resulted in a number of successful cooperative ventures. The St. Louis (Missouri) City Schools have developed a cooperative partnership with fifty-five community businesses for the purpose of expanding program options for the city's youth (St. Louis Public Schools 1981).

A significant number of school districts are now involved with business and industry in cooperative work/study opportunities for their students. In this arrangement, students are enrolled in classes related to their part-time work at a training station and earn credit for their on-the-job experience. Programs are generally offered in distributive education, office occupations, home economics, and occupations related to food service. The number of students enrolled and the supervision required are key factors in calculating the costs or savings of this activity.

The Griffin-Spaulding County School District (Georgia) has a cooperative program with a local chamber of commerce called "Future Stock." The program is designed to increase communication between the school and community, expand educational opportunities for students in using community resources, increase business and industry involvement in the schools, and provide volunteer services to the schools. The program is governed by a steering committee of twelve members, six of whom are selected by the chamber of commerce and six by the board of education. The program has been in operation for three years and both district officials and industry representatives report that it is highly successful in meeting the program's objectives.

In the Bartlesville Public Schools (Oklahoma), the district has agreed to participate with a local beverage company in a unique program in which the district allows the company to use their name in a promotional activity. Their motto is "Boost Bartlesville." The advertisement encourages people to buy beverages distributed by the company to help support the schools. Fifty cents for every case of the product sold during the month goes to the public schools. The district realizes $20,000 to $30,000 annually, which is applied to general district expenses.

RESEARCH ON NONTRADITIONAL FINANCING METHODS (NTFM)

Despite the above-mentioned activities in the areas of nontraditional financing methods, only one comprehensive study has been undertaken to determine the types of activity in present practice and the present or potential impact of them on school districts. This study, "An Examination of the Types of Non-traditional Financing Methods and Their Present and Potential Impact on Public School Districts" (Meno 1983), reviews the NTFM activities of fifty-nine national school districts, selected at random, and yields some significant findings.

Potential of NTFM Activity in Revenue Development and Cost Avoidance

The 1983 study shows that, in the districts studied, NTFM activity can be highly effective in developing new revenues and avoiding or shifting expenditures. The study reveals that an organized effort to implement NTFMs could potentially result in a 9 percent positive budget impact by a district that is not presently employing any NTFM activity.

While the study reveals that no single district was experiencing this level of positive fiscal impact, neither was any sampled district undertaking an organized, systematic attempt to exploit the full range of NTFM activity. Quite to the contrary, most districts' efforts were reactive to immediate budgetary problems and contained no central focus. This was compatible with the study's preliminary finding of a relationship between perceived level of fiscal stress and level of NTFM activity.

Limitations on Implementation of NTFM Activity

A number of factors inhibit the implementation and constrain the growth of NTFM activities. First, administrators and community members interviewed in the study almost unanimously expressed the belief that public schools should not be involved in profitmaking activities or be in competition with the private sector. District administrators consistently rejected the term "profit" when used to describe the result of an activity that would be described as "profit" in the private sector. This no-profit mentality over public schools provides an explanation of why the enterprise activities reported were so constrained. In many cases, these activities were camouflaged as public-service activities, such as the sale of meals to private nonprofit organizations.

Second, there is a belief among public school administrators that public schools should be free schools. Even in those districts that charged student-user fees, a vast majority of those interviewed expressed concern about the practice. The prevailing feeling was that such fees constrained participation and would, therefore, be inappropriate if there were any other way to fund the activity or program. There was universal agreement that the fees should not be charged for the basic instructional program, but the definition of basic instructional program was not uniform. Meno, therefore, concludes that belief in the provision of a free public education by educational administrators will constrain, at least to a degree, the growth of some types of NTFM activities.

Third, utilization of NTFM activities, especially the donation and cooperative types, will require an increase in the sharing of public school governance, at least in the broad sense of the term. The study's findings convey the clear impression that donation and cooperative NTFM activities are not to be implemented without a price to the district. Second-party members support these activities because the activities also enable them to meet their goals. In the districts studied, special-interest groups such as colleges, businesses, and service clubs cooperated with school districts in activities that specifically resulted in perceived benefits to them. This can be mutually beneficial when their goals are compatible with the purpose of public schools. However, the range of mutual compatibility is not unlimited and, in some areas, severely constrained. Conceptually, this should provide natural limits for the expansion of activities in this area, but the boundaries are not yet clear.

Fourth, the changing structure of our society limits the development of NTFM activities. As the American family has changed from the two-parent family with the wife as homemaker to one with markedly increased female participation in the workforce, fewer mothers are available for school volunteer activity. This nonavailability severely constrains the extent of volunteer activity reported in numerous districts studied.

Development of Successful NTFM Activity

NTFM activity cannot be developed in isolation. If the community is to play a financial role in public school operation beyond providing tax support, the community will have to be allowed greater overall participation in the schools. The two districts in the study with the highest level of NTFM activity success reported that this success was a result of an organized attempt to involve the community in traditional revenue development and overall district operation, rather than specific NTFM activity. Understanding and knowledge of the workings of the school district, not guarded secrecy, create an environment in which donation and cooperative NTFM activity are more likely to take place. Therefore, the first step in implementing NTFM development could well be the systematic increase of community involvement in school district operation.

Multisector Public School Operation

Public schools have always been viewed as operating in the public sector, that is, to provide public services. In recent years, however, public schools appear to be having increased difficulty funding all of their activities through traditional tax-supported methods. As reported in Meno's study, districts are engaging in a number of NTFM activities and the trend appears to be increasing. In some cases, districts are employing activities more closely aligned with the private sector in that they sell specific services or goods for a profit.

Further, districts are also involved in what Weisbrod (1977) describes as third-sector private nonprofit activity. These are activities that cannot be clearly identified as providing common goods, but rather benefit a substantial group of less than a majority. Increased NTFM activity may signal the movement of public schools from a single-sector to a multisector operation in order to respond to the increased heterogeneity of district population and the increased scope and type of community expectations.

Under this conceptualization, the public-sector operation of public schools supported by tax revenues would become more constrained and include only those areas clearly providing for the public good. Other activities that are less clearly placed in the public domain would be supported through NTFM activities by those in the community that value or require the service. In order to support these activities, school districts would employ private nonprofit and private-sector behaviors to provide a viable construct for viewing the fiscal strain, the tax limitation movement, and the growth of a NTFM activity dynamic.

Level of NTFM Activity Potential across Districts

An important question to be considered is whether the fiscal impact potential of NTFM activities is equal across school districts. If it is found to be unequal, will it alleviate or aggravate existing disparities in school district funding? The 1983 study finds significant differences between districts in NTFM activity potential in specific activity areas. For example, in districts serving predominantly poor populations, user fees have less fiscal impact potential than districts with well-to-do populations. Districts that have universities or industries within their boundaries have a higher potential for cooperative activities. Districts with foundation headquarters in or nearby to the district appear to have a better opportunity of receiving grants for their schools. These disparities in activity type were apparent in the data compiled.

However, Meno's data were not adequate to determine whether such disparities are holding true across the total plain of NTFM activity. This is not surprising since the study was designed to identify existing NTFM activity, not overall fiscal impact potential. Certainly, the study revealed a wide disparity of fiscal impact on the districts studied—from $1.57 to $76.57 per student enrolled in the district. However, whether this is a result of differentiated district NTFM potential, district leadership, or yet to be identified limitations, was not determined by this study.

It should be noted, however, that even in the case where NTFM potential fiscal impact was inversely related to traditional funding wealth, the theoretical 9 percent fiscal impact identified in this study as potentially available from NTFM activity would not be adequate to overcome present disparities in school district funding. While it can be stated that the fiscal impact of NTFM activity has the potential for generally improving school districts' finances, its impact on existing disparities in school funding is unclear.

IMPLICATIONS FOR EDUCATIONAL ADMINISTRATION

Nontraditional financing methods have significant implications for the educational administration profession. The first implication is that practitioners will need, to a greater extent than ever before, to internalize the basic mission of public education. In the past, external controls have been imposed to assure appropriate public education and public-sector practices. With the growth of NTFM activity, many of the old rules and traditions of public education will be modified or changed. Educational administrators will have to answer to a multitude of matters and yet retain the essential elements of the public school mission. It will be necessary for preservice and inservice programs to provide, through rational thought, the purposes and goals of public education. Otherwise, NTFM activity could become a vehicle for dismantling public education instead of a valuable tool in maintaining its continued viability.

Second, educational administrators will have to formulate new guidelines for appropriate practices, where there are presently none, if increased NTFM activity does signal a movement by school districts into multisector operation. Educators will have to give careful consideration to the reasonable limits that should be placed on NTFM activities so that these activities remain appropriate and productive for public education. For example, if it is going to become common practice for districts to allow the use of their names in product promotion, what guidelines should be utilized for determining product appropriateness?

Third, educational administrators will have to develop new skills in order to exploit the potential of NTFM activity effectively. The successful implementation of donor, enterprise, and cooperative NTFM activity will require many new and different skills and levels of understanding. Operating an activity for a profit, fund raising in the donor market, and cooperative activities with business and industry are not typical activities in present educational administrative practice. If the trend of increasing NTFM activity continues, educational administrators will have to be trained in taking the best advantage of this potential.

THE NEED FOR ADDITIONAL NTFM STUDY

There are a number of areas where further study of NTFM is needed. But in order to examine the relative fiscal impact between districts for NTFM activities, an accurate method of comparison must be developed that will provide a measurement of degree of impact. Net impact as a percentage of total budget is not accurate enough. The composition of local school district budgets varies significantly from state to state in that some include fringe benefits, salaries, and other items, while in other districts these expenditures are reflected in the state budget. This means that school district budgets reflect, to varying degrees, an accurate picture of actual per-student educational costs and expenditures. Since all districts utilize similar methods for determining total student enrollment, per-student fiscal impact appears in dollars by the reported student enrollment. A suggested starting point for further research would be the testing of this costing logic to determine its limitations, if any.

While a reasonable effort was made in Meno's study to validate the accuracy of reports from districts, data was generally accepted as valid and accurate unless obviously contradictory. In some cases, official's reports were based on estimates of level of activity and fiscal impact. This was particularly true in activities such as indirect donations (support organizations), donation of goods, and cooperative efforts with private nonprofit organizations. It would be a productive field of inquiry to undertake a detailed study of one or more districts to determine the discrepancies, if any, between reported and actual levels of NTFM activity and fiscal impact.

Inherent in NTFM activity are negative consequences to traditional concepts of school board control and school district governance. As NTFM activity grows, educators will have to make decisions on whether or not the fiscal benefits of certain NTFM activities are worth the potential damage or modification to present practices of school district governance. Research designed to identify the specific school district governance consequences of each type of NTFM activity is needed to enable educational administrators to make intelligent use of NTFM potential.

CONCLUSION

With increased national attention being paid to the performance of public schools and the resulting expectations for increased school programming without corresponding increases in tax-supported funding, school districts will feel increasing fiscal stress. These are exactly the conditions that encourage the growth of NTFM activity. Nontraditional funding methods hold both significant promise as an additional revenue resource as well as numerous possible negative consequences. The growth and accompanying impact of NTFMs will merit close monitoring by educators over the next decade.

REFERENCES

Brames, Fred. 1980. "School Building Construction through Private Funds in a Small School District." Paper presented at the Annual Meeting of the Association of School Business Officials, New Orleans, Louisiana, October, pp. 1-7.

Burbank, C. William. 1980. "What to Do with Surplus School Space." *American School & University* 52, no. 6 (February): 36-38.

Committee for Recreation/Education Cooperation of California. 1981. *Let's Cooperate II—The Costs and Benefits of Cooperation Between Recreation/Park and Education Agencies.* Sacramento, California.

Council of Educational Facility Planners. 1980. "An Interesting Proposal." *CEFP News and Views* (July): 10.

Institute for Educational Development. 1969. *Partnership High School—The Search for New Ways to Cooperate*, Industry and Education Study No. 2. (October), pp. 1-44. New York: IED.

Jefferson, Arthur. 1979. *New Directions for Business, Labor and Education: Programs in Operation 1978-79* (October), pp. 1-22. Detroit: Detroit Public Schools.

Maeroff, Gene I. 1982. "Schools Seek Private Funds." *New York Times* (November 9): p. C1.

Meno, Lionel R. 1983. "An Examination of the Types of Non-Traditional Financing Methods and Their Present and Potential Impact on Public School Districts." Ph.D. dissertation, University of Rochester.

National School Resources Network. 1980. "School Community Cooperation: Oakland's Adopt-a-School Program." *Technical Assistance Bulletin* (January), pp. 1-4. Washington, D.C.: NSRN.

Ritz, Joseph R. 1983. "Reville Taps Panel to Probe Management of City Schools." *Buffalo Evening News* (February 6): Section 7, p. 2.

St. Louis Public Schools. 1981. "New Programs Expand Options, Promote Integration." *School & Home* (May/June).

Schergens, Becky. 1982. "Business and Schools Form a Fruitful Alliance." *Enterprise Magazine* (June): 24-25.

Schomp, Katherine. 1980. "Use It, Sell It or Lease It—What To Do With an Old School." *1980 National School Boards Association Annual Convention Review* Clinic E-77 (April). Washington, D.C.: NSBA.

Scott, Charles. 1979. *A Guide to the Community Resources Information Bank 1979-80.* King of Prussia, Pennsylvania: Upper Menon Area School District.

Smith, Norbert C. 1983. *National Association for Exchange of Industrial Resources.* Northfield, Illinois: The Exchange.

Vocational Foundation, Inc. 1981. "New York City Lower Manhattan Business Community Helps Design Magnet School for Business Careers." *You and Youth* 3, no. 11 (November): 1-8.

Weisbrod, Burton A. 1977. *The Voluntary Nonprofit Sector.* Lexington, Massachusetts: Lexington Books.

7 INSURANCE AND RISK MANAGEMENT
Trends in Asset Protection and Fiscal Efficiency

Bettye MacPhail-Wilcox

During the last ten years, risk management has evolved from a simplistic notion of procuring, managing, and protecting insurance policies to a much more sophisticated and technically complex process. The responsibilities and options associated with the current concept of risk management have expanded in response to the need to do more with less. The resulting changes in school business practices promise to improve fiscal operational efficiencies, the quality of the work environment, and employee goodwill.

A study of insurance management in 104 Virginia school systems suggests that knowledge and skill in risk management among school business executives is distressingly inadequate (Sweeney 1978). In fact, a study sponsored by the Association of School Business Officials supports contentions that practices in property appraisal, planning the district insurance package, and the use of alternative risk management strategies actually jeopardized effective risk management in school districts (Moyer and Bartages 1977).

As practices associated with comprehensive risk management are diffused and operating costs continue to strain instructional budgets, school business executives must acquire a wider range of skills associated with planning, analyzing, procuring, economizing, and optimizing cash flow. Professional development activities and higher education training programs for school business officials must provide better risk management training if schools are to contain the costs protecting district assets without siphoning dollars from instructional budgets.

Although school districts must contend with a wide range of risk exposures related to property, various forms of liability, and criminal activities, the purpose of this chapter is not to review the major categories of risk exposure in school operations.[1] Rather, the chapter will review problems and changes in risk management that have important implications for school districts and school business officials. An expanded concept of risk management will be introduced and used as a basis for discussing prominent strategies in handling school district risk exposures. Within this framework, emerging trends in school risk management and the insurance industry that are likely to become stable practices in the 1980s are capsuled.

AN EXPANDED CONCEPT OF RISK MANAGEMENT

A number of concurrent forces are providing the impetus for more creative and comprehensive approaches to risk management in school administration. Among these are the rising costs of insurance and related services, extraordinarily inflated and rapidly changing replacement costs, reduced levels of funding, and fear of default in long-standing systems such as social security. The drive for efficiency in the insurance industry also has served to stimulate change. Deregulation, consolidation of types of coverage offered, more efficient data processing, and stiff competition among independents and large insurance companies are but a few of the forces affecting the industry, and subsequently, the schools (Hill 1983: 10-20).

Earlier definitions of risk management hinged on transferring the effects of loss to an institution other than the school district, usually an insurance underwriter. More recently, alternatives to insurance have been applied to reducing the probability of loss and the economic burden of protection from loss. These alternatives include risk avoidance, loss prevention and control, and retention of risk or some portion of it. A comprehensive risk management program will include all of these risk management strategies. The management of risk currently demands substantially more expertise of school business officials in risk analysis and treatment than it did previously. Today, the focus extends beyond procuring insurance coverage to conserving district assets and generating income for the school district by controlling losses from pure risks and optimizing cash flow.

Effective risk management requires commitment, analysis, evaluation, and treatment. These activities are continuous in that the entire risk management program is constantly evaluated for efficiency and effectiveness. Yet, many local school districts do not have a risk philosophy, nor do they have a systematic process for discovering risk, evaluating risk exposures, or selecting the appropriate tools or strategies to be used in dealing with each risk. In the main, many treat risk by renewing insurance contracts annually, some of which are unnecessary, and attempting to negotiate lower premiums with the same carrier. Practices such as these, in conjunction with relying on the sole advice of a few insurance agents, prevent school districts from enjoying the advantages of an increasingly competitive insurance market.

Commitment

A comprehensive risk management plan requires that the local board of education develop a risk management philosophy along a continuum anchored by aversion and tractability. The philosophy should incorporate considerations of legal requirements affecting risk management in the school district, fiscal conditions in the school district, and satisfaction with current risk control strategies. Legal considerations, for example, specify whether coverage of certain kinds of risks and strategies are mandatory, prohibited, or permissive. These mandates should be incorporated into a statement of commitment to a set of risk management objectives for the district. Other considerations include the amount of risk a district is willing or able to retain by covering losses from operating funds or reserve funds.

The role of school business executives in the development of a district risk philosophy is critical. They must act investigatively to identify all risk exposures in the school district and evaluate less experience as well as less potential. They must then develop a comprehensive plan of risk treatment from a pool of possible strategies that seem to change monthly in number and completion.

Discovery

Regardless of the risk management philosophy of the district, a thorough audit of risk exposures should be conducted and presented to the board. These risk exposures, in combination with legal demands or constraints, trends in risk expenditures, and losses within and outside the district, provide the substance for analyzing loss potential from various perils and hazards.

Identification of risk exposures can be facilitated by the use of historical records, insurance policy checklists, risk analysis questionnaires, flow charts of district operations, the analysis of financial statements, systematic onsite inspections, and the like (Athearn 1981: 28; Vaughn 1982: 37-38). Some districts suggest that consultants, insurance agents, brokers, and advisory committees be used as resources in the identification of manifest and latent risk exposures (Lenz 1982: Rakich 1982).

Risk Evaluation

When risks have been identified, potential losses resulting from each must be evaluated in terms of magnitude and probability. The severity of loss is usually approximated on the basis of cash and replacement values. It is strongly recommended that professional appraisals be used to establish property values. In practice, risk managers must ensure that property is neither undervalued or overvalued. For example, errors in valuation related to the use of overly simplistic measures like square feet in a building, are not uncommon. Neither are errors of omission and depreciation in property schedules.[2] Both can be costly to the school district.

The probability of loss is based on an analysis of the frequency of loss reflected in historical records or statistics for similar school districts. Data pertaining to the magnitude and probability of potential losses, as well as legal considerations, should be used to construct criteria by which risk exposures can be prioritized. This stage of the planning process leads directly to a systematic consideration of alternative risk management strategies.

Risk Management Strategies

The tools for dealing with known risks include avoidance, loss prevention and control, retention, and transfer. Avoidance requires the separation of the school district from the risk. This might entail prohibiting or curtailing certain activities, substituting plexiglass for glass, restricting access to certain areas or kinds of equipment, as well as eliminating various activities or kinds of equipment from the curriculum (Natale 1981).

Loss prevention and control strategies are aimed at reducing the probability of loss or minimizing the severity of loss. Efforts to reduce loss may include, for example, the installation of burglary alarms and sprinkler systems. The "engineering approach" to loss control focuses on the removal of hazards from the environment and encompasses such activities as clearing grounds of unsafe hazards. The "human approach" to the control of risk exposures often takes the form of training employees and clients in matters pertaining to safety and hazard awareness. The increasing incidence of civil rights and malpractice suits, for example, suggests that intense training in due process and knowledge of both the legislation and litigation surrounding it can reduce professional liability claims like those described by Gander (1982).

Both loss prevention and control strategies are used to curb financial loss, improve the work environment, and encourage insurers to lower premiums. Control strategies are viewed even more positively by insurers when they are accompanied by a systematic plan of inspection, review, correction, and training (Hester 1981; Rakich 1983).

Risk retention strategies require the district to assume all or some part of the burden of potential losses. This area of risk management has gained substantial prominence as rising insurance costs cut into the fiscal resources of school districts. As of 1979, nineteen states had adopted legislation enabling newer techniques of risk retention, and twenty-six had abolished sovereign immunity for the state or enacted a torts claim act.[3] One result of these activities is that many school districts can now create insurance reserves (Natale 1981: 151).

Generally, risk retention techniques are used when expected losses over a period of time are small relative to the cost of insurance and can be predicted with a reasonable degree of certainty. They often take the form of "no insurance," large deductibles, coinsurance, self-insurance, stop-loss coverage, "unbundling," "pooling," or some combination of these. Trends in the adoption of each of these techniques by schools will be described in the next section of this chapter.

Risk management strategies that rely on shifting the financial burden of risk through contractual agreements are known as transfer techniques. Surety bonds, subcontracting, and insurance are common examples of transfer strategies. Risks can be transferred only if they are pure risks.

Pure risks differ from speculative risks in that they are insurable and the probability of loss is not under the control of the insured. Rather, the probability of loss is based on large numbers of homogeneous exposures to the same period. Potential losses are calculable and unlikely to affect all of the insured simultaneously. Hence, the probability of loss from pure risk can be approximated. If a risk exposure does not meet these criteria, it is uninsurable on the basis of economic feasibility.[4]

When environmental conditions and hazards enhance the severity and susceptibility to peril, transfer of risk is often recommended. The school business official should consider this treatment when the following conditions prevail: (1) catastrophic exposures to loss exist, and the cost of protection relative to loss is low; (2) risk potential is unpredictable, and the district wishes or is required to level the risk over a period of years; and (3) services, like claims processing or program administration, can be handled more cost efficiently and satisfactorily by an agency other than the school district (Revzan 1983: 35).

Webb (1979) has translated these warning conditions into a set of useful principles. If a loss can be financially devastating, it should be transferred regardless of the probability. A mistake made by some risk managers is to confuse the fact that the probability is remote with the financial catastrophe that would result should the loss occur. A second principle, based on the odds of loss, has important implications for the cost of coverage. Since insurance companies profits are based on average probabilities, high probabilities of loss will not be transferred economically. In such cases, school districts are urged to adopt loss prevention and control activities that may make coverage less costly (Vaughn 1982: 40-43).

Another principle requires the comparison of the cost of services from an external agency with the cost of the same services if provided within the school district. The efficiency and personalization of claims administration can affect employee and community goodwill, a factor of no small consequence in times of bad press and low morale.

CURRENT TRENDS IN RISK RETENTION

Retention strategies currently receiving substantial attention include "no insurance," coinsurance, the assumption of larger deductibles, stop-loss coverage, self-insurance, and "pooling." Each has the potential for saving the district money, and some have the potential for generating extra dollars for instruction or other aspects of operations.

"No insurance" is the riskiest retention strategy. In essence, the school district retains liability for financial losses. They are treated as daily business risks and covered out of operating funds or reserves. Selection of this strategy should be based on a careful historical assessment of school district losses and similar data for comparable school districts. When funds are not held in reserve, the decision not to insure should be limited to risk exposures small enough to be absorbed from operating budgets. Generally speaking, this strategy would only be viable in very large or wealthy school districts (Westran 1962).

Coinsurance, a method of spreading the risk between the insurer and the insured has gained in popularity. Generally, a reduced rate is offered in exchange for the individual insured to cover a percentage of the total claim. For example, a 20 percent coinsurance plan on some medical packages requires that the individual pay 20 percent of the approved cost of services.

Risk retention through large deductibles is similar to "no insurance" and coinsurance in that the insured party retains a part of each net loss. With deductibles, losses accrue to a fixed dollar amount before the coverage provided by the policy is invoked. Coinsurance often accompanies a deductible provision and provides that the insured will retain a percentage of each net loss. Both strategies hinge on the insurance principle of avoiding first-dollar coverage, and both can yield substantially lower premiums for coverage.

Stop-loss coverage is a risk management strategy that in principle amounts to acquiring an individual or aggregate deductible large enough to cover risk exposures that are undesirable or devastating beyond a certain level. Small school districts or groups with less claim certainty should consider individual stop-loss coverage, while large districts should consider aggregate stop-loss coverage. If risk aversion is high, both should be considered.

Stop-loss coverage is often used in conjunction with self-insurance plans to limit the maximum amount of loss possible given an unforeseen catastrophe or in the early stages of developing self-insuring capacity. It is patterned after the reinsurance strategy used by private agencies who cede part of the risk they have underwritten to another company in order to protect themselves from devastating losses. This enables them to underwrite particularly large amounts of coverage that they might otherwise be unable to handle.

Basic considerations in adopting the above strategies include the amount of loss that a school district can afford from operating or reserve funds relative to the probability of loss and the overhead and adjustment costs to the insurer. It makes little sense to pay for first-dollar coverage for minor school bus damages when the district has a fully staffed garage capable of such repairs. Likewise, first-dollar coverage on roof leaks or other small maintenance jobs is not necessary in a district with a fully staffed maintenance department. In such cases, coverage is economically inefficient.

Without a comprehensive definition of self-insurance, each of the foregoing retention strategies might be classified as a type of self-insurance. However, the concept of self-insurance that has emerged as a trend in school business affairs refers to the process in which the district provides its own insurance rather than transferring the risk to a private insurer. The usual practice is to divert a predetermined annual appropriation into a fund that accumulates both principal and interest. The practice continues until the fund is sufficiently large to cover those risk exposures that are to be phased out of commercial insurance coverage. When the fund is stable and has a healthy reserve, premiums can be reduced, or in some cases eliminated, and excess dollars can be diverted to other aspects of district operations.

Self-insurance as an alternative retention strategy for school districts hinges foremost on whether, and under what conditions, the state law permits it. Other salient factors that school business officials should consider include: local school board and employee support; the magnitude of the spread of risk within the district; comparability of coverage by category of risk exposure; the likelihood of multiple losses resulting from geographic proximity; the order in which various risk exposures will be transferred to the self-insurance plan; the probability and magnitude of future losses; strategies for covering losses that would be devastating to the fund; and district ability to maintain the fund at adequate financial levels (Candoli et al. 1978: 263-277).

In planning for self-insurance, costs other than claims must be considered. Administrative, collection, publicity, inspection, and audit expenses, as well as protection for new acquisitions and renovations, should not be overlooked. The numerous factors that must be considered make it wise to conduct a thorough feasibility study with a reputable company specializing in assembling self-insurance coverage before instituting such a program.

"Pooling," or spreading the risk in order to take advantage of the law of averages, is a strategy closely related to the conceptual basis on which insurance companies operate. In practice, groups of small school districts pool resources for protecting themselves against devastating risk exposures.

Operational Self-Insurance and Pooling Programs

The popularity of self-insurance for school districts is most evident in the areas of workers' compensation, health insurance, and property damage. Important considerations pertinent to operating programs of self-insurance in each of these areas are described in the following text.

Self-insurance of workers' compensation plans has paid handsome dividends to numerous school districts. Meneffe and Keenan (1980) report an immediate 20 percent savings in administrative costs and overhead for self-insured school districts in California. Participating districts experienced a bonus in expeditious and personalized services and have a net 5 to 15 percent savings on claims payments. Meneffe and Keenan also report that personalization associated with self-insured school districts reduced employee inclination to abuse insurance claims and improved the quality and quantity of information reported by witnesses.

In a study of self-insured industries, Hunt (1979) identifies additional unexpected benefits from self-insurance programs. He observes fewer compensation claims litigated among self-insured industries than among those who contracted for insurance, and he also notes shorter durations of disability among self-insured industries. Both would offer additional benefits to school districts.

Some districts in California, Pennsylvania, and New York have pooled resources to provide self-insurance for workers' compensation. Menefee and Keenan (1980) have suggested that districts with less than $200,000 in annual premiums for workers' compensation join a pool. The authors contend that pools can be economically operated with a group of districts having approximately $500,000 in total premiums. Participant districts contribute 80 to 90 percent of their usual annual premium initially. Over time, pools are able to declare dividends or reduce premiums paid by members.

One such pooling assignment was put in operation among nineteen Pennsylvania school districts in 1979. Each district pays 10 percent of an amount determined by the district size, payroll, and loss record to a Claims Service Organization that in turn pays compensation losses. Each district is billed monthly to cover the cost of claims up to the amount of exposure that each district retains. Beyond this level, claims are paid from a Central Fund created by district contributions based on payroll and loss experiences. Accounting and legal fees, surety bonds, and other operational costs also are paid from the Central Fund. Stop-loss coverage is purchased to cover claims in excess of $5 million. In addition to realizing approximately 20 percent savings in the first year, districts have acquired cash-flow advantages that were otherwise unobtainable. Savings and investments promise additional savings as premiums are reduced in response to Central Fund growth (Palley Simon Associates 1980).

In New York, a workmens' compensation pool that began in 1970 with sixteen school districts, in 1979 expanded to provide a self-insured health benefits plan (Spataro 1981). In addition to savings and earnings, benefits of this plan included the districts' ability to design unique health benefits packages. The major disadvantage reported is the amount of time required to administer such self-funded programs.

Positive reports similar to those attributed to pooling arrangements for workers' compensation have been made by school districts operating life and health self-insurance programs. One Pennsylvania district instituted a plan in which state-mandated budget funds for annual sick leave (sick pay, substitute teachers, and income protection insurance) were invested and allowed to accumulate in a special fund. As a result, costs for the same protection dropped from $42,000 over three years to $400 per year (Stubbs 1975). Similar savings were reported by Gara (1974) for a life and health insurance plan in a school district of 7,600 students. The two forms of coverage were combined to reduce administrative costs, and the district acted as the underwriter while accepting bids for claims administration. Purchase of a life insurance policy that did not require high reserves led to cash savings of $200,000.

An Illinois school district cut administrative claims overhead in half by implementing a medical self-insurance programs (Jenkins 1980). The district opted for a third-party claims administrator who has improved coordination of benefits between multiple insurers to yield $100,000 annually from other primary insurers on certain cases. The plan was so profitable that premium increases were unnecessary for the first four years of operation.

In California, Delsol (1980) reports a plan similar to that in Illinois. The program earned the district interest, provided lower and more stable costs for coverage, and gave dollar rebates to employees who stayed well. The plan provided for the purchase of a high deductible policy for individual claims exceeding $500. First-dollar coverage up to $500 is provided by a district-administered program in which unused funds accrue to each employee on an annual basis. These accumulations are retained until such time as the employee leaves the district. When this occurs they are given a check for accumulated unused coverage as severance pay, and the district retains the interest earned during the accumulation period.

Though the magnitude of savings resulting from this "stay-well" plan of self-insurance has been criticized, the fact that it can save dollars for the district and provide additional revenue for the district has not been disputed (Harroun 1980). In fact, criticism of the plan can be used to guide the analysis of economic efficiency associated with self-insurance. For example, as Harroun has noted, savings can be effected only if the dollars spent for self-insurance are less than the dollars spent for standard insurance or if self-insurance generates dollars that would otherwise not have been available. Harroun also has cautioned administrators to consider the probability of liability suits resulting from withholding interest earnings on employee funds and encouraging employees to ignore first-dollar health problems in order to gain financially.

It should be noted that such analyses of economic efficiency as those advanced by Harroun do not account for quantifying non-economic benefits such as employee good-will. Self-insurance plans seem to pay handsomely in cases of good-will. For example, the medical self-insurance plan adopted in Florida's Lee County school district has been very positively received by both employee and hospital accountants (Klein 1980). Both groups praised the reduction in red tape and increased efficiency in payment that accompanied the self-insurance plan. The first year of operations saved the 29,370 pupil district $500,000 in claims, which were processed by a local insurance agency. Stop-loss coverage is used as a safety net for protecting the fund solvency. In order to protect the fund from inflation, a 10 percent premium increase was approved by the local school board for the second year of operation.

Throughout the various plans reported, it is evident that some of the traditional insurance services and coverages can be a part of a self-insurance plan. The strategy of separating and assigning various aspects of the insuring process to different entities is known as "unbundling." When services and coverage are unbundled, some services can be provided by established insurance companies, others by contract with specialty firms, and others can be retained and provided by the school district (Jenkins 1980). Companies that specialize in providing a limited range of services or coverage have proliferated as a result of competition and the attendant drive toward specialization.

The savings that this strategy can effect are most evident among school districts electing to handle their own claims administration program. Rakich (1982) reports that as much as 40 to 50 percent of the overhead and management costs associated with comprehensive contract insurance can be saved by districts that perform the tasks usually covered as overhead expenses in insurance contracts. Meneffe and Keenan (1980) find that California school districts obtained more personalized claims administration for approximately 5 percent of previous costs by contracting with a specialty firm. Regardless of whether districts use "unbundling" as a part of a self-insurance plan or as a bidding strategy, they should take extra care to guard against duplicating coverage on the same risk exposure. Standardized insurance contracts make this an easy mistake, thereby negating the economic efficiency gained by "unbundling."

Traditional insurance services also can be combined with the "pooling" concept described earlier in this chapter. Large school districts can use a cost-center approach for calculating protection needed. This strategy treats particular categories of risk on an actuarial basis. That is, the probability of loss at any one cost center (school site, for example) is spread across the district on some rational and probabilistic basis. This results in the computation of a lump sum of coverage for the district that is based on the probability that occasional large losses are not likely to occur at all sites simultaneously and are as likely to occur at one site as another. A share of the large loss is assigned to each site such that total coverage for an individual site is less than it would have been if only one such exposure existed in the district. While this technique is to some extent appropriate for most exposures, except those that involve catastrophic losses, it appears particularly useful for districts in which there is only a small variation in expected losses over time. The amount of risk that will cover losses in excess of those usually experienced by the entire group is transferred (Larson 1962; Natale 1981: 15).

In several ways, the cost-center strategy reflects the basis of state property programs that are self-insured. South Carolina began operating a state insurance program that included public school buildings in 1900. By 1976, five states were operating related programs. While each state's plan varies in the percentage value of property insured, the types of coverage provided, and whether participation is mandatory or permissive, each has resulted in substantial savings to participating school districts. Hypothetical modeling of state self-insured property plans in other states based on loss-ratio experience indicates that the method would be cost efficient for other states as well. Projected costs appear to undercut private insurance rates and eventually reduce or discontinue premium payments (Brown 1976).

Summarily, school districts that seek to self-insure some portion of pure risk related to workers' compensation, life and health insurance, or property coverage stand to improve economic efficiency. They also gain increased revenues from fund investment and accumulation that can be used to defray operating costs or can be shifted to instructional functions. Careful and comprehensive planning with the appropriate use of stop-loss coverage, unbundling, and pooling can enhance the efficiency and effectiveness of self-insurance programs of risk management.

CURRENT TRENDS IN THE TRANSFER OF RISK

If protection from risk exposures is not possible through avoidance, control reduction, and retention, risks are subject to transfer. When risks are shifted to an insurance underwriter, a contractual agreement insulates the district from devastating losses.

Because the transfer of risk has become more complex with ever-increasing policy nuances and a highly competitive market, it is advisable to seek assistance with this form of risk management. Brokers can be contracted to negotiate, plan contracts, or conduct feasibility studies. Historically, these specialists have been paid a percentage of the premium; however, a more recent trend is to pay on a fee-for-service basis. Though some states prohibit retainment of brokers, insurance placement boards of professional organizations such as the Public Risk Insurance Management Association, the Insurance Institute of America, or the Risk Management Society can provide useful information about insurance to school business officials. The information provided can be used for planning comprehensive approaches to risk management that will enhance both coverage and savings to school districts.

Operating Transfer Programs

In addition to the techniques of "unbundling" and the purchase of stop-loss coverage described earlier, the transfer of risk is characterized by several other trends. Two of these involve bidding for insurance coverage and the selection of policies with features that allow the district to optimize its cash flow.

"Bidding" insurance has become more common in the last five or ten years. Although many school districts traditionally have obtained coverage from local insurance companies for political reasons, the need for economy in operations has motivated many to adopt a bid process.[5] When using the bidding process, school districts should adopt more comprehensive acceptance criteria than the lowest bid. Service range and reputation, endorsements, conditions, exclusions, and deductions should be studied carefully for utility, economy, and satisfaction (Candoli et al. 1978: 266; Vaughn 1982: 46-48; Rakich 1983: 8-14). Bid specification should be defined well enough to encourage easy comparison across respondents, but loosely enough to allow innovative and cost-saving approaches derived from retentions and cash-flow optimization.

Retrospective ratings and extended payment plans are policy options that can provide improved cash-flow conditions when school districts transfer risk. Reduction in outlays for losses and premiums, combined with extended payment plans, allows more funds to be invested for longer periods of time.

Some companies now base premiums on incurred losses such that the insured pays an amount within a predetermined range that is divided into multiple payments throughout the year. Other companies with similar packages base premiums on fixed administrative costs and losses that the underwriter usually pays. Security for the difference between paid and incurred losses is often required. Overall, these approaches differ in the way administrative costs are handled and the way premiums are collected. These plans, in conjunction with a cash-flow optimization strategy, can earn extra dollars for school districts (Revzan 1983: 39).

SUMMARY AND IMPLICATIONS

Whether school boards and business officials prefer traditional insurance approaches or the more current and comprehensive approaches to risk management, scarce dollars can be conserved and new dollars earned as a result of better risk management practices. Self-insurance can be applied successfully to coverage for workers' compensation, life, health, and property insurance. Unbundled coverage and services, stop-loss coverage, and pooling risks and resources offer the potential for savings, security, and economic efficiencies to large and small school districts alike. As more courts and state legislatures act to discontinue school district immunity, and as insurance costs continue to escalate, school business executives must apply newer concepts and strategies of risk management to acquire reasonable professional liability, casualty, and property protection. Already, such efforts are reported in California (Menefee and Keenan 1980: 16).

Because the cost of insurance depends heavily on the spread of risk and the probability of loss, more states will adopt self-insurance programs for the various risk exposures associated with schools. In the interim, districts will form pools to serve the same purpose.

Local boards that continue a philosophy of strict risk aversion and rely heavily on the transfer of risk also can benefit from the more competitive insurance market that exists today. To do so, they must take advantage of unbundling, bidding, and cash-flow optimization. Lastly, but perhaps most importantly, if risk management programs are to be successful and efficient, school business officials must obtain the training and expertise needed to plan, implement, and oversee such programs.

NOTES TO CHAPTER 7

1. Interested readers are referred to Lloyd E. Rogers (1977) or California State Department of Education (1977).
2. Golz (1980) describes three gross valuation errors: inconsistent valuation procedures, phantom assets, and improperly classified buildings, contents, or exclusions.
3. The number of states was derived from Conley (1980).
4. For more on this and related subjects see Athearn (1981) or Vaughn (1982).
5. Rakich (1983) provides an excellent overview and format for the bidding process.

REFERENCES

Athearn, James L. 1981. *Risk and Insurance.* New York: West Publishing Company.

Brown, Richard, Jr. 1976. "Isn't It Time to Turn Insurance Dollars into Instructional Dollars?" *Journal of Education Finance* 1, no. 3 (Winter): 391–396.

California State Department of Education. 1977. "Administration of the School District Risk Management Program." Sacramento, California: Bureau of Management Services.

Candoli, Carl I.; Walter Hack; John Ray; and Dewey Stollar. 1978. *School Business Administration: A Planning Approach.* Boston: Allyn and Bacon, Inc.

Conley, Dennis. 1980. "Municipal Liability Legislation, 1977, 1978, and 1979." New York: American Insurance Association (May). Mimeo.

Cornelius, Robert. 1981. "Risk Management Needs Hands-On Attention." *Nation's Schools Report* 7, no. 3 (October): 2–3.

Delsol, Louis. 1980. "Self-Insurance Plan." *The School Administrator* 37, no. 9 (October): 7.

Gander, Peggy. 1982. "Protecting Against 'Errors and Omissions' Law Suits." *The School Administrator* 38, no. 9 (October): 1, 18–19.

Gara, Robert. 1974. "Self-Insurance Saves $200,000." *School Business Affairs* 40, no. 1 (January): 15-16.
Golz, William, Jr. 1980. "Minimize the Risk in Risk Management." *School Business Affairs* 46, no. 5 (April): 10-11, 39-40.
Harroun, Leon E. 1980. "The Negative Sides of 'Stay-Well' Insurance." *Executive Educator* 2, no. 12 (December): 19-20.
Hester, Dwight. 1981. "Loss Control: An Effective Management Tool." *School Business Affairs* 47, no. 5 (April): 30-32.
Hill, Thom. 1983. "Insurance Industry Consolidating." *News and Observer*, Raleigh, North Carolina (October 25): pp. D1-D2.
Hunt, Allan. 1979. "Worker's Compensation System in Michigan. A Closed Case Survey." Kalamazoo, Michigan: Upjohn Institute for Employment Research.
Jenkins, Harvey L. 1980. "A Self-Insured Medical Program May Be the Answer." *School Business Affairs* 46, no. 5 (April): 26-29, 33.
Klein, Ken. 1980. "This System Saved a Bundle When It Opted for Self-Insurance." *American School Board Journal* 167, no. 8 (August): 23, 40.
Larson, William A. 1962. "The Actuarial Treatment of Corporate Exposures." In *Identifying and Controlling the Risks of Accidental Loss*, edited by J. Blood, pp. 39-60. New York: American Management Association.
Lenz, Matthew. 1982. "Managing Your Risks." *American School and University* 54, no. 10 (June): 38-42.
Menefee, Gerald R., and John R. Keenan. 1980. "California Schools Save by Self-Insuring." *School Business Affairs* 46, no. 5 (April): 14-16.
Moyer, Ralph W., and Paul Bartages. 1977. "Results of ASBO Risk Management Survey." *School Business Affairs* 43, no. 6 (June): 139-141.
Natale, Joseph. 1981. "Economics In School Insurance." *School Business Affairs* 47, no. 5 (April): 14-17.
Palley Simon Associates. 1980. "School Districts Form Association to Fund Self-Insured Worker's Compensation." *School Business Affairs* 46, no. 5 (April): 36.
Rakich, Ronald. 1982. "Risk Management." *The School Administrator* 30, no. 10 (November): 1, 10-13.
Rakich, Ronald. 1983. "Taking the Mystery Out of Insurance Bidding." *The School Administrator* 40, no. 9 (October): 8-14.
Revzan, Henry A. 1983. "The CFO's Perspective on Risk Management." *Financial Executive* 51, no. 11 (November): 33-39.
Rogers, Lloyd E. 1977. *School Business Management Handbook No. 2*. New York: State Education Department, Division of Management Services.
Spataro, Anthony. 1981. "Self-Funded Health Benefits Program: An Idea Whose Time Has Come." *School Business Affairs* 47, no. 5 (April): 35.
Stubbs, Donald R. 1975. "Premium For Sickness-Health Insurance: Zero." *School Business Affairs* 41, no. 6 (June): 135-136.

Sweeney, James. 1978. "Is Your School System Dangerously Under-Insured?" *American School Board Journal* 165, no. 7 (July): 33-34, 41.

Vaughn, Emmett J. 1982. *Fundamentals of Risk and Insurance.* New York: John Wiley and Sons.

Webb, L. Dean. 1979. "Taking the Risk Out of Risk Management." *School Business Affairs* 45, no. 4 (April): 16-17, 40.

Westran, Roy A. 1962. "A Planned No-Insurance Program." In *Identifying and Controlling the Risks of Accidental Loss*, edited by J. Blood, pp. 78-84. New York: American Management Association.

8 PROVIDING, FINANCING, AND MANAGING SCHOOL TRANSPORTATION

Robert Gresham

Since Massachusetts, in 1869, passed legislation that provided transportation services for public school students, transportation has become an essential and growing service of public schools throughout the nation. Both the numbers of students served and the costs of providing such services have continually and dramatically been on the increase.

As shown in Table 8-1, during the 1929-30 school year, 7.4 percent of the public school students were transported at public expense, at a per-student cost of $28.81. During the 1979-80 school year, the percentage of students transported had risen to 57 percent and the cost per student was at $175.83. By 1979-80 the total cost, nationwide, for public school transportation was requiring 4 percent of the total expenditures for public elementary and secondary schools—$3,833,145,000 out of a total of $95,961,561,000 (National Center for Education Statistics 1982). Additionally, while the 1979-80 public school enrollment had decreased by nearly 4,000,000 students from a high of 42.2 million students in 1971-72, the percentage of students transported in 1979-80 was nearly 11 percent higher than the percentage transported in 1971-72.

While the student population has been on the decrease since 1972, projections are for a gradual upturn in student population beginning in about 1985. By 1990, the student population may well be at the level of 1972. At the present percentage of the total number of stu-

Table 8-1. Number and Percent of Public School Pupils Transported at Public Expense and Current Expenditures for Transportation: United States, 1929–30 to 1979–80.

School Year	All Public School Pupils	Pupils Transported at Public Expense — Number	Pupils Transported at Public Expense — Percent of Total	Expenditure of Public Funds — Total, Excluding Capital Outlay (in thousands)	Average Cost per Pupil Transported
1929–30	25,678,015	1,902,826	7.4	$ 54,823	$28.81
1931–32	26,275,441	2,419,173	9.2	58,078	24.01
1933–34	26,434,193	2,794,724	10.6	53,908	19.29
1935–36	26,367,098	3,250,658	12.3	62,653	19.27
1937–38	25,975,108	3,769,242	14.5	75,637	20.07
1939–40	25,433,542	4,144,161	16.3	83,283	20.10
1941–42	24,562,473	4,503,081	18.3	92,922	20.64
1943–44	23,266,616	4,512,412	19.4	107,754	23.88
1945–46	23,299,941	5,056,966	21.7	129,756	25.66
1947–48	23,944,532	5,854,041	24.4	176,265	30.11
1949–50	25,111,427	6,947,384	27.7	214,504	30.88
1951–52[1]	26,562,664	7,697,130	29.0	268,827	34.93
1953–54[2]	25,643,871	8,411,719	32.8	307,437	36.55
1955–56	27,740,149	9,695,819	35.0	353,972	36.51
1957–58	29,722,275	10,861,689	36.5	416,491	38.34
1959–60	32,477,440	12,225,142	37.6	486,338	39.78
1961–62	34,682,340	13,222,667	38.1	576,361	43.59

1963–64	37,405,058	14,475,778	38.7	673,845	46.55
1965–66	39,154,497	15,536,567	39.7	787,358	50.68
1967–68	40,827,965	17,130,873	42.0	981,006	57.27
1969–70	41,934,376	18,198,577	43.4	1,218,557	66.96
1971–72	42,254,272	19,474,355	46.1	1,507,830	77.43
1973–74	41,438,054	21,347,039	51.5	1,858,141	87.04
1975–76	41,269,720	21,772,483	52.8	2,377,313	109.19
1977–78	40,079,590	21,800,000[3]	54.4	2,731,041	125.28
1979–80[4]	38,234,000	21,800,000[3]	57.0	3,833,145	175.83

1. Data on pupil transportation for 1951–52 are based on enrollment.
2. Data for 1953–54 and subsequent years are based on average daily attendance.
3. Estimate from SCHOOL BUS FLEET (December–January issues).
4. Preliminary data.

Source: National Center for Education Statistics. Digest of Education Statistics. 1982. Washington, D.C.: Government Printing Office.

dents being transported, this could well mean an additional two million students to be transported, thus compounding the student transportation problem already faced by many districts today.

PROVIDING TRANSPORTATION SERVICES

In the early years of public education, transportation was recognized as a responsibility of the parents of the students being served. However, as the geographic size of school attendance areas increased, and as schools consolidated, the local districts began to provide such services. The need for publicly supported pupil transportation was accentuated by the increased activity of states in reorganizing school districts and consolidating school attendance areas which continued throughout the 1940s and 1950s. School district reorganization resulted in the closing of many small schools, particularly in rural areas. As these schools closed, it was necessary to transport students to larger units.

Fifty years after Massachusetts passed its legislation, all forty-eight states and the then territory of Hawaii had enacted their own legislation providing transportation for students who were beyond walking distance of their schools. However, many of these early transportation laws operated only in instances where the schools closest to the child's home had been closed or the district had contracted to send the child to another district. Some of the legislation had also limited the amount that could be spent for pupil transportation (Stollar 1971).

State involvement in school transportation varies. Some laws mandate that all students living beyond prescribed distances from their schools must be transported; other states stipulate that the provision of transportation services be completely voluntary on the part of a local school district. For example, in Illinois, free school transportation is required for students who live more than one and one-half miles from school, while in Colorado, the provision for student transportation is completely voluntary. Some states combine the voluntary and mandatory provisions. In Nebraska, the local school district has the option of offering transportation services. If the local district opts to provide transportation, it must bus all students who live over four miles from school.

In recent years, three major pieces of legislation have caused significant increases in the extent of transportation services required. With the passage of Public Law 92-142, many handicapped students are required to be transported, and in some local districts, "special education" students may be the only ones being furnished transportation.

Under desegregation laws, the courts have also mandated racial balancing in schools and so ruled that students must be bussed to achieve a racial balance.

A third piece of legislation offers transportation services to students of parochial or private schools, but this provision varies considerably from state to state. In certain states, parochial or private students may be transported only on previously established public school routes, getting on at the regular stop nearest their residences and getting off at the established stop nearest their schools. In other states, local districts are required to transport parochial or private school students directly from their residences to any parochial or private school in the county or other specified area.

FINANCING TRANSPORTATION

Since schools were first established on a local basis, it was natural for the financing of schools to be considered a local problem. Some New England towns began very early in their history to use property taxes to help finance education. Massachusetts and Connecticut were leaders in this field. As the westward movement of settlers accelerated and the number of local districts began to multiply, the acceptability of the local property tax as the mainstay of school finance increased. By 1890, all of the states were using property taxes as the main source of school revenues.

Although various state governments took on the responsibility for education rather readily, their acceptance of financial responsibility was slow in developing. In fact, little attention was given by the states to their role in providing financial support to local districts until the late 1920s. A study by George D. Strayer and Robert M. Haig (1924) of the New York State School System led other states to look at the equalization of educational opportunity through a foundation or a minimum program of school finance.

As state support for education evolved, most of the state support prior to the 1940s was based on grants to local districts based on the number of students enrolled or on average daily attendance. These grants were general aid and not earmarked for specific purposes. Thus transportation was financed completely from these general funds, both local and state. By mid-century, although some states had recognized transportation as a specific service that needed special financial support, Johns (1949: 49) reported that "the development of sound practices for the apportionment of state funds for school transportation has been neglected in most states."

In the next quarter century, expenditures for transportation increased considerably, primarily because of rising costs for fuel, labor, and equipment. More importantly, by the 1970s there was increasing recognition that pupil transportation needs do not concern all districts equally and that these differences should be provided for in the state school support program (Jordan and Hanes 1978).

Currently, the amount of support given for transportation in the fifty states, as well as the method of allocation, varies considerably. Some states (e.g., Delaware, Hawaii, New Mexico) support the total cost of transportation through state funding. Others, such as Nebraska, provide minimal state support. Generally, state funding is cooperative and based on a specified amount per unit of service, such as mileage or students transported (flat grants); as a proportion of locally approved costs (percentage grants); or as a formula that includes such variables as density, route miles, or number of pupils transported (Augenblick 1979).

In recent years, as resources have declined many states have had difficulty maintaining school support programs. Several states have had to reduce either the actual level of state support or the relative state share of financial support for the schools. In several instances, the transportation program has been a prime target for reductions. Such reductions have resulted in lawsuits such as *Seattle School District v. The State of Washington*, which was brought about when Washington reduced the city's share of the transportation formula to 59 percent of required funding in 1978. The suit was brought on the basis of the provision (Article IX Section I) in the Washington State Constitution that states: "It is the paramount duty of the State to make ample provision for the education of all children residing within its borders." Similar cases are before other state courts.

Also in response to reductions in funding, many districts have looked carefully at who should be a transportable student. The appropriate "walk-in" distances, especially at the junior high and senior high levels, have been reconsidered, and in many instances, these distances have been increased, thereby decreasing the number of students being transported.

Other districts have considered charging the families of transported students for this service. One such district, the Millard School District in Omaha, Nebraska, is charging for the transportation of junior high students who live more than two miles but less than four miles from the school. By Nebraska law, all students who live over four miles from the attendance center must be transported.

In many of the metropolitan areas that encompass several individual districts, there is considerable duplication of transportation costs. This has led to the concept of regional transportation services in instances where buses of one district traverse through other districts. A regional transportation program servicing several districts could thus transport students of the region to their individual schools at a significant savings of route mileage and costs.

MANAGING TRANSPORTATION SERVICES

The primary goal of transportation management is to move students to and from their homes safely and efficiently. During periods of sufficient resources, this operation generally has not received the attention that has been given to the safety aspects of the program. However, the past few years have witnessed declining resources, and the efficiency of the transportation program has become a major concern in the management of transportation services. Budgetary restraints have caused departments to study all aspects of transportation costs, and new concepts in routing, vehicle acquisition and maintenance, and general operations have been and are being developed and geared at reducing overall transportation expenses.

Routing

Common patterns of routing in the past generally provided for almost door to door service for the students. Buses were routed up and down residential streets making one or more stops on every block. To limit the time that students were being transported, buses often ran routes with few passengers and, it was common to see a sixty-five-seat bus running a route with only twenty students.

Two new concepts of routing have been developed to bring greater efficiency to the transporting of students. One concept is based on the grid or perimeter pattern similar to city busing routes. Buses run on established routes that traverse major arteries and make designated stops. If the schools being transported to have similar starting times, students at multiple levels can be driven together. If school starting times are staggered, the same route can be traversed at different times by the same bus to pick up students for each school.

Center routing, a second concept being utilized, picks up large numbers of students at a designated stop. The center stops are usually established at parks, greenbelts, or school sites with the students living within a prescribed area walking to the designated stops. Under this concept, a bus may carry its full capacity at a single stop.

Staggered starting and ending times in schools also allow for back-to-back routing. Since high schools are normally larger and lie nearby junior high and elementary schools, when times are staggered a bus can cover a high school route, move immediately to a junior high route near to the senior high and then follow a nearby elementary route. This significantly reduces the "dead-head" distance, that distance between the end of one route and the beginning of the next.

With the advent of computer technology, routing is now done via the computer in many districts. Accurate maps of the district can be placed on the computer so that a program can develop routes that will pick up near-capacity loads while traversing the least distances. Districts utilizing computerized routing have been able to reduce the number of buses needed as well as reducing the transportation mileage significantly.

Vehicles

Early school buses were simply truck chassis with covered bodies behind the engine compartment. In most cases, the seating was longitudinal. These buses were all about the same size, looked alike, and traffic safety was not a major concern. Most of these early buses were owned by private individuals who contracted with school districts to transport the students to school.

As times changed, school buses changed. The increase in traffic caused safety to become a prime factor in their design, and considerations for safety brought about body construction of metal frames and panels that would not cave in on impact. During the 1950s and 1960s, states became involved in specifications for body construction that would give ultimate protection in the case of an accident. The federal government also became involved in recommending and even mandating specifications for construction, seating, and safety accessories. Many regulations have issued and are continuing to issue from the National Highway Traffic Safety Administration.

As the number of students transported increased, the need for different sizes and kinds of buses became apparent. School buses were kept unchanged to haul large numbers of students (84 to 90), but in some situations smaller buses were designed to accommodate only a few regular passengers. The transportation of handicapped students brought about the need for buses equipped with lift doors and special tie-downs for wheelchairs. For extremely handicapped passengers, individualized compartments were built.

Generally, these improvements and additions to school buses have added to the unit cost. During periods of increasing resources, providing these costly vehicles did not appear to be particularly problematic. But the cost of new school buses in the last decade has more than tripled. With the advent of lessening funds it is, therefore, difficult for individual districts to finance the capital costs of new buses. The magnitude of the capital outlay cost has become a prime concern to school administrators and has led to questions over the longevity of service of these vehicles and their on-line maintenance. One possible way of cutting the unit cost of these new buses is through large volume bidding. Several states presently bid on buses for the entire state, allowing the local district the opportunity to purchase from this bid. In such cases, the savings to the local district can be substantial. In Florida, where state bidding is prescribed, because of the large number of units bid by the state the savings to the local district is thought to be about 25 percent.

School buses have traditionally been replaced after ten years or 100,000 miles. During the late 1970s, as fleets began to run greater mileages annually, some were being replaced at a lesser vehicle age.

However, with declining resources, fleets are beginning to keep their buses for longer periods of time. A 1982 survey (Henke 1983) shows the average replacement age and mileage for all buses to be 10.4 years and 117,957 miles. As funds continue to be tight, buses will be kept in service for increasing periods of time and will be run greater mileages. However, buses can be kept in service longer only if they have been properly maintained. Daily inspections and periodic preventive maintenance give longer life to body and chassis components. While vehicle maintenance has always been an important part of fleet operation as a safety requirement as well as a day-to-day operation, the need to prolong the useful life and mileage has made good fleet maintenance doubly important to the overall cost of the transportation program.

Greater longevity and mileages on vehicles has brought added aspects to maintenance work. Although good operational maintenance will increase the life expectancy of vehicles, there eventually comes the time when a bus chassis must be repowered or a body refurbished. Repowering and refurbishing a bus may extend the longevity to fifteen years or longer at a cost that is a fraction of a replacement. Owners of larger fleets have, therefore, begun hiring mechanics qualified to repower or refurbish buses and have begun developing maintenance facilities that allow space for engine and drive-train replacement as well as body reconditioning and painting.

Unfortunately, many school districts are small and cannot provide either the facilities or the personnel necessary for anything other than day-to-day operational maintenance. However, a new concept, known as maintenance co-ops, might aid these smaller fleets and it is being introduced in some states. A maintenance co-op program allows two or more districts to share and administer jointly a single maintenance facility large enough to economically provide the necessary maintenance operation. Such a program is being developed under state funding in the state of Washington (*School Bus Fleet* February/March 1983). Another example of this concept is the Kern County (California) facility that services thirty-five districts (*School Bus Fleet* June/July 1983). Such maintenance co-ops can provide specialized facilities, personnel, and parts inventory that were impossible for an individual district to supply. Further, these co-ops can provide service at a cost less than it would cost to contract out to commercial facilities.

Alternative Fuels

Fuel is a major cost associated with operating buses. The most common fuel has been, and continues to be, gasoline, and until recent times, it has been in great supply and relatively cheap in cost. Recently, however, the availability of gasoline has come into question. Because the crude oil from which gasoline is derived is a nonrenewable resource, experts have been telling us that the world supply is limited and that if its use is continued at the present rate, the supply will be exhausted early in the twenty-first century. Experts in the field also predict that, as the supply of crude oil is utilized, the price of gasoline will continue to increase dramatically. These concerns are exacerbated by the fact that much of the world's supply of crude oil is subject to the control and manipulation of foreign powers. The availability of gasoline and its high cost raise serious doubts about our dependence on gasoline as a fuel.

With the concern for cost, supply, and the pollutant effect of gasoline as a fuel, alternative fuels are being studied and adapted for use in the internal combustion engine. One of the first alternatives to be utilized was diesel fuel. Diesel fuel is derived largely from crude oil, as is gasoline, but has advantages over gasoline in terms of costs. Until recently the cost of diesel fuel was normally less than gasoline. A gallon of diesel fuel would also run an engine nearly twice the mileage as would gasoline.

As a result of the perceived cost savings associated with diesel fuel, over the past decade many school bus fleets have converted to the use of diesel fuel either through purchasing new buses equipped with diesel engines or by replacing gasoline engines in older buses with diesel ones. A recent survey showed that 13.2 percent of the nation's school buses are now diesel-driven (Henke 1983), and while diesel-powered buses have a higher initial cost than gasoline-powered buses, the savings in fuel pay back the difference in about two years.

In the past, it had been thought that diesel emissions did not contribute significantly to the pollution problem. More recent thinking is that diesel emissions do indeed play a major role in those areas where pollution is most severe. Consequently, diesel engines are targeted for some type of pollution control. This raises the question of the continued or increased use of diesel power for school buses, and since school buses are constantly in the public eye, public relations may dictate the curtailment or discontinuation of diesel power.

The most popular alternative fuel to gasoline and diesel is propane. Propane is a derivative of natural gas which, before its advantages were discovered, was considered a wellhead waste product. It has served as fuel for motor homes and portable stove heaters for a number of years, and it has been used as a vehicle fuel in European countries for over two decades.

Gasoline engines can be converted to use propane as a fuel at a relatively small cost. It offers a high octane that burns cleaner and pollutes less than either gasoline or diesel fuel. The cleaner burning also causes less engine wear which, in turn, lowers maintenance costs. The cost of a gallon of propane is generally about 60 percent less than the cost of a gallon of gasoline. A recent industry survey showed that 3.8 percent of all student transportation vehicles are fueled by propane (Henke 1983). The world reserve of natural gas is huge compared to the reserve of crude oil, and propane, as a derivative of natural gas, will be in great supply long after the crude oil reserve has been dissipated. The price is not expected to rise as rapidly as either gasoline or diesel fuel.

Natural gas is yet another alternative fuel. Stored in cylinders at up to 2,700 pounds per square inch, compressed natural gas can be used as a fuel in any gasoline-powered engine. Compressed natural gas is not a new idea as an engine fuel; its use as fuel was first achieved in 1869, about a decade before the gasoline engine was invented, and it has been used in cars and trucks in this country since the late 1960s. It was first used to power a school bus in 1980 when the Eaton (Colorado) School District converted its fleet of sixteen buses to utilize compressed natural gas. Since that time, it has been used as a fuel for school buses in many places throughout the country. The *School Bus Fleet* (Henke 1983) industry survey showed that one-half percent of all transportation vehicles are, at present, utilizing compressed natural gas as a fuel.

The costs of compressed natural gas is less than half of that of gasoline or diesel. It is also cleaner burning than these fuels so the pollution factor is nearly nonexistent. As with propane, the cleaner burning means less engine wear, cuts down on maintenance costs, and gives longer engine life.

Whether compressed natural gas will remain the least costly of fuels is open to question. At the present time, natural gas is under federal price controls as a result of the Natural Gas Policy Act of 1978. On January 1, 1985, 40 to 60 percent of the supply will be decontrolled. Legislation decontrolling brings about a rapid price increase for a period of time, regardless of supply and demand factors. Presently, projections are that when deregulation occurs the price will increase and then stabilize.

Some experts feel that the "fuel of the future" will be methanol, commonly called wood alcohol. Methanol is distilled from the burning of any organic material including wood, coal, or even refuse. It has been used for years as the primary fuel in racing cars. Methanol is now being used as a vehicle fuel in several European countries, South Africa, New Zealand, and Brazil. Brazil has had a huge conversion program underway for some time. Despite all this, though, there has been limited experimentation with the use of methanol as a fuel for school buses.

The amount of methanol presently manufactured is minimal compared to the amount necessary for its use as a primary fuel. In addition, its cost is equal to or greater than that of gasoline. To become a viable alternative, the methanol industry will have to expand greatly. Such expansion will probably reduce the cost.

Probably no one alternative fuel will become the common fuel, such as gasoline has been over the years. One would expect each alternate fuel to capture a share of the market, but the share will be determined largely by both the cost and the distribution system for providing the fuel. Even though propane is more expensive than compressed natural gas, undoubtedly the ease of obtaining propane through its distribution system gives this alternative fuel the greater popularity of the two in terms of future use.

SUMMARY

The transportation of students to the public schools has increased nearly eightfold in the last half century. In fact, although overall public school enrollments have decreased during the past decade, the number of students transported has continued to rise. Projections are that enrollment will begin to increase by 1985 and reach the all-time high enrollment of 1972 by the early 1990s. Even if the percentage of students transported remains stable, the number of students transported will increase by two million, thus adding significantly to the already expanding costs of public elementary and secondary education.

Since transportation financial support is, in many places, being reduced, this increase in transportation means finding ways to reduce costs. All aspects of the transportation program will have to be carefully scrutinized to find ways of reducing these costs.

This chapter has explored several aspects of the transportation program that lend possibilities for cost reductions. Greater "walk-in" distances lower the numbers of students to be transported, and more efficient routing of buses reduces routes, thus cutting costs. Better maintenance extends the life of the vehicles, thus cutting down on initial outlays for vehicles. Experimentation with alternative fuels has shown the possibility of significant savings.

REFERENCES

Augenblick, John. 1979. *School Finance Reform in the States: 1979.* Denver, Colorado: Education Commission of the States.
"Economics of Scale." 1983. *School Bus Fleet* 28, no. 3 (June/July): 27–31.
Henke, Cliff. 1983. "Survey Reveals Industry Still Strong, but in Transition." *School Bus Fleet* 28, no. 1 (February/March): 23, 25.
Johns, Roe L. 1949. "Determining Pupil Transportation Costs." *Nation's Schools* 43, no. 2 (February): 48–49.
Jordan, K. Forbis, and Carol E. Hanes. 1978, "A Survey of State Pupil Transportation Programs." *School Business Affairs* 44, no. 5 (May): 133–136.
National Center for Education Statistics. 1982. *Digest of Education Statistics 1982.* Washington, D.C.: U.S. Government Printing Office.
Seattle School District v. the State of Washington, 585 P.2d 71.
Stollar, Dewey H. 1971. *Planning to Finance Education.* Gainesville, Florida: National Education Finance Project.
Strayer, George D., and Robert M. Haig. 1924. *The Financing of Education in the State of New York.* New York: The Macmillan Company.
"Washington Co-op Holds Line On Costs." 1983. *School Bus Fleet* 28, no. 1 (February/March): 12–13, 16.

9 SCHOOL FOOD SERVICES
Issues and Trends

Lloyd E. Frohreich

INTRODUCTION

The ageless adage that you can't teach a hungry child, among other rationale, has prompted school food service programs to be established and survive years of debate over their existence and funding. There is considerable support for the statement that child nutrition programs, as provided by schools and other agencies, have been a major factor in combatting malnutrition in this country. Sociological and economic changes have caused the family structure to be redefined whereby schools have assumed a greater role in taking care of children of two-career and single-parent families. What originally was a subsidiary feeding program in schools has evolved into a large business operation. School food service programs trail only McDonalds and Kentucky Fried Chicken in pure volume of business.

The debate in school food service programs continues on a variety of issues including whether this country ought to provide a universal free lunch, the requirements for participation in free and reduced-price food programs, the role of food service programs in teaching nutrition education, and the share of support that should come from local, state, and federal sources. This chapter will address some of

---

The author gratefully acknowledges the assistance of Rachel W. Schultz in the development of this chapter.

these issues and others in the following sections. While a comprehensive treatment is impossible given our limitations, it is hoped the reader will gain a reasonably accurate perspective of the programs, issues, and trends that are the concern of food service personnel in schools across this country.

GOVERNMENT-SUBSIDIZED PROGRAMS

It is first necessary to offer a brief program description that will provide the reader with a basis for understanding the issues to be presented later in this chapter. It would not be overstating the case to suggest that present school food service programs have evolved because of federal legislation and a dependency on federal funds. How the absence of federal funding would affect food service availability in schools and other institutions is not known. Whether states would assume the funding slack or local school districts would support programs entirely also is not known. But an absence of federal support would likely mean a substantial reduction in food services, particularly for disadvantaged and economically deprived children.

National School Lunch Program

The National School Lunch Program (NSLP) was established in 1946 as a measure of national security to safeguard the health and well-being of the nation's children and encourage the domestic consumption of nutritious agricultural commodities and other food. Further, its purpose was to serve participating children with nutritious, low-cost lunches and contribute to their physical and mental development. The federal government offers (1) financial assistance for each lunch served, (2) technical assistance and guidance to establish and operate a program, (3) donated foods or cash, and (4) additional financial assistance for each free or reduced-price meal served. The federal government adjusts the reimbursements annually according to changes in food costs in the consumer price index. Table 9-1 is a presentation of the per-meal federal reimbursements for contiguous states in each class of meal served under the auspices of the National School Lunch Program for FY 1982 through FY 1984. These reimbursement rates pertain to districts serving less than 60 percent free

Table 9-1. Per-Meal Federal School Lunch Reimbursement, FY82-FY84.

	Fiscal Year		
Meal Class	1982	1983	1984
Paid Lunches	$ .105	$ .11	$ .115
Reduced Price	.693	.75	.803
Free	1.093	1.15	1.203

and reduced-price meals. The reimbursement rate increases by two cents for each category if more than 60 percent of the lunches are served to eligible students at free and reduced prices.

Any public and nonprofit school is eligible to participate in the school lunch program. Also eligible are public and licensed nonprofit private residential child-care institutions such as orphanages, homes for retarded children, and temporary shelters for runaway children.

Lunches must meet minimum meal pattern requirements. Each lunch must consist of specific amounts of lean meat or alternate, two or more vegetables and/or fruits, whole grain or enriched bread or bread alternate, and fluid milk served as a beverage. This lunch is designed to provide about one-third of the recommended dietary allowance (RDA) for nutrients each day as recommended by the Food Nutrition Board of the National Research Council and National Academy of Sciences. In 1975, the "offer versus serve" plan was required for high schools by the USDA and was made optional for middle schools and junior highs in 1977. In 1982, it was extended to elementary schools. Under the "offer versus serve" plan, children must take at least three of the five foods that schools must offer (see above) to qualify for federal reimbursement. Somewhat controversial when it became required, the "offer versus serve" plan has been reported by food service managers to contribute to less food waste and to reduced meal costs.

State agencies are required to make onsite evaluations of participating school districts once every four years to ensure compliance with program and nondiscrimination regulations. The Assessment, Improvement, and Monitoring System (AIMS) is the management improvement system used in the NSLP and the Commodity Food Program, and the NSLP has many more specific and detailed provisions that monitor school programs.

A child is eligible for free meals if the child's family earns no more than 130 percent of the federal poverty line, and a child is eligible for reduced-price meals (40¢ or less) if the family earns no more than 185 percent of the federal poverty line. Regardless of family income, students who participate in the NSLP receive a subsidized lunch under the program. All NSLP districts receive a federal reimbursement in cash and USDA commodity subsidies worth about 12 cents a meal.

Substantial federal budget cuts between FY 1981 and FY 1982 caused much consternation among local school district food service officials. More than 2,700 schools were reported to have dropped out of the NSLP in FY 1982 as a result of these budget cuts. There was an estimated 3 million student daily drop in school lunch participation in FY 1982 when participation fell from 26 million to 23 million. Most of the decline (estimated two-thirds) was in the paid category. Since parents were required to submit their social security numbers with applications for free and reduced meals in FY 1982, this may have been the cause for decreased numbers applying for free and reduced-price meals. Federal expenditures for the NSLP were $3.29 billion in FY 1981, $2.84 billion in FY 1982, and $3.21 billion in FY 1983.

School Breakfast Program

The School Breakfast Program was begun as a pilot program under the Child Nutrition Act (CNA) of 1966 and was made permanent under Public Law 94-105 in 1975. Breakfasts must meet USDA nutritional standards which means that schools must serve fruit or juice, milk, and bread or cereal. A high-protein food must also be served as often as possible. Schools and institutions must offer breakfast to every child, and a child cannot be discriminated against by making the child sit alone, eat a different meal, be served from a different line or at a different time because of race, color, national origin, or inability to pay.

The School Breakfast Program guidelines are similar to those of the NSLP regarding principles of operation, eligibility for free and reduced-price meals, state approval, and administrative provisions.

Table 9-2. School Breakfast Federal Reimbursement, FY82-FY84.

Participation Category	Fiscal Year		
	1982	1983	1984
Paid Breakfast	$.083	$.088	$.090
Reduced Price	.285	.300	.328
Free	.570	.600	.628

Federal payments for contiguous states are shown in Table 9-2 for each category of participation for FY 1982 through FY 1984.

The above reimbursement rates are for school districts in which less than 40 percent of the meals served are free or reduced-price. Rates are 10 to 12 cents higher for reduced-price meals and 10 to 13 cents higher for free meals if more than 40 percent of the breakfasts served are in the free and reduced-price category. Breakfast programs are served in more than 34,000 schools to about 3.4 million children who would otherwise not receive a nutritious meal at home before coming to school each day. About 90 percent of the participating children receive free or reduced-price meals.

Special Milk Program

The Special Milk Program was initiated in 1954 for public and nonprofit schools of high school grades or under, camps, and licensed nonprofit residential and nonresidential care institutions such as nursery schools, child-care centers, settlement houses, and orphanages. Schools are not required to provide a milk program, but if it is provided, it must be available to all who request it. Schools must use the federal reimbursement to reduce the selling price to all children.

In FY 1982, for the first time, the Special Milk Program was restricted to schools and institutions without other federal meal programs (i.e., the NLSP and the Breakfast Program). This provision greatly curtailed local school district milk programs. Schools currently receive 9.25 cents reimbursement for each half-pint of milk served, and the program served a total of 1.2 million children at a federal cost of $20 million in FY 1983.

Food Distribution Program

Food Distribution Programs have been in existence since 1935. To aid American farmers and to provide excess commodities to existing food service programs, the USDA buys food under price-support and surplus-removal legislation and makes this food available to the following approved programs.

1. Children in the NSLP, the Child Care Food Program, and the Summer Food Service Program.
2. Indian reservations and those households that participate.
3. Needy people in charitable institutions.
4. Elderly people and their spouses authorized by Title III of the Older American Act.
5. Pregnant and breast-feeding women, infants, and children up to six years of age who live in areas served by the commodity supplemental food program.
6. People who live in a declared disaster area.

The USDA pays for the initial processing and packaging of food and for transporting the food to designated points within each state. State distribution agencies are responsible for storing the food, transporting it throughout the state, and distributing it at the local level to eligible organizations. Processed USDA food is believed to provide the following benefits.

1. Removing excess inventories of various commodities.
2. Putting hard-to-use donated foods into more acceptable ready-to-use end-products.
3. Increasing the variety of food items available for the School Lunch Program and Breakfast Program.
4. Saving these programs and institutions money by decreasing prices paid for end-products.

Because of the nutritional needs of participants in the NSLP, Needy Family, Elderly Feeding, and Commodity Supplemental Food Programs, the USDA always purchases specified foods and amounts so that directors of these programs can depend on their availability.

Commercial and institutional facilities process foods that the USDA donates by converting foods into different end-products and repackaging them. The price of the end-product is reduced by an amount equal to the value of the donated foods the end-product contains. State distribution agencies must approve processors' contracts. The state also allows schools and other institutions to enter into contracts with processors. The processor may then make the products available to any school or institution that is eligible to receive donated foods. The USDA has recently introduced a national commodities processing system that is making lower priced, processed foods available to schools and institutions. The new system allows schools to take greater advantage of the surplus USDA commodities because of the availability of a wider variety of finished products.

In 1982, the USDA provided over $760 million in commodities to lunch programs, $417 million in entitlement, and $345 million in bonus commodities. USDA-donated foods are estimated to provide about 20 percent of the food used in the school lunch program. Until dairy support is curtailed or the program is redesigned, the supply of dairy products will always probably exceed demand. A commodity study sponsored by USDA is currently underway and involves ninety school districts. The pilot program allows one-third of the districts to receive cash instead of commodities, one-third to receive a letter of credit to purchase specified foods, and one-third to receive the actual distribution of commodities. This pilot program and study will end in 1985. Initial reaction is that there is a preference for cash in lieu of commodities, but the counterargument is that such a system will not likely remove surplus foods from the market.

SCHOOL FOOD SERVICE SURVEY

A survey of the current status and issues surrounding food services programs was prepared especially for this chapter. A random sample of school food service directors was chosen from across the country, and districts of all sizes were included in the study. The survey asked for information on enrollment, food service expenditures, food service revenue sources, program participation, average daily participation in major programs, and responses to selected food service issues.

Table 9-3 displays the survey results for food service revenues for all programs by percentage of support. All school districts responding

Table 9-3. Food Service Revenue: Percentage by Source.

Revenue Source	Percentage of Support
Federal	36.7
State	14.5
Participant	26.6
Local Tax	17.4
Other Revenue	4.8
	100.0

to the survey participated in the National School Lunch Program. Only 13.5 percent of the districts participated in the Special Milk Program, 75.7 percent indicated they participated in the past but no longer participate, and the remaining 10.9 percent do not participate now and will not do so in the future. The School Breakfast Program currently operates in 40.5 percent of the school districts, 16.2 percent of the districts indicated they participated in this program at one time but no longer do, 8.1 percent said they do not participate now but likely will participate in the future, and 37.8 percent do not participate now and will not likely participate in the near future. Only 13.5 percent said they participated in the Summer Food Service Program with most of the others indicating they do not participate now and do not intend to participate in the near future.

The Donated Food Distribution Program included 83.8 percent of the districts sampled, whereas 16.2 percent indicated they do not participate and have no plans to in the near future. A total of 51.3 percent of the school districts participated in the Nutrition Education and Training Program. Participation in the Elderly Nutrition Program was only 5.4 percent, and 48.6 percent indicated they had some kind of independent or other type of food service program for children and adults.

Twenty-eight issues were addressed in the survey. Most of them dealt with the management of food service programs and this will be discussed under the issue of management and operation. The response scale ranged from strongly agree (1) to strongly disagree (5). Two questions related to participation were included in the survey, and respondents were asked whether student participation in school lunch programs was decreasing. Responses averaged a 3.3 scale score, which is between "neither agree nor disagree" and "somewhat disagree." A 3.5 average scale score indicated that districts also were somewhat ambivalent on whether breakfast programs should be implemented by all school districts.

ISSUES AND TRENDS

The issues and trends in school food services extend over a variety of topics and programs. Our discussion will begin with the state agency role and responsibilities and will conclude with some related research findings. Intervening considerations will be given to local management and operation with an extensive discussion on the issue of delivery systems. Additional sections will address the problems of training and certification, the commodities food distribution program, and contracting food services to outside companies. Interspersed throughout these topics will be a presentation of our survey findings related to each issue.

State Education Agency Responsibilities

State Education Agencies (SEAs) have overall responsibility for all contracts with local school and private food service programs in a state. Generally, this authority rests with state departments of public instruction and covers any institutions or agencies included in federal acts and policies reimbursed by federal funds and receiving commodity distributions. SEAs interpret laws, provide technical assistance and training, give guidance and direction to local program administrators, and approve local programs for operation and for reimbursement from state and federal levels.

The Assessment, Improvement, and Monitoring System (AIMS) was established by USDA and the Food and Nutrition Service (FNS) to ensure that a sufficient degree of accountability is present in local programs. Winawer (1983) suggests that the emphasis in child nutrition programs over the years has shifted from nutrition to fiscal integrity to accountability. As the SEA is responsible for monitoring aspects of AIMS, it has created a source of conflict with local education agencies (LEAs), in that the state has shifted its role from being a partner and assistant in the food service function to one of evaluation. It is the opinion of many that a state's AIMS responsibilities have interfered with the state's technical assistance, training, and its job of nutrition education. SEAs must process the flow-through funds to local programs. SEAs do not have direct authority over local district operations of child nutrition programs. Noncompliance penalties may only be imposed on local programs by an assessment on overclaims and a suspension of program agreements.

Winawer (1983) emphasizes the need for SEAs to create statewide credibility. An effective public relations program and a high degree of trust are necessary to make local and state program interactions run smoothly and efficiently. Auditing, monitoring, supervising, and other nondiscretionary accountability requirements tend to dampen SEA and LEA relations. Overall, the goal should be to expand child nutrition programs, increase participation, and improve the quality of existing programs. The debate between accountability and nutrition program assistance will no doubt continue as long as the federal AIMS requirements are in effect.

The USDA recently gave states the option of assuming responsibility for the transportation of surplus commodities to the state. USDA will give states money it would have cost the federal government to ship the food. There have been criticisms of the commodity distribution system since it began in the 1930s. States and local districts have complained for years about shipping schedule conflicts, over-shipments, under-shipments, poor handling, and lack of controls on the quality of food at delivery points. Many state authorities believe that the new plan will give states more control over delivery schedules and handling standards.

The survey asked food service directors whether the recent changes in the documentation of free and reduced-price meal applications has proved to be a deterrent in under-reporting incomes for application verification. The average scale response was 3.4, which indicated that directors were somewhere between "neither agree nor disagree" and "somewhat disagree" on this question. Evidently, food service directors do not believe this requirement is having the intended effect of retarding the practice of mis-reporting family income. Another survey statement suggested that food service reporting requirements are not excessive and do not require an inordinate amount of time. An average response of 2.5 indicated respondents were between "somewhat agree" and "neither agree or disagree" on this item. It is apparent that food service directors are not particularly unhappy with state reporting requirements as these requirements stand now.

Training and Certification

Hardly an occupation or profession is not in a recurring debate over its entry requirements and maintenance of competencies once a person is certified. As food service directors are being employed with more extensive education and experience than was evident a few years ago, there is a trend toward upgrading certification requirements. Economy in school food services begins with the personnel. Educated and well-trained staff save money by knowing how to purchase, store, prepare, and serve quality foods. Therefore, a high-quality training program and thoroughly trained personnel are indispensable.

The School Food Services Foundation of the American School Food Services Association (ASFSA) certifies directors, managers, and assistants of food service programs and requires applicants to complete specified continuing education credits prior to initial certification. Training standards also exist to maintain certification after an initial three-year license is granted (Ricks and Kannwischer 1982). ASFSA has also established recommended competencies for personnel in school nutrition programs. A few school districts are even requiring national and/or state certification as a prerequisite for promotions or salary increases.

There still exists much disparity in the kinds of jobs and responsibilities granted to men and women in the food services industry. A survey of employees found that 90 percent of the women respondents worked in institutional food service, yet 90 percent of the commercial restaurant executives were men (Prentiss 1979). Prentiss reports that education is increasing in all segments of the food service industry, and since strong similarities exist in the roles of institutional and commercial restaurant personnel, education could be similar. Coursework and education should, therefore, be transferable from one field of study to the other.

On the question of certification, our survey of food service directors was disappointing. An average scale response of 2.6 indicated that respondents were somewhere between "somewhat agree" and "neither agree nor disagree" on the question of whether there ought to be state mandated certification/licensure programs for food service managers. The training and certification of food service personnel will likely continue to be a controversial topic in the future.

Commodity Food Distribution

The Commodity Food Program (CFP) has been a mixed blessing for most school districts since it was adapted for school use in 1946. Products donated to schools appear to be beneficial, but the burdens of poor quality, poor delivery timing, storage problems, and processing fees are significant problems for some school districts. Food service directors have suggested that purchases by USDA are based on the lowest price and this is reflected in food quality, which is often inferior to what directors would normally purchase on the open market. Schools are also often faced with increased storage costs and excess costs and excess inventories of food commodities they cannot consume.

These criticisms have been leveled at the CFP for as long as it has existed, but changes in recent years seem to be alleviating the problems somewhat. There now exist three methods of processing commodities. The first is based on recipient agency contracting, which means the local school district takes delivery of commodities and processes them into salable foods for consumption. The second method allows state agency contracts with a company to process commodities into a variety of food products that are then sold to school districts. School districts receive a rebate for the value of the donated commodity contained in the food product. The third method, new as of July 1983, is called the National Commodity Processing System. The USDA contracts with processors as the state does in method two. The advantage of method three is that there is less paperwork involved and transportation is not as great a problem. In addition, a few states do not use state processing contracts and leave many local school districts with only the first method of accepting and processing commodity food distributions. Commodity-processing contracts provide an opportunity to not only use commodities in convenience food products, but also to develop new products and attract student customers (Gilroy 1983). Purchasing national- or state-processed products allows many additional food items to be added to the menu, which has proven to be an asset in increasing student participation. It also is much easier to specify and standardize the nutrient content of processed foods than when school districts process their own commodities.

Still, the processing of commodities is not without its problems. As the use of convenience foods has increased, the need for local labor has declined and made local food service personnel and unions unhappy. Perhaps in too many cases the work has expanded to fill the time rather than an appropriate reduction in labor hours. A few school districts have refused to participate in the CFP despite its improvement. They claim that their money is better spent on purchasing food rather than on state handling charges, processing, delivery, and extra personnel to do the paperwork. They also claim they can buy and serve the same product throughout the year at a more consistent level of quality. Another criticism is that government processing contracts result in a 50 percent loss of commodity entitlements due to processing costs alone.

It is likely that the CFP will be with us for years since it is one of the most viable means of reducing the nation's extensive surplus of farm commodities, particularly milk products. The FNS of the USDA, with its seven regional offices, has overall authority of CFP. State education agencies take title of commodities distributed to the state and provide for distribution to eligible participants. States charge participants anywhere from nothing to the total cost of distributing the food and administering the program.

Our survey of food service directors indicated fairly strong agreement (1.8 on a 1 to 5 scale) with the statement that the National Commodity Processing System will help reduce food costs for local school districts. Likewise, respondents agreed that state processing contracts also will mean lower recipient costs (2.0 average scale score). There was less agreement that donated commodities processed by local districts will cause increased local labor costs (3.2 average scale score). Respondents were equally ambivalent about the benefits of "cash in lieu of commodities" (3.2 average scale score) and "letter of credit to purchase commodities" (3.0 average scale score) that were mentioned under a description of the commodities program earlier in this chapter. Finally, a suggested statement in the survey that the CFP is fine as it stands led to a 3.1 average scale score response. Clearly, there is much disagreement among local food service directors across the country over the value of this program.

Contracting Food Services

Maintaining local district food service programs has become more difficult because of cutbacks and taxpayer discontent. Food costs continue to climb as do employee salaries and benefits. Many school districts have, therefore, turned to outside management companies to operate their food service programs. Most of these school systems are operating at a deficit, want to be freed of daily operational problems, and want to improve overall program quality. The decision to use an outside company reflects an emphasis on economy, convenience, shifting complex problems, and a de-emphasis on local control and the educational and health role of good nutrition.

The advantages to contracting food services are touted by management companies and those school districts that have had successful experiences with such ventures. Generally, the following are suggested reasons for contracting with outside companies.

1. Expertise in such areas can develop systems designs, computer applications, cost controls, lay-out and equipment designs, and financial analyses.
2. Larger companies can economize because of economy-of-scale purchasing, inventory control, menu planning, and shipping costs.
3. Contractors can use factory and assembly line production techniques to prepare and process food.
4. Contractors are more likely to have extensive training programs, technical assistance, and merchandising expertise.

Contracting, however, is not without its faults. The following are possible reasons for being cautious about entering into contractor arrangements.

1. Communications must be kept open between contractors and the school district at all times. Contractors insensitive to the needs of the district may become lax in providing for the needy, treating students fairly, addressing local needs, and pricing meals that will attract adequate student participation.
2. Local districts lose some internal control because of the need to relinquish duties and obligations in negotiating a contract.
3. Contracting may not be appreciated by local employees and taxpayers who feel threatened because of the loss of jobs and the exporting of local tax revenue.
4. Poor attitudes by local administrators may develop toward profitmaking outsiders. It also is possible that dependency relationships may develop after a contractor has been retained.

Most food service experts agree that highly trained professionals are the key to an effective program, whether a school district employs these people through a contract company or recruits its own professionals. Until the early 1970s, outside contracts were not allowed. It may be argued that smaller districts cannot operate a food service program as efficiently as a contractual arrangement, but most agree that large school districts can employ quality personnel and retain economy-of-scale features that allow the operation of an effective and efficient food service program. In our survey, food service directors strongly disagreed (4.21 on a 1 to 5 scale) with the idea that contracting with food service management companies will ultimately save money, and a greater consensus was found on this item than any other in the survey.

Management and Operations

Managing and operating a food service program requires knowledgeable professionals who are highly trained not only in foods and nutrition, but also in personnel management, fiscal management, and many other areas that require their oversight. A few of the problems, issues, and trends about which food service managers must be knowledgeable and which require daily decisionmaking to operate an effective and productive food service program are discussed below.

Delivery Systems. Delivery systems must be selected according to local district characteristics and needs, so it is unreasonable to expect that all districts would choose the same system. Delivery systems include bulk service and transportation, onsite preparation and service, hot- and cold-pack transportation and service, and preplated hot- and cold-pack service. A discussion of each of these systems would be too extensive for our purposes and beyond the scope of this presentation. Therefore, our attention will dwell primarily on the following areas: satelliting, "offer versus serve," and à la carte service.

Satelliting. The practice known as satelliting has grown in recent years, particularly in districts of sufficient size to take advantage of the increased efficiency it provides. In satelliting, foods are prepared for consumption at a central kitchen and then deliveries of bulk foods, preplated foods, or hot- and cold-pack foods are made to sites for consumption. Factory-like central kitchens can prepare foods much faster and with lower labor costs than onsite preparation. With less than 300–400 meals served at a site, it is difficult to justify the traditional onsite preparation of all foods because of high labor costs (Van Egmond-Pannell 1983).

Satelliting is a system that improves efficiency, maintains quality, standardizes meals served, and allows for more administrative control. Preplating foods allows for automated partitioning, better enforcement of quality standards, fewer labor hours, and less duplication of equipment. In addition, satelliting warrants the use of more limited-term employees, shared management, and cooperation.

Satellite food service systems appear to be a trend whose time has come and our survey results supported its adoption. Respondents to the survey question of whether satellite feeding helps reduce food service costs indicated that most somewhat agree (2.1 average scale score) with this statement. A related question on whether shared management of cafeterias will help reduce costs elicited less but still somewhat positive agreement (2.4 average scale score).

"Offer Versus Serve." There has been considerable controversy surrounding the "offer versus serve" concept when it was implemented a few years ago by USDA. Essentially, "offer versus serve" allows any student participating in the NSLP to choose at least three and up to five of the major ingredients in a Type A lunch that qualifies a district for federal reimbursement. Those looking at this program from a cost-effective and management viewpoint are generally pleased with the plan. They argue that it reduces plate waste, reduces the per-meal cost, and allows students to select from à la carte items that add revenues to the food service budget. A contrary viewpoint might be taken by nutritionists who suggest that children are not getting one-third of their minimum daily requirement of necessary nutrients. Furthermore, nutritionists are concerned that children are reducing their consumption of milk and vegetables.

The survey of food service directors generally supported these viewpoints. They tended to agree that "offer versus serve" has decreased food costs (2.1 average scale score) and that greater choice through à la carte service may mean children are not eating nutritionally balanced meals (1.8 average scale score). No doubt the cost side and nutrition side of this debate will not diminish in the near future as food service people continue to argue the "offer versus serve" issue.

À la carte Lunches. Critics of the traditional Type A lunch have been saying for years that it has failed to recognize changing food preferences, its reimbursements are too low, it has reduced participation, and it is not cost-effective. Advocates of à la carte service suggest that this particular service is more popular, produces higher participation rates, is more profitable, and is more acceptable to parents. If you cannot keep a student pleased with the quality and choice of foods being served, they will go to local fast-food restaurants and you will lose them as customers.

School districts are experimenting with a variety of à la carte approaches, including combo meals, soup bars, sandwich bars, potato bars, walk-up windows, and the use of signs, posters, and announcements to advertise their products. The reports on à la carte service are enthusiastic and tend to support the advantages mentioned above. Many report that à la carte service has saved the food service program from financial disaster.

À la carte service is not without its critics who suggest, as with the objections to "offer versus serve," that students will not select a nutritious meal if they only eat à la carte items. À la carte is less popular in low socioeconomic areas where students must choose the Type A lunch if they wish to eat free or at a reduced price. To combat the low-nutrition argument, FMS has restricted the sale of à la carte items along with a Type A lunch if the item contains less than 5 percent of the recommended daily allowance of eight nutrients. The restriction applies to such items as soda water, water ice, gum, and selected candies until after lunch service is over. School districts may petition that non-nutritious items be removed from the restricted list under certain circumstances. The restrictions apply to any district participating in the NSLP or the Breakfast Program.

Respondents to the survey generally agreed that à la carte service enhances the revenue of a food service program (1.7 average scale score).

Marketing Food Services. Decreasing enrollments, competition from fast-food chains, and tight budgets are forcing school districts to look for ways to enhance their products and increase participation. Even an attractive and nutritious product may not sell itself. School districts increasingly are using marketing techniques as a solution to these problems. School districts who begin by conducting a marketing survey generally find that food service programs have a poor image and are criticized for poor environments (Kavulla 1983).

A number of sources suggest the following strategies for marketing a food service program.

1. A marketing survey is important to find out what students like and dislike about the current program and what they would like to see in future programs.
2. An ongoing advisory board made up of students, parents, and teachers will help food service managers keep abreast of current problems and needs.
3. An extensive advertising campaign should make use of posters, signs, and articles in the school newspaper, and announcements should be used to extoll the virtues of eating a school lunch.
4. Incentives, such as plaques for highest participation and most attractive lunchroom, awards of free deserts, and convention trips for outstanding employees, should be used to engender some enthusiasm in the food service program.
5. Efforts should be made to make cafeterias more attractive and provide a more intimate and conversation-inducing environment.

Almost everyone agrees that school cafeterias are dingy, noisy, and are too often combined with gymnasiums providing unwanted aromas. Federal and state officials have failed to recognize and support monies for the improvement of eating environments, including sound control. Food service people often argue that proper eating environments are as important as libraries and other areas. Respondents to our survey generally were supportive of a strong public relations campaign (1.8 average scale score) and the use of marketing techniques to increase student participation (1.9 average scale score).

Food Storage and Warehousing. There probably is no one best answer for every school district to the question of how they should manage the storage and distribution of large quantities of food. Size can be a factor since larger districts probably have more to gain by establishing a warehouse system. Smaller districts face a number of problems, including the cost of constructing space for food, the unavailability of local food distributers, and the handling of large quantities of food commodities. Experts have suggested that several small school districts may want to organize a cooperative warehousing and distribution system. There is no doubt that storing and transporting food is an expensive proposition, particularly if a district must pay someone else to provide these services. The general consensus seems to be that districts without adequate storage and warehouse space and who must rely on private storage and more frequent deliveries should make a feasibility study before increasing their warehouse space. District-owned warehousing does provide for more local employment opportunities, and there are considerable savings from larger deliveries at less cost per unit.

Controlling warehouse operations, food inventories, and planning delivery schedules can become a major problem without proper training and experience. Respondents to our survey neither agreed nor disagreed with the statement that controlling and maintaining a food supply inventory is not a difficult management problem (2.5 average scale score).

Fiscal Management. Fiscal controls, reports, and analyses necessary to operating an efficient and profitable food service program are perhaps the areas in which food service managers have the most difficulty. Extensive federal and state laws and policies on food service programs do not make this responsibility any easier. The USDA recently eliminated the requirement that schools maintain separate cost accounts for their breakfast, lunch, and other nonprofit food service operations. Schools now are required only to maintain their revenue and expenditure records to document the use of funds and the nonprofit status of their programs. Still, this does not minimize the need to maintain separate cost records on local programs so that an analysis may be done on each program's financial status.

Food service in schools is essentially an enterprise fund that is self-supporting, and all expenses, revenues, overhead, and indirect costs are attributed to it. A full-cost accounting system is required to maintain accurate cost analysis data for each program, delivery system, and meal pattern. Separate analyses should be done on food cost and labor cost. Variables such as food cost as a percentage of income, labor cost as a percentage of income, number of meals served per labor hour, income per meal served, food cost per meal served, labor cost per meal served, and percentage of paid, free, and reduced-price meals served are necessary to perform an adequate internal analysis of each program (Friese 1981). If food service managers do not know where costs and revenues are, they can hardly analyze problems as they arise. Whether paid for or not by food services, joint or shared costs such as administration, utilities, insurance, maintenance, computer services, and depreciation of equipment should be identified.

Measuring profitability may not be a difficult task, but if a program is found to be unprofitable, determining "why" requires more extensive data and analysis. Bryan and Friedlob (1982) recommend that food service managers use variance analysis to determine exactly where plans and standards vary from actual operations. They also suggest the use of quantity variance, collection variance, and price variance comparisons in studying program plans and results.

Several survey questions dealt with this area of fiscal management and operations. One question asked whether the elimination of the USDA requirement for separate program accounts had reduced administrative staff hours. An average scale score of 2.9 indicated that respondents neither agreed nor disagreed with this statement. Perhaps the most agreement was obtained on a statement that further federal funding cuts will be a problem in offering the NSLP (1.6 average scale score). On the other hand, responses to the question of whether federal reimbursements are too low to maintain a cost-effective school food service program without losing student participation drew a 3.0 average scale response. A statement that local tax dollars should be used to subsidize food service operations drew an average scale score of 1.8 or very slight agreement.

Another related question asked whether verifying the eligibility of free or reduced-price meal applicants is an appropriate role for school administrators. An average scale score of 3.3 indicated somewhat mixed reactions to this question. A question on whether collective bargaining for food service personnel will have a harmful effect on food service program costs resulted in a slightly positive response of 2.5 on a 1 to 5 scale.

RESEARCH ON FOOD SERVICE PROGRAMS

LaChance (1978) notes that studies of nutrient status conducted at various universities over the years supported the premise that nutrients delivered benefit the general performance of children. He suggests that breakfast increased student attention span, and school milk consumption has demonstrated positive learning benefits. There is a relationship between economic need and higher participation, grade level (lower participation at the secondary level) and food preference (higher participation in à la carte programs). Further, LaChance says that the relationship of food delivery programs to food and nutrition education and the significance of nutrient delivery programs to educational performance and health benefits rarely have been recognized and never systematically considered as significant in American educational planning.

A recent USDA-sponsored study found that school lunch participation makes an important contribution to the diets of children of all ages (Plewes 1983). Other findings indicated these children were getting a higher daily percentage of eight of the eleven important nutrients. Because of federal subsidies it is difficult to find a meal as beneficial as a school lunch for the same price. The same study estimated that the federal government subsidized about 51 percent of the total cost of the NSLP in FY 1982 as compared to a 25 percent share in FY 1970.

Research has also shown that it is less expensive to buy a lunch at school than bring a lunch from home and that lunches from home lack variety, nutrition, appropriate sanitation, and tend to be discarded more frequently than school lunches. School lunches are, in addition, more nutritious and much less expensive than lunches at fast-food restaurants.

A study conducted by Frost & Sullivan, Inc., and reported in *School Business Affairs* (1980), indicates some of the following trends in school food service programs.

1. Greater impact of nutrition research, nutrition education, and dietary goals on menu design and cooking methods.
2. Greater use of commissaries and automation in food production and delivery.
3. More systematic analysis of daily costs through cash registers and computer systems.
4. More bacteria testing and nutrition analysis of meals served.
5. Greater use of frozen or chilled foods, fresh fruits, microwave ovens, disposable utensils, and fast foods.
6. More attention to appearance, taste, and variety of foods served.

SUMMARY

LaChance (1978) comments that the child must be viewed as a human resource crucial to the nation, and the health of all citizens should be the greatest concern since the productivity of the nation is related to the productivity of its people. A delivery system should include concern for food, nutrition, and health maintenance. Schools are the only available institutions nationwide by which nutrition education programs can be adapted and reach such a large portion of the population. The education aspects of food and nutrition have so far not been a mandate of either the School Lunch Act or the Child Nutrition Act. School food service directors are not considered members of the teaching faculty but rather a member of the service staff. Too many educators perceive the role of food programs as merely a service function and not one of education. Somehow school food programs must be brought into the mainstream of education as an important contribution to health, general well-being, and a long and productive life.

REFERENCES

Bryan, E. L., and G. T. Friedlob. 1982. "Management Accounting in School Food Services." *School Business Affairs* 48, no. 12 (November): 50.

Friese, J. C. 1981. "Menu, Personnel and Money Management." *School Business Affairs* 47, no. 12 (November): 24.

Gilroy, S. K. 1983. "Commodity Foods Contain Costs and Create Customers." *School Business Affairs* 49, no. 11 (November): 34.

Kavulla, T. A. 1983. "Marketing School Food Services." *School Business Affairs* 49, no. 11 (November): 24.

LaChance, P. R. 1978. "U.S. School Food Service Programs and Prospects." *School Food Service Research Review* 2, no. 2: 73.

"Major Chances Forecast For School Feeding Systems in 1980s." 1980. *School Business Affairs* 46, no. 12 (November): 31.

Plewes, M. S. 1983. "Updating the National School Lunch Program." *School Business Affairs* 49, no. 11 (November): 18.

Prentiss, B. R. 1979. "Selected Public School Food Service and Commercial Administrators: Personal Attributes, Management Characteristics, and Scope of Position." *School Food Service Research Review* 3, no. 2: 90–92.

Ricks, J. F., and M. D. Kannwischer. 1982. "Training For Today and Tomorrow." *School Food Service Journal* 36, no. 4 (April): 33.

Van Egmond-Pannell, D. 1983. "Satelliting School Lunch Production." *School Business Affairs* 49, no. 11 (November): 20.

Winawer, H. H. 1983. "Child Nutrition Programs: Interaction Between SEAs/LEAs." *School Business Affairs* 49, no. 11 (November): 26.

10 MANAGING TOMORROW'S FACILITIES

C. William Day

INTRODUCTION

Educational facilities can no longer be considered in simple terms, but as a complex response to an even more complex set of circumstances. Not many years ago it was common for an educator to hand an architect a list of required rooms on a few typewritten sheets, perhaps supplemented by a set of building standards developed by the maintenance department, and then say, "Here is everything you need to know about our new elementary school." The business manager or maintenance department was expected to superintend that building for the next fifty years without any major problems. If those wonderfully simple days ever really existed, they are gone forever. Educators, architects, school board members, and citizens who are planning and managing our schools today have a heavy responsibility. By their actions they will either limit education through inadequate planning or free it by designing facilities that serve the educational needs of students today and tomorrow.

Many ingredients go into planning and managing excellence. Creativity, imagination, and invention are essential in directing a facility that anticipates the future, makes effective use of the limited dollars available, and provides an environment that excites the imagination and challenges the abilities of the professional staff, students, and patrons who use it.

Knowledge, background, and research must become part of the planning and management process if the facility is to be an adequate home for education. The educational program itself must be based on an understanding of community needs, the traditions of the area, and research into the nature of future needs. The facility, in turn, must be based on an equally broad foundation of knowledge if it is to become a meaningful environment for education. There must also be an understanding of the needs of the child, stated with functional and visual grace so they become eloquent ambassadors of education. Judgment will help eliminate the nonessentials and direct planning and management toward the true imperatives of education.

Willingness and determination are thus indispensable, and without a clear-cut set of objectives, the entire process of providing education may fall by the wayside. Facility management must join this growing parade in the quest for excellence. Those who participate in education must face up to the vital and exciting tasks and challenges before them.

During the past fifty years of American public education, school facilities were built, operated, and replaced with little concern for the best way to accomplish these tasks. With a few notable exceptions, educators and lay people did not bother themselves with the long-term problems of school facilities. During our early years, school boards often divided themselves into subcommittees, as many boards of trustees of the nation's colleges still do. One of these subcommittees would be responsible for buildings and grounds and for directing the business manager in the day-to-day care and repair of the plant. However, as school boards were reduced in size and their tasks made more numerous and complex, attention to plant activities was restricted. By the baby-boom years of the 1950s and 1960s, the school boards' plant-related activities were almost exclusively limited to planning and constructing new facilities, consolidation, and bond issues. Planning and construction of new facilities became of prime concern, overshadowing all operating and maintenance aspects of facility management.

Facility management is not confined merely to the activities of the physical plant director's department. It requires that school boards develop community support and an operating policy of facility management that adequately cares for the physical plant entrusted to their keeping; that administrators give supporting leadership and guidance; and that faculty/student groups react to services rendered.

The policy implemented by each local school system and school building staff controls substantially the degree to which the plant benefits the program, how costly the plant will prove to be to the community, and how long it will be before buildings become obsolete and need replacing.

Today, 12 to 13 percent of all educational expenditures are devoted to the plant and plant-related services (Deriso and Lane 1983). Given the magnitude of the dollars involved, boards and administrators must constantly seek more positive management techniques with which to secure the maximum and most economical output from this fundamental educational resource. Without good buildings—and especially without good buildings that are economically operated—opportunities for teachers to teach and for children to learn are greatly reduced. The modern concept of facility management is one of the most demanding developments in current educational business management.

In the years ahead, facility management will depend more and more on the use of computers. The computer will enable us to place all maintenance- and custodial-related information into a data bank and to utilize this information in making a variety of decisions. Equipment inventories, service schedules, maintenance and operations needs, job descriptions, personnel records, purchase documents, and other similar items are all examples of the kinds of computer-held information that can assist educational business managers with decisions.

Unfortunately, many school districts have, for one reason or another, not yet implemented a modern policy of facility management. This chapter is directed toward assisting those school districts and those school business officials who need to re-evaluate their facility programs. The major issues and policy considerations currently involved in facilities management are discussed. In addition, selected strategies and processes are identified which school districts of all sizes might initiate to take better advantage of the educational opportunities made possible through competent and economical facilities management.

THE PURPOSES OF EDUCATIONAL FACILITIES

Everyone knows that schools are built to teach pupils. But that is where public understanding seems to stop. It is therefore imperative that school board members, administrators, and faculty effectively inform taxpayers of the nature and importance of the school building itself.

The educational plant that has been adequately designed, constructed, and operated with constant effort toward achieving the best educational setting possible is one equipped to stimulate all of the human senses. Such facilities are environments that enable the eyes to work accurately without unnecessary fatigue or injury; that acoustically enable the ears to have discriminating access to all of the sounds that need interpreting; that provide room space in which to work and relax comfortably without unduly interfering with the activities of others; that are healthy and stimulating thermal environments for a variety of physical activities; and that are aesthetically pleasing environments that contribute to an atmosphere of learning.

MAKING BETTER USE OF EXISTING FACILITIES

Today, with much public interest being directed toward the costs of education and the resulting impact on taxes, it is understandable that school officials have devoted their attention to seeking possible economies in all phases of school operation. Capacity or utilization, maintenance programs, modernization, and energy usage are areas being given particular attention.

Increased Utilization

Fuller use of the existing school plant is one way of avoiding the expense of building new school facilities. Extension of the school day, the school week, and the school year are proposals that have this as an aim. Extending the school year from the prevailing thirty-six-week calendar would result in an immediate increase in plant efficiency, and lengthening the school day can also increase capacity and utilization. However, either of these plans frequently meets with resistance from parents and school personnel. In other school districts, increased utilization of facilities, particularly for high schools, could be achieved by use of a computer for the scheduling of space. In other instances, the merger of schools and adjoining schools districts in order to take full advantage of existing space could also be beneficial. Unfortunately, even when certain actions could obviously provide economical and better use of what we have, customs, traditions, and politics sometimes prevent implementation. Any proposal calling for merging or reorganizing is almost guaranteed to arouse public debate and is generally considered political suicide. Hence, the prospect of any significant amount of merging taking place in the near future is limited.

Deferred Maintenance and Facility Preservation

One result of the majority of capital funds having been put into new construction during the 1950s and 1960s (when pupil enrollments were rapidly increasing) was the neglect of older facilities. Now, with that growth period over, school districts are faced with serious problems in older facilities and they are having great difficulty in acquiring capital funds to deal with them. Although no one really knows the precise extent of this deferred maintenance problem, it has been estimated at close to $50 billion for elementary and secondary schools. The problem is serious and certain and will haunt educators for years to come. Unless some system for addressing the problem is soon devised and implemented by facility managers at the local, state, and national levels, today's deferred maintenance problems will be slight in comparison with those in the early part of the twenty-first century.

Given the need for maintenance of older facilities and the number of newer facilities, school districts must develop a maintenance policy that will contribute toward the best use of the community's investment over a long period of years. Generally stated, such a policy is one that includes (1) periodic inspections to locate maintenance needs before emergencies occur, (2) scheduled expenditures for meeting these needs, and (3) provision of well-trained and experienced maintenance personnel with adequate tools and equipment.

While some reliance may be placed on budding principals to requisition many of the needed items of maintenance, a policy should be adopted that demands periodic surveys of the condition of all facilities. Qualified maintenance personnel of the local school system or outside technical help such as facility planners, architects, and engineers, may be employed. Once a complete facility survey has been conducted, very little time, effort, and expense is required to keep the survey updated on an annual basis. Such a survey of needed repairs is valuable in the preparation of budget estimates, since it serves to strengthen the case for a budget request. Keeping school district patrons informed, on an annual basis, of the condition and needs of all buildings will increase public support when needed.

School administrators should recognize that maintenance and operation costs are almost a total and direct function of the physical plant—the space to be cleaned, maintained, heated, and cooled. Maintenance and operation costs have very little to do with the enrollment in a district. The following are general suggestions for reducing cost outlays and the level of cost increases associated with the maintenance and operation of school facilities:

1. Review recommendations arising from energy audits conducted within the previous three or four years.
2. Re-evaluate the feasibility of using microcomputers for load-shedding and building management.
3. Investigate the feasibility of using maintenance "generalists" as opposed to journeymen or the traditional trades.
4. Analyze each custodian's required "noncleaning" activities, and eliminate or assign them to more appropriate personnel.
5. Begin building capital reserve funds for costly maintenance projects that may be required in the future.
6. Consider the use of consultants to assist in achieving further reductions in maintenance and operations expenses.
7. Find out how other districts are reducing costs.

Modernization

Modernization of a school building may involve one or more processes normally used for bringing buildings up to present standards: rehabilitating to restore to good condition; remodeling or the process of making over; and face-lifting, a superficial change to improve appearance. A number of considerations may guide the facilities manager in deciding whether to modernize or to replace existing buildings. The following questions should, however, first be answered:

1. Where does this building fit into the long-range plan? Does the long-range forecast reveal a need for this type of facility in this general location?
2. Can this building be modernized to meet current and future educational needs?
3. Are the needed changes economically and educationally feasible? Can the site be enlarged if necessary? Can a building addition be built at the place where it would function? Can instructional spaces be rearranged to meet current and future educational needs?
4. How many years will the estimated life of the building be prolonged by the proposed changes? Will changes that cannot be made cause educational obsolescence to recur within a few years?
5. What will be the comparative costs? (Perhaps the best basis for judging this is to find the unit cost per pupil per year, both for the modernized building and for the new building that would replace it.)
6. What will the community support? (See Boles 1965).

By 1985, as construction dollars become harder to obtain, 50 percent of all construction dollars will be spent on additions and modernization of existing educational facilities. Given the colossal expenditures for previous construction, administrators will be faced with the challenge of protecting their investment in existing facilities. In addition to the ever-changing demands of curriculum and the increased use of schools for other activities, educators will be forced to upgrade existing structures. Thousands of dollars will be needed to replace obsolete equipment and to purchase computers, printers, audio-visual equipment, and more. *Now* is the time for the prudent school administrator to develop a program for evaluating all buildings in the school district in order to determine what could be accomplished in the next few years that would not only extend the useful life of the buildings but make them better educational environments. One simple approach involves computing the current replacement cost of all educational facilities and comparing that to the modest budget required each year to upgrade current buildings. Unfortunately, educators in the past have tended to wait until major problems with existing facilities occurred before attempting to convince the board of education or the public of the need for additional monies for improvements. It is hoped that school administrators and school boards will learn that a small dose each year goes down easier than the entire bottle in each of several years.

Energy Conservation and Energy Management

Energy conservation will continue to be an important trend in the development of educational facilities. Since operating costs can exceed capital costs within a few years, some educational institutions will elect to replace excessive energy consumers with more efficient systems. The public demand for more efficient and cost-effective energy systems is intense. As a result, new and better systems are continually appearing on the market. We will continue to see greater use of active and passive solar energy systems, alternative fuel sources, and new mechanical-electrical concepts such as heat recovery, heat pumps, and heat storage. Energy conservation will therefore be a key element in the design of new facilities with more consideration given to building orientation and microclimates. Experimentation and innovation will continue to be a part of efforts to achieve better results. Thus far, few buildings achieve all energy goals using dependable systems. But the competition to provide more efficient energy sources and systems is there. Research into energy conservation is intense and it will undoubtedly provide successful results in the end.

Energy management, on the other hand, considers not only energy-consuming systems, but also the function they perform and the way the function affects or is affected by the systems. The goal of energy management is to use energy to enhance performance without waste, but the basic precepts of energy management are often overlooked because energy conservation is paramount. For example, one can reduce the number of lamps installed to save energy dollars, but one soon finds that the cost of the extra central heating needed to make up for the lost light heat results in a net increase in energy costs. Technological advancements have brought increased efficiency to energy management as they have to energy conservation. In the future, microprocessors assisting with energy management will be as much a part of the school as students and staff.

RETRENCHMENT POLICIES

The problems related to retrenchment have been trumpeted throughout the country for several years. Although there is a tendency when dealing with this problem at the local level to think of it as unique to that area, the problem is, in fact, being faced by public schools across the country. Beginning in the late 1970s, school officials were forced to recognize that the school-age population and its need for facilities were declining rather than growing. School boards and facility managers found themselves attempting to maintain programs already in existence, rather than improving or expanding programs. Districts caught in a financial crisis became more concerned about closing or using surplus school space than about opening new buildings or housing a new group of students.

There has been a feeling of guilt associated with all of this, that there is something "un-American" to the concept of decline. Most of us have lived in an era of increasing numbers of students, teachers, buildings, services, and resources. Suddenly those conditions have changed. School district retrenchment has been a painful experience for school officials and community members alike. All parties involved were slow to realize what was happening and, ultimately, the results. It seemed natural to some to blame school officials for a lack of management and to hold them personally responsible for failing to foresee the pending consequences of an era of retrenchment. While this may be an easy response, it is not a rational one.

The problems associated with a supposed failure to anticipate a need for retrenchment have not been limited to the public schools. Some would advance the notion that the giants in the automotive industry did not, or could not, read the signs portending a period of retrenchment; jumbo jets have been parked for the same reason; the utility interests were unable to plan for certain external forces that have ruptured relations with the consumer; and real estate interests have likewise been thwarted by unpredictable external conditions.

The three facility problems related to retrenchment are: excess buildings, excess rooms, and excess space or land purchased in the predecline period. Decline in the number of facilities can take the form of complete closure and building sale, "mothballing," leasing, partial closure, joint occupancy, or use by a district for other educational programs. Each of these options has its own problems and benefits. The challenge to school administrators is to assess each option accurately and to provide data necessary for thoughtful decisionmaking.

At the same time that school boards, educators, and the public are attempting to deal with the problems associated with decline, they cannot ignore the projections of a mid-1980s expansion of the school-age population. Thus, school officials are faced with the dilemma of establishing policies and procedures that will solve the immediate concern of district contraction and surplus space while planning for the possible expansion of their pupil population in the mid-1980s. These seemingly contradictory problems will demand imaginative, new, and often parallel or concurrent solutions. A unified program that will meet the immediate concern, but allow for viable short- or long-term alternatives for the future, must be adopted to deal with current facility surplus and future facility shortage.

Closing Schools

It has been said that it is easier to move a graveyard than it is to close a school. Thus, among basic skills required of administrators in a district of declining enrollment are those necessary for the closing of schools. Educators must be able to consolidate and still maintain public support. School closing is one educational challenge that should be approached cautiously and systematically over several years. Talking about the possibility creates fears, hostility, and organized opposition. While community conflict cannot be avoided, it can be controlled by the intelligent leadership provided by educators and the board of education. The art of controlling conflicts is one that requires a great deal of time, effort, and patience, and assistance from many segments of the community is required. What may be effective in one community may not be effective in another. Decisions must be made at the very outset of any discussion or proposal for closing schools as to:

1. The types of information that need to be generated;
2. The use and involvement of citizens' committees;

3. The use of current professional staff;
4. The involvement of the media;
5. How the finished product will be disseminated.

If prior experience tells us anything, it is to take time to consider all factors before making a decision. School patrons do not like surprises when it comes to closing schools. Efforts should be made to visit and talk to as many service clubs, PTA/PTO groups, and other agencies as possible concerning the need to consolidate some schools. Educators have a wealth of information available that is hardly ever shared with the school community. The following indicators of the cost of decline should be shared with the community, on a per-building basis: (1) enrollment trends over the past five years; (2) utility costs per square foot; (3) maintenance costs per square foot; (4) personnel costs per student; (5) utility costs per student; (6) maintenance costs per student; (7) student/teacher ratio; (8) loss of state aid, if any; (9) mandated program costs, if any; and (10) other new program costs, if any.

Pavline and Pitruzzello (1982) suggest the following to administrators involved in school closings:

1. Don't tell the public that school closing will save money.
2. Don't count on overwhelming support for your plan from people in areas where no schools are slated to be closed.
3. Don't hold anything back.
4. Don't allow residents to claim that they were not heard during reorganization deliberations.
5. Don't become overconfident.

Adaptive Reuse of Surplus Space

The need for school systems to look creatively and earnestly for methods of using school buildings for purposes other than traditional instruction has become a concern for school boards and facility managers across the country. The strategy of adaptive reuse has become popular because it offers positive benefits in both economic and social terms. Adaptive reuse is the recycling of a facility for some purpose other than that for which it was originally constructed and includes leasing and joint occupancy, as well as other arrangements.

Depending on the condition of the building, costs of recycling the space and bringing it up to modern codes are often considerably below those of comparable new construction.

Leasing or renting an entire building can be a viable method of eliminating surplus school space for some districts. However, certain community and legal questions often must be answered before lease or rental agreements are made. The school community may well react, especially if it is their neighborhood school, with a hostility equal to that of the sale program. Many states and some municipalities have laws regulating rental and lease agreements concerning public buildings. Renting to service agencies—public or private—such as the Y.M.C.A., mental health, family counseling, day-care or health-care centers, or agencies of municipal or county governments normally will not meet the same social or legal restrictions as when private businesses are considered. Zoning and code (electrical, mechanical, and fire) requirements must be researched and met by the renting school district (renovation and remodeling costs may be assignable to the occupant through the lease agreement). The per-square-foot rent should be established and procedurally consistent. A rental program might well be established and based on the nature of the program housed within the facility and the fixed costs applied by user type. Finally, the lease agreement must be written to protect the community and school district while ensuring the building's availability in the future.

A concept entitled "space sharing" or "joint occupancy," if at all workable within the specific circumstances of a local district's space situation, appears to offer the most positive and supportable use of surplus school facilities. A school district considering a joint occupancy program must address five major concerns: (1) determining what constitutes surplus space, (2) assigning administrative staff to oversee joint occupancy, (3) ranking types of tenants according to their "desirability" to the school system, (4) setting up a fee structure for renters, and (5) writing a lease that clearly describes the responsibility of both landlord and tenant.

A joint occupancy arrangement may be entered into with either public service agencies or with business or private enterprise. The rental or lease of space to a private business is the most cost-effective use of surplus space since it offers the justification of higher rental/lease agreements than with public service agencies. This end of the conceptual spectrum faces the stiffest resistance from teachers, parents, school boards, educators, and businesses alike.

Joint occupancy provides effective use of facility space and returns revenue to the school system for use of that space. Facility managers should always retain an imaginative outlook for these types of possibilities.

Interagency Use of Public Facilities

During the past decade, seven thousand school buildings and hundreds of other government-owned buildings were closed. The closure of school buildings is largely attributed to declining enrollments; the closure of governmental buildings to the consolidation of offices and reduction in financial support. The impact of this phenomenon has been enormous. The public investment in the closed schools alone is over $5.6 billion (assuming a conservative estimate of 40,000 square feet per building and a value of $20.00 per square foot). A conservative estimate of the current cost of providing the same square footage (at $70.00 per square foot) is $19.6 billion. If we also consider the value of the other public facilities affected, the total becomes astronomical. The disposition of the public's investment in these facilities is of concern not only to citizens, but also to the institutions that serve them.

The problem is not just one of excess or surplus space, but of lack of coordination and information. For example, in one city recently, at the same time the school system had more than 250,000 square feet of excess space, four other public agencies were paying over $1 million annually to rent slightly less than 250,000 square feet of privately owned space, more than half of which was used for child-care, recreation, counseling, and other social services.

Interagency use of public facilities is a possible response to these unnecessary costs. Many agencies have begun to recognize the possibilities and advantages of these shared arrangements and have formed new cooperative ventures to facilitate such efforts. Such responses, however, are complicated by numerous legislative, political, economic, and social issues. The situation cannot be addressed by one organization working alone or in isolation from others mutually affected.

The concept of interagency use of public facilities may not be appropriate in all situations; but citizens, public administrators, and decisionmakers alike need to become more informed about the concept in order for them to better address contemporary public concerns in the present era of limited resources. The efficiency and utility of the public sector in the future may well depend on how wisely public resources are shared and used.

ASSET MANAGEMENT

Most school districts do not capitalize on their many assets. That is, they do not have a planned, aggressive program for generating income from all available school properties when they are not in use (which in most school districts is a considerable portion of the time). Consider just a few of the moneymaking possibilities available to most schools today. Kitchens could be leased to catering firms during vacations, off-hours, or weekends. Pools could be leased to private clubs for several hours a week to produce a considerable amount of income. Computers, hardware, and software, could be leased during off-peak hours. Gymnasiums could be available on Saturdays and Sundays for all types of functions. Auditoriums and theaters could be leased for many different activities. Buses, print shops, carpentry shops, auto-body repair shops, and general classrooms are all areas that offer potential leasing revenue.

School districts need to develop a comprehensive plan for identifying available assets, and then an aggressive plan to market them should be initiated. The process of developing an asset management plan must start, though, with the agreement of the superintendent and school board to commit the school district to its development. Once this commitment is made, the following steps should be taken (Brown 1983):

1. Review state and local laws and ordinances;
2. Review inventory assets;
3. Identify times when assets are available;
4. Develop a list of possible clients;
5. Develop a marketing plan;
6. Develop a set of general guidelines; and,
7. Establish specific, detailed guidelines for users.

Time will be required to make an asset management program work smoothly, and certain problems will of course arise. Some of the most common problems to be expected involve inconvenience, property damage and personal injury, municipal ordinances and state laws, neighborhood opposition, parking, and conflict of interest. However, even with the possible problems, the plan is worthy of the consideration of school boards and school administrators.

THE SHAPE OF SCHOOLS TO COME

As the twenty-first century approaches, the question is often asked, "What will educational facilities be like in the year 2000?" Many currently existing facilities, and new ones designed much like them, will be used. The same kind of teachers will be teaching many of the same courses and perhaps with less money to spend. Change will come, but as always, it will be slow. Administrators will devote more time to the educational programming of facilities. Due to public demand for more accountability, the amount of money available, and the uncertainty of demographic projections, architects will give more attention to form, shape, surfaces, and materials. Additional effort will be put into master planning, protection of the natural environment, creation of more humanistic surroundings, and low maintenance facilities (Day 1983).

Great Spaces

For years, educational facilities have projected an image of being cold, gray, and impersonal institutions. Today, such innovations as atriums, skyways, student malls, and outdoor learning laboratories are emerging that provide warmer, more personal spaces. In parts of this country, compact buildings have become the rule and architects are feeling the need to provide spatial relief for the users. Where climate permits, clusters of smaller buildings can take advantage of natural lighting and ventilation at a more economical cost.

Regional Style

There was a time when buildings could be readily identified as schools. Recently, more and more school buildings are being designed to reflect the flavor of a geographic area rather than to fit the public image of what a school should look like. Regional characterization, designing a building with strong consideration for local materials, traditions, values, and climate have become, and will continue to be, a high priority as architects design the schools of the future.

Organizational Patterns

Many conflicting claims have been made in recent years over the relative advantages and disadvantages of grade organization. To most, except the purist, grade structure has little to do with student achievement. The building administrator and faculty will have more to do with student achievement than will the manner in which grades are organized. In the future, we will become much more dynamic, at the local level, with regard to grade organization. Declining secondary enrollments will provide an opportunity to move additional grades into high school facilities. Additions to some buildings will permit bringing kindergarten through eighth grade under a single roof. An addition can permit joint-use areas to separate the lower grades from the upper, thus permitting one building to house two schools. Flexibility and openness to change will be essential.

SUMMARY

Moving toward the twenty-first century, a rearrangement of our educational facilities, resources, and people will be paramount. Capital expenditures of the past must be protected by placing more dollars into deferred maintenance, modernization, and additions. The search for economical and efficient energy systems will present a challenge to facility managers. Grade organization patterns will change periodically as school districts attempt to keep large expensive buildings operating. Buildings will have multiple uses and will be adaptable to retain commercial value when they are no longer needed as schools. Money will be tight, needs will be great, and significant changes will be necessary. Educational planners have an imposing, though interesting, challenge ahead of them.

REFERENCES

Boles, Harold. 1965. *Step by Step to Better School Facilities.* New York: Holt, Rinehart and Winston.

Brown, Oliver. 1983. "Aggressive Asset Management is Earning Our Schools $125,000 in New Money." *The American School Board Journal,* 170, no. 4 (April): 42-45.

Day, C. William. 1983. "The Shape of Schools to Come." *American Schools & University* 56, no. 3 (November): 7-8.

Deriso, Jerald L., and C. Jerome Lane. 1983. "Maintenance & Operations Cost Study." *American Schools & University* 55, no. 7 (March): 39-46.

Pavline, Lawrence, and Philip Pitruzzello. 1982. "You Can Close Schools Without Enraging Everyone—Here's How." *The American School Board Journal* 169, no. 7 (July): 21-22.

11 PURCHASING WITH LIMITED RESOURCES

Lloyd E. Frohreich and Joyce E. Ferguson

The title of this chapter is concomitant with the theme of this yearbook—managing with limited resources. Gensemer (1981) found that purchasing personnel resources accounted for about 80 percent of school district budgets, which means that 20 percent or less of supply, equipment and service purchases are under the control of the purchasing department. Although 20 percent is not a major portion, it still is substantial enough to devote the time and energy to ways of making each purchasing dollar buy more resources.

Educators may well be aware of the need to establish accountability for the process of education, but they are not as likely to be aware of the potential for establishing accountability for the expenditure of funds for materials and services. Accountability in industrial purchasing is more pronounced because of the profit motive, but purchasing in education does not have this driving force to make it accountable. Unfortunately, the savings that can be generated by an effective and efficient purchasing function have not been emphasized, except in a few larger school systems across the country.

The primary responsibility of the purchasing department has been to process purchase requisitions, request bids or quotations, issue purchase orders and check shipments against orders and invoices.

The authors gratefully acknowledge the assistance of Rachel W. Schultz in the development of this chapter.

Education has focused extensively on the competitive bid as a means of saving money, but bidding also encourages purchases strictly for requirements and neglects the development of an integrated purchasing function which suggests there are a multitude of tools available that school districts need to utilize as circumstances change. There are techniques that will optimize inventories, decrease paperwork, increase satisfaction with purchases and also save money.

This chapter is devoted to the idea that there are methods educational institutions can use to buy more with their purchasing dollar and make their purchasing operations more cost effective. The next section discusses very briefly a typical purchasing operation and suggests that the purchasing function should become more automated and make more extensive use of computer configurations. Specialized buying techniques are discussed and it is proposed that educational institutions consider such techniques as blanket orders, stockless purchasing, systems contracting, visits to vendors, and cooperative purchasing if they want to make their operations more cost effective. Finally, this chapter closes with a discussion of the current issues and problems in the purchasing world. Issues related to bidding, school board policies, evaluation, ethics and other topics are treated.

PURCHASING FUNCTION AND AUTOMATION

Call (1968) stated rather well the objectives of purchasing in academic and educational institutions:

1. To maintain continuity of supplies that support teaching and research activities.
2. To make a minimum investment in a materials inventory consistent with the institutional function and budgetary implications.
3. To avoid duplication, waste, and obsolescence with respect to materials.
4. To maintain standards of quality in materials based on suitability for use.
5. To procure materials at the lowest cost consistent with the quality, service required, and the preferences of users.
6. To obtain the maximum value for the budget dollar.

Throughout the literature on purchasing one can find references to saving and economics, assumedly with the idea of converting savings to more appropriate instructional ventures or buying more of a needed commodity. Figure 11-1 presents a traditional framework for the purchasing function as perceived by most school districts. The specialized buying techniques discussed later bypass one or more of these steps and would be viewed by a few districts and school boards as too radical.

The steps in this flow of material and forms is as follows:

1. Requisitions are sent from school buildings and departments to purchasing office.
2. Purchasing office verifies approval and availability of funds and sends purchase order to vendor.
3. Purchasing office sends copy of requisition and purchase order back to person or building of origin.
4. Vendor ships merchandise to building, district warehouse, district receiving office or wherever district requests.
5. Vendor sends invoice to purchasing department for processing and payment.
6. Receiving personnel verify shipment and packing list and forward information to purchasing department.
7. Purchasing department matches and verifies invoice with purchase order and packing list and forwards to accounts payable for payment.
8. Authorized person signs voucher and payment is sent to vendor.

The availability of computers in recent years has meant that school business offices have management tools and resources to help them with their paper flow problems and with all the accounting records associated with the purchasing function. Any school district of reasonable size (2,000 or more students) can now afford the computer hardware and software packages that will reduce significantly the manual processing and paperwork involved with purchasing. If a district is of insufficient size, it can turn to a multitude of regional, cooperative, private or public school districts that provide data processing services.

Following are examples of the assistance a computer can provide the purchasing function.

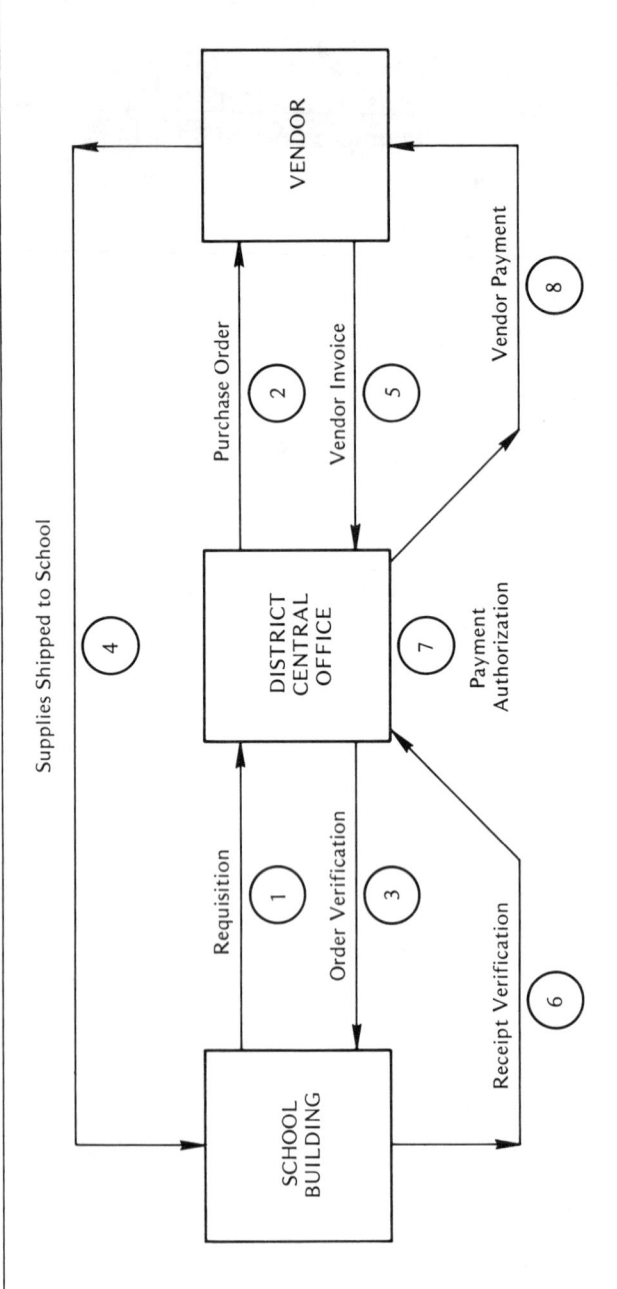

Figure 11-1. Purchasing Flow Diagram.

1. Compare requisition amount with availability of funds in affected accounts.
2. Write purchase order if funds are available and approval is given.
3. Encumber affected accounts for the amount of the purchase order.
4. Reconcile shipping report with vendor's invoice.
5. Print the check when approval is given.
6. Update and print appropriate accounting, budget and financial records such as encumbrance records and balances, purchase order updates, check registers, budget status reports, and district financial statements.

Temkin and Shapiro (1982) argue persuasively that school districts spend too much time typing and using calculators when many purchasing office operations can be done on a computer. They suggest that a complete list of supply and equipment item specifications can be permanently maintained and updated on a computer with word processing capability. A current catalog with complete specifications can be printed and made available to all school personnel with minimal effort. A computer can work from a master list of supplies with specifications and write bids or purchase orders. Following evaluation and decisions on bids, awards are made by entering the bidder's name, brand, quantity, and price into the computer, which prepares purchase orders and delivery schedules as programmed. The more explicit are supply specifications, the less uncertainty there is among vendors on bid items and the less confusion about what the school district needs. Good specifications require constant review and revision and the computer can be of great assistance in keeping specifications current.

SPECIALIZED BUYING TECHNIQUES

There are specialized methods of purchasing which may be appropriate for school organizations and cooperative arrangements. Among those techniques which may hold promise for certain school districts or joint arrangements are stockless purchasing, systems contracting, sole sourcing, the blanket order, small order purchasing procedures, and cooperative purchasing.

Marsh (1971) found that specialized buying techniques are being used extensively by the educational institutions he studied. He found that the blanket order was being used by all the educational institutions in his sample and that there was a trend toward the use of stockless purchasing and systems contracting. The educational institutions he studied were large public K-12 and private and public institutions of higher education.

The blanket contract, stockless purchasing, systems contracting and small order purchasing procedures which make use of blanket contracts are outside the traditional purchasing methods. They acquire materials at an agreed price and they provide the purchasing department the opportunity to use expert methods in executing the details of a contract.

Stockless Purchasing

An agreement is entered between a buyer and a vendor for a pre-priced group of materials in preestimated quantities that a buyer will use in a given time period. When an item is needed, it is delivered to the school within 24 to 48 hours. Normally, a higher price is paid, but for the higher price the school has no warehousing or space requirements for extensive inventories, a reduction in paperwork on small irregular purchases, increased user satisfaction, reduced product shrinkage (theft) and the school is not tying up cash flow dollars before they are actually needed. A buyer can order at any time, knowing that the vendor will have an agreed upon item in stock.

Stockless purchasing, as with most specialized buying techniques, is a means of circumventing or at least reducing the need for a large amount of inventory space. Caswell (1961) addressed the advantages and disadvantages of warehousing school supplies. He concluded that the per dollar cost of warehousing supplies in a school district is uniformly much greater than commercial warehousing the same supplies. The disparity in costs is more than double in most instances, and more than three or four times as much in others. Aljian (1966) computed the carrying charges to be between 18 and 25 percent of the value of the stores inventory for public agencies.

England (1970) characterized stockless buying as a blanket-type contract with designated approximate quantities, specified time periods, prices, provisions for adjusting prices, delivery procedures, simplified billing procedures, and a catalog of all items covered by the contract. England suggested that this system reduces paper handling costs for the buyer and seller and has been a help in solving the small order problem.

Systems Contracting

A systems contract is an agreement between the buyer and the vendor in which the vendor agrees to provide a catalog of supply items for a specific time period with delivery made 24 to 48 hours from the writing of the original requisition (Munsterman 1978). The school district is purchasing the expertise of the vendor in maintaining a warehouse, a delivery system, a purchasing system, and a quantity control system. Again, the school district may pay a fee for this service, but there is a corresponding reduction of paperwork, warehousing, inventory control and personnel costs associated with these responsibilities. The objective in systems contracting is not only to avoid carrying an inventory of goods but also to relieve the buyer of the chore of having to order the material.

School districts need to do an analysis of their supply categories and needs with respect to items that are of low value but purchased repeatedly. For this process to be successful, standardization of products is necessary as well as the use of brand trade names in specifications. Systems contracting reduces paperwork because anyone in the school district who serves as requisitioner uses a standard catalog to place an order and a standard requisition form serves as purchase order, packing slip, delivery verification and invoice. Systems contracting is not a panacea and should not be used by all school districts, but it is an alternative that deserves consideration before new commitments are made for new warehouse space or a redesigned purchasing and inventory system.

Sole Sourcing

It is important when selecting equipment for purchase that a district try to procure more than one bid. If the sole source vendor goes out of business, the district may be left with no options for adding to equipment and no service maintenance on existing equipment. However, there are times when sole sourcing is necessary. Normally these are times when the district is expanding on existing equipment such as the mainframe computer system, word processing equipment, language labs, and so forth. Many times only one vendor or source is able to bid on such equipment. To provide for these instances, school board policy should address the question of sole sourcing. The purchasing administrator should have absolute proof that only one source is available to bid the equipment. In so doing the purchasing agent should determine if the product or service is unique and if the vendor possesses exclusive and/or predominant capabilities. The purchasing official must also determine that the price is fair and representative (Council of State Governments 1975).

It is wise to ask for financial statements or bid or performance bonds in instances of sole sourcing. Should the vendor go out of business for any reason, the district will be protected. In addition, a list of references to be contacted regarding equipment dependability and service quality is advisable. If the school board is convinced that all avenues have been explored, permission to purchase will be given much more readily.

The Blanket Order

The blanket order is an agreement to provide a designated quantity of specified items for a period of time at an agreed price, or it may be an agreement to furnish all the buyer's needs for particular items for a designated period of time (Westing, Fine and Zenz 1969). The blanket order or continuing agreement is a very appropriate alternative to the single-purchase, fixed-price order. The primary purpose of a blanket order is to purchase a variety of items from which there are frequent deliveries from one source, The blanket order is most appropriate for items with low unit value, but high annual usage, whose rate of usage cannot be accurately determined.

Prices on blanket orders may be negotiated, bid, set at market price, or include a method of determining a price that is satisfactory to both buyer and seller. The advantages of a blanket order as follows:

1. Purchase orders are reduced which means less clerical work, less accounting, and less paperwork.

2. Lower prices may be achieved through grouping requirements and quantity discounts.
3. A purchasing manager's routine work is reduced.
4. Once a contract is made, the supplier knows the stock requirements, selling costs are almost eliminated, and paperwork is significantly reduced.

Most specialized buying techniques relate to maintenance, repair, and operating supplies that tend to be large in the numbers of different items purchased but small in value relative to total purchases. The cost in terms of purchasing manpower and paperwork tends to be disproportionately high for these items. The continuing contract or blanket order can be extended for as long as it is mutually agreeable to both parties. With a continuing agreement both the buyer and seller are saved the expense of rebidding and the associated paperwork of new contracts.

Advantages to educational institutions exist if blanket contracts can be negotiated, the institution or institutions involved have sufficient buying capacity to obtain a price advantage, and price fluctuations are not a constant economic occurrence.

Small Order Purchasing Procedures

Young (1971) lamented over the fact that auditors frequently found insufficient small order systems among smaller school districts. Emergency, rush and small orders typically are more expensive and lack accountability controls. A number of solutions have been offered for both recurring and nonrecurring purchases. For recurring purchases, blanket orders, family buying, traveling requisitions, annual service contracts and computerized buying have been suggested. For nonrecurring purchases, petty cash systems, C.O.D. orders, telephone orders, charge account orders, combination purchase order/requisitions, and check payment orders have been suggested. Generally, the dollar value of an item will be the determining factor in a system of classifying small orders. An analysis of purchasing behavior will be necessary to determine what items are consuming time and costing the school district a disproportionate amount of the purchasing dollar.

The small order purchasing procedures mentioned above are too numerous to expand on in this chapter, however, the blanket order system is often mentioned as one procedure to help solve the problem of frequent small order purchases. Another that's mentioned frequently is the purchase order draft payment system, which provides for payment, ordering and delivery all on one set of forms. All school districts make use of petty cash accounts for handling small, emergency needs, but these must be strictly controlled under a very specific set of procedures and policies.

Cooperative Purchasing

Perhaps the most promising means for smaller school districts to save their purchasing dollars is through cooperative purchasing. School districts may cooperate independently or form with a regional agency to purchase supplies, equipment and services. Too few regional service agencies in a state devote enough time and resources to the concept or implementation of cooperative purchasing. Lehman (1973) developed a conceptual model for cooperative purchasing. Generally, each school district needs to examine its own status with respect to how much of an item is needed in a given time period, but Lehman concluded that as district size and purchasing volume decline, the advantage of volume buying in a cooperative arrangement improve.

The advantages of cooperative purchasing have been enumerated by many sources and include, but are not limited to the following:

1. Price advantage at higher volume of purchase.
2. Improved testing and selection.
3. Time savings for both administrators and classified staff.
4. Standardization of specifications.
5. Reduction in sales visits.
6. Cooperation among districts that can borrow from each other when supplies run short.
7. Reduction in overall paperwork caused by placing many small orders.
8. Increased knowledge among purchasing agents through shared ideas about purchasing, writing specifications, and legal matters.

Cooperative purchasing is not without its critics. For each of the above advantages, there are those whose experiences can turn each of the above into a disadvantage. Vendors may argue, for example, that the kind of support they provide through logistics, expert advice on new products, and warehousing, is lost in a cooperative arrangement. Vendors have some legitimate criticisms of cooperative purchasing but a well-coordinated cooperative program should be able to overcome most of these criticisms. Perhaps the disadvantage most often heard is the problem of agreement among districts on quality and specifications of products. School districts should not join cooperatives if their expectations on quality are significantly above or below other cooperating districts.

As example of cooperative purchasing is operated by the Rocky Mountain School Study Council. This council is comprised of sixteen school districts located along the front range of Colorado. These districts represent approximately 80 percent of the student population of the public schools of Colorado. The steering committee of the study council is comprised of the superintendent of each member district. Among several committees operated by the Council is the Cooperative Purchasing Committee. This committee is made up of the purchasing administrators of each of the sixteen member school districts. The committee meets on a monthly basis, year-round, to cooperatively bid for a vast variety of products. The products and items that presently are bid cooperatively are: (a) tag-board; (b) fine paper; (c) newsprint; (d) construction paper; (e) tissue paper (art); (f) duplicating paper; (g) athletic balls; (h) duplicating supplies; (i) pianos; (j) typewriters; (k) ribbons; (l) lamps (custodial); (m) lamps (audio visual); (n) plastics; (o) file cabinets; (p) storage cabinets; (q) envelopes; and (r) office supplies. The committee is now working on writing the specifications for computer paper, computer printer ribbon, and diskettes.

As a result of cooperatively purchasing these products, member districts have realized significant savings. The smaller districts benefit from belonging to the Rocky Mountain School Council because they are able to take advantage of large dollar savings by virtue of bidding with large districts. Some districts have saved as much as $1,800 on just one piano. This committee has even surpassed the bid price received by the State for some items.

Each member district is responsible for evaluating certain bids and making recommendations for award of bids to the committee. All bids are computerized and sent out through the University of Denver Bureau of Educational Research. Each year the Director of the Bureau of Educational Research appoints a graduate student as secretary to the Cooperative Purchasing Committee. This student is responsible for coordinating activities of the committee and the University of Denver Computer Staff in sending out bid documents.

Because of their volume, some bids are done on a semiannual basis to accommodate the districts' storage and space needs. The bids that are bid semiannually are for office supplies and paper. Other items are bid annually and the vendors honor their prices for one year. Ordering all items at one time can eliminate the problem of having to deal with small bids that have to be bid often. However, for a district considering entering a cooperative arrangement, only a thorough study of all purchasing and storage considerations can tell which items should be purchased annually in bulk, which items should be purchased on a more frequent schedule (even at extra cost), and which items to buy on an *ad hoc* basis (Wallace 1971).

In addition to the activities involved in actual cooperative purchasing, the committee cooperates by sharing: (a) new vendors; (b) bidding documents (other than cooperative bids); (c) purchase order documents; (d) expertise concerning the techniques of purchasing; (e) knowledge concerning dangerous products, and; (f) board policies and procedures. The committee also holds equipment showings for such things as copiers, file cabinets, and athletic equipment. Once the equipment is available, the committee or sub-committee critically evaluates every aspect of the equipment and shares the evaluation with all committee members.

Visitation to Vendors

The purchasing administrator should take advantage of invitations by local vendors to new equipment showings. The showings allow the purchasing administrator to see many models of equipment at one time, and make it easier to compare the advantages and disadvantages of each piece of equipment. Do not hesitate to actually make these comparisons at the showing. When bid specifications are written, it helps if one is able to indicate specific features desired on a specific piece of equipment. It also demonstrates to the vendor that the administrator's homework has been done. In addition, experience indicates that when the buyer has evaluated equipment at the vendor site, their very best price quote will usually be received because the vendor is aware that the buyer has probably seen the competition's equipment as well.

It is helpful for purchasing administrators to tour the maintenance facility of the vendor whose equipment may be purchased. Purchasing administrators can view the sophistication of the service center and whether or not adequate staff is available to handle the amount of equipment being sold.

PURCHASING ISSUES

Earlier sections of this chapter addressed a few of the issues found in the literature on purchasing, notably those related to the extent to which computers should be used, the value of specialized buying techniques and cooperative purchasing. The rest of this chapter will be devoted to more isolated issues with particular emphasis on the advantages and disadvantages of bidding, the value of school board policies, the purchasing handbook, the use of evaluation procedures, the place of ethics in the role of purchasing, and several less profound issues.

Quotations and Bidding

There is some controversy among the purchasing profession as to the value of bidding, obtaining quotations or buying on the open market. It has been suggested that school districts are too involved with the idea of bidding or that states are too strict with respect to what items and at what cost level items must be bid. On the other hand, there are many proponents who advocate bidding because it is saving school districts money and it is the free enterprise concept of competition at its best.

A basic principle that all purchasing managers should follow is that a phone quotation, a written quotation or a formal bid should be used for every major item or group of items purchased by a school district. The controversy arises over the cost level at which any or all of these procedures are implemented. There can be no doubt that a formal bid requires considerable time, paper work, and processing costs, so the savings must be greater than the costs of bidding. States that impose statutory dollar minimums on bidding are not doing their school districts any favors. As inflation forces higher prices, school districts are compelled to bid at cost levels which result in few savings and, in fact, may cost a district more after savings have been subtracted from the cost of the bidding process.

Jaret and Jaret (1982) argued that business philosophies generated by personal contact have been seriously eroded by institutional bidding. They suggested that the bidding process is too impersonal, too legalistic, and too competitive for either the school or the vendor to be winners. For every low price, something must be sacrificed—quality, service, or delivery schedules. The time necessary for both the school and supplier to prepare for bidding and make the bid on a $100 item is not cost effective, particularly when a phone quotation likely would succeed as well. The costs of bidding are ultimately passed on to the consumer. Vendors recommend that if districts must bid they should simplify procedures, write exact specifications and be vigilant and firm when bid deliveries do not meet the standards and specifications set forth in the bid.

The State of Kentucky enacted a version of the Model Procurement Code developed by the American Bar Association (Macaluso 1982). The code sets forth administrative and judicial remedies for the resolution of controversies relating to public contracts. It also defines a set of ethical standards governing public and private participants in the procurement process. The alternative contract formations adopted by Kentucky that allow school districts to set price are as follows:

1. *Competitive Sealed Bid*—must meet all legal requirements as to form and substance.
2. *Competitive Negotiations*—do not require definitive specifications but define what a product is to accomplish and are used for more technical products.
3. *Negotiations*—after a competitive sealed bid does not meet specifications or exceeds available funds.
4. *Noncompetitive Negotiations*—are used when it is not cost effective to bid or there is an emergency; a single item, licensed and professional services or replacement parts are needed.
5. *Small Purchase Procedures*—are used for an item or items which will aggregate to less than $5,000 annually.

The Kentucky statutes set procedures for resolving protests, sets ethical standards, and removes all restrictions for cooperative purchasing among government units and agencies.

These writers are in some accord with these procedures except the final item that sets an aggregate cost guideline on small purchase procedures. Furthermore, there is a sixth category which might be added and entitled competitive quotations. There is a need for school districts to have the flexibility to ask for simple written quotations when it is determined that a competitive bid would serve no useful purpose and would not be cost effective.

In the final analysis, it is the school district which, in the absence of specific state bidding requirements, must determine its own pricesetting procedures. Experience and working with suppliers should be the determining factors in the decision on whether to go through formal bidding, seek written quotations or ask for quotations on the phone. The decision hardly can be the same for every school district in every state, which implies the need for more flexibility and latitude in state bidding statutes.

Board Policies on Purchasing

School board members often lament that much of their time at board meetings is spent on bonds, buses, beans, and buying—euphemistically called the four B's in some boardrooms. The four B's often consume more of the board's time and energy than the critical problems of education. Unfortunately, too many school boards do not address these problems through policies that allow them to use their time more efficiently. If a school board can convert its unwritten and unofficial decisionmaking procedures relative to purchasing into written policies, it may find the time it needs to deal with the more critical issues of planning, curriculum improvement, evaluation, and others.

The market place today is marked by unrest and fierce competition. It is, therefore, absolutely necessary that good judgment and sound bidding and procurement practices are followed. Existing school board policies and procedures should be evaluated to determine whether or not they adequately spell out the guidelines under which the purchasing personnel must operate. In the event updates and revisions are needed, such suggestions should be shared with the chief administrative officer and passed on to the school board for consideration.

When school board policies are reasonable and clearly written, the purchasing administrator can follow the guidelines to the letter. It is particularly important to have clear bidding policies. When a district has clear policies which are followed, the school board will typically stand behind the decision of the purchasing administrator in the awarding of bids. It can be very embarrassing to all concerned when these policies are not followed and an unhappy vendor appears at a board meeting and effectively undermines the recommendation of the purchasing administrator in a bidding situation.

The National School Boards Association (1969) surveyed its members a few years ago regarding participation in purchasing and found: (1) 92 percent were involved in the actual decision to purchase products or services for schools; (2) 77 percent said they have a voice in specifying a particular brand of product; (3) 80 percent said they make the final decision as to a special brand or service selected; and (4) nearly 20 percent indicated they initiated the idea for a possible purchase of a product or service. The disparaging part of this report is that the text which accompanied these data lauded school board members for their extensive participation in the purchasing process. We believe that extensive involvement in buying decisions is not something of which school boards can be particularly proud. Many matters relating to purchasing would be better placed under the purview of the business manager, purchasing manager, or superintendent. The whole purchasing department and its personnel would operate more efficiently under the control of a well-conceived and tightly designed set of board policies. Too many school boards pay their administrators a reasonable salary and then abrogate their decisionmaking powers. Administrators cannot be held accountable if their decisionmaking is compromised by school board infringements in areas which are of less than critical importance.

The Purchasing Handbook

A purchasing handbook is a useful tool to all users and will eliminate many time-consuming phone calls to the purchasing department. Each time a phone call is prevented and the routine order of the office can proceed without interruption, the district saves money.

In addition to communicating with users, a well prepared and up-to-date purchasing handbook can serve a variety of functions. It is almost a prerequisite to computerization of the purchasing function. The needs and objectives of a system are the first things a systems analyst studies in designing any computer system. It is important to have a complete description of all present procedures and documents before computer programs can be either purchased or developed. Perhaps most importantly, the purchasing handbook provides the framework for the overall evaluation of the purchasing operation since it contains a description of the various objectives, relationships, activities, and responsibilities (Munsterman 1978).

What purchasing topics should a school board address in a set of policies? There is insufficient space to relate all those topics which might be included, but the following will serve as a point of departure:

1. *Philosophy of purchasing*—a discussion of the purposes of purchasing, receiving, storing and distribution of supplies, equipment and services; the function of the purchasing office; intent to be cost effective; and, where operation of the purchasing function should reside.
2. *Purchasing authority*—a designation by the board as to who has purchasing authority.
3. *Purchasing responsibilities*—a detailed list of those responsibilities and operations which the purchasing department and its employees are to perform.
4. *Purchasing limitations*—the administrative leeway on purchasing powers of individuals in terms of bidding and quotation cost guidelines.
5. *Standardization and quality control*—policy guidelines with respect to procedures for setting specifications, analyzing products, and evaluating user satisfaction.
6. *Evaluation*—expectations of the school board with respect to performance levels and accountability criteria applied to the purchasing function.

Evaluation of Purchasing

How does a school district and school board determine whether the purchasing agent or purchasing department is performing at an adequate level? In the history of management few questions have intrigued the executive mind as much as the question of how to measure performance. The work of the purchasing agent and purchasing department is so complex, somewhat rational and subtle in its benefits, that evaluation of performance is exceedingly difficult. It is not feasible to evaluate a function until the nature of the services needed and expected has been determined.

One of the first steps in any evaluation is to secure some agreement on what a job is and what priorities should be given to its various responsibilities. Does the purchasing department make decisions on what to buy, when to buy, where to buy, how much to buy. and how much to pay? If so, the degree to which these are performed should have some part in forming an evaluation strategy. A school district has at least three choices in evaluation:

1. Using the personal opinion and judgment of supervisors and other administrators.
2. Audit, examination, and review to assess conformance to or variance from established standards and objectives.
3. Appraisal or evaluation of measurable results that are regularly reported or recorded in some form.

Too often evaluation of purchasing is based on personal opinion and judgment. The purchasing department and its employees must understand what is expected of them. Standards of performance along with performance objectives should be established. One standard often used for purchasing departments is the cost of purchasing per dollar of purchases and per order written. Other performance standards can be based on simple volume or count comparisons over time. For example, the purchasing department may be analyzed on the basis of the number of sales interviews, number of quotations or bids, number of requisitions processed, or number of purchase orders sent. Other evaluation methods and criteria include but are not limited to:

1. Amount of savings made through purchasing.
2. Comparison of actual purchase price to some standard.
3. Measuring variance of operating costs from budget.
4. Analyzing vendor relations, delivery time, quality of product, service, and employee satisfaction.

Evaluation of a school district's purchasing operation has often been ignored in the past. A cost effective and efficient purchasing function should be the goal of every school district. It is an area in which money can be saved if appropriate evaluation techniques and criteria are used to assess its effectiveness.

Ethics in Purchasing

No personnel of a school district are as susceptible to the temptation of vendor gratuities as are the employees in a purchasing department. The interaction between purchasing agents and vendors is a daily occurrence and business is transacted in a variety of circumstances and locations. In an effort to please or persuade district officials to buy their products, vendors often send gifts or offer to buy meals for purchasing employees. It is a practice that is reasonably widespread and school districts need to have a definitive policy on how employees are to react in such circumstances.

To this end, sound policies must be consistently applied (Council of State Governments 1975). Purchasing administrators must never allow themselves to be placed in a compromising position or in a position that could cause a conflict of interest to arise. This can happen very subtly when one does not pay attention. Marketing people can unintentionally cause this to happen just because of their enthusiasm in selling their product or intentionally through the careful care and cultivation of purchasing personnel. Conflict of interest statutes in most states cover both intentional and unintentional acts and their consequences.

The reason that ethics is being discussed in this chapter is that a viable policy on accepting vendor gifts can affect product costs. Obviously, a policy of unlimited acceptance of vendor gratuities would cause the greatest increase in prices. However, we support a policy that does not allow employees of the school district to accept from vendors gifts of any value. This is the official policy of the Association of School Business Officials and it is ascribed to by most professional purchasing organizations and officials. There can be no hint of favoritism or unethical practices when school district employees are dealing with private business. Public officials are buying products with taxpayer money and all transactions with vendors should have no trace of unprincipled behavior. Even though the practice of accepting vendor favors is not likely to add appreciable amounts to the cost of purchased goods, it is a practice that needs to be monitored and controlled.

OTHER ISSUES

Too many school districts have a tendency to keep their employees uninformed about the purchasing process. The requisitioning and purchasing process should not be a dark secret; in fact, it is to the purchasing department's advantage to keep employees as well informed as possible. Knowledgeable employees ask less questions and need less assistance on purchasing matters. A purchasing manual, product descriptions, specifications and purchasing procedures generally are nonexistent or outdated in too many school districts. Computers with word processing capability are one answer to this problem. Purchasing departments should have no excuse for not preparing current and descriptive purchasing manuals for their employees.

Relationship with Users

The availability of the purchasing administrator to all other administrators and personnel is important. The purchasing administrator should make a special effort to visit all buildings or departments in the district and communicate an interest in learning more about their special needs. If the purchasing department is to do the best possible job in obtaining needed equipment, supplies or services, this is vital. The rapport that is developed between the purchasing administrator and other administrators, secretaries, and the custodial staff will allow for honest feedback on products and equipment. The end user, after all, is the one who really knows the product. If the user is dissatisfied with the product, it probably will not be used and different products may be ordered in its place. This wastes dollars.

One area in which user involvement is particularly important is the testing of products. Not all districts have the luxury of being able to test a variety of products. However, for those products that can be tested, the purchasing administrator should take responsibility for developing appropriate evaluation forms that are easy to understand and easy to complete. The documentation collected can then be used to evaluate products for purchase. The information collected can also be helpful when dealing with vendors. It gives the vendor insight into which areas the company can improve and in the long run both the company and the district benefit.

Product Quality

Attention to the factors mentioned above will help alleviate the common criticism of lack of control over product quality. The blame for this problem rests with both educational institutions and suppliers. The first prerequisite for quality is a clearly defined set of product specifications. School districts tend to be too lax in setting product standards. This is a signal to suppliers and manufacturers that schools are willing to accept almost any minimally acceptable subsitute product. Cost-conscious and profit-motivated producers will provide low quality products as long as schools are willing to accept such products. School districts need to demand higher quality supplies and equipment through tighter specifications. Specifications too often are written without the advice and counsel of the users. Purchasing departments would be well advised not to write specifications in the isolation of their offices and without some input from those knowledgeable about a product's performance qualities.

Receipt and Verification of Deliveries

Educational institutions need to tighten controls on receipt and verification of supply and equipment deliveries. Too often the system of receipt and verification is spread over too many people and the result is poor accountability with respect to both the count and condition of delivered goods. Poorly controlled systems also leave a district open to theft and fraud. Below are some simple rules which should be followed.

1. A central receiving location for all deliveries is best for most school districts.
2. Receiving personnel should be trained on what to look for when receiving shipments, i.e., quantity, condition of goods, and verification of purchase orders.

3. Personnel who write purchase orders should not be allowed to receive goods.
4. Accurate records and standard forms should be required for purchase orders, receiving tickets, inventory control, and voucher payments.
5. Duties should be segregated when possible to prevent fraud. Different people should process forms, e.g., the person who makes account receivable entries should not receive checks and make bank deposits.

Payment of Vendors

Another issue relates to payments of vendors. Vendors and suppliers often have complained that school districts are being unfair when they delay payments for goods or services. Our experiences and observations verify the truth of these complaints. Many school districts take the position that payments should be made as late as possible or up to the point of avoiding legal action. There is considerable support for the notion that such a philosophy is only adding to the purchase price. In dealing with a slow-paying district, vendors are justified and often add to the price of a product because delayed payments increase the supplier's cost. Vendors have cash flow problems as do school districts and other businesses. They must borrow short-term if their inventory is depleted and must be replenished. School districts should make every effort to pay for goods and services within thirty days of receipt. The relationship with suppliers will be improved and the vendor's ability to keep prices in check will be enhanced greatly.

Disposal of Surplus and Obsolete Material

Another responsibility of the purchasing department that often comes under public scrutiny is the disposition of obsolete property. In the area of disposal of property, as in others, the prudent purchasing administrator should operate from a set of very clear and concise written policies which specify where the authority and responsibility lies in identifying items as surplus and in determining the most appropriate method of disposition (Council of State Governments

1975). For example, procedures may specify that the building or department administrators be required to send a memo to an associate superintendent or department head in their area for permission to declare an item obsolete. The associate superintendent or department head would then notify the purchasing administrator that it has been approved for disposal.

Trade-ins. An optimum way for disposing of obsolete equipment is to trade it in for new equipment. This allows equipment to be traded for a small profit to the district and does not cause any alarm to patrons. Even when equipment has no trade-in value at all vendors may be willing to take it in order to sell their equipment.

Auctions. When a trade-in or other arrangement is not possible, an auction is usually a profitable way to move old equipment. The district does make some profit and the patrons are usually satisfied that equipment was not "just thrown away!" Professional auctioneers are usually hired to handle the proceedings. In choosing an auctioneer, some items that should be considered are: (a) obtaining settlement from the auctioneer at sales end; (b) holding the auctioneer responsible for any bad checks; (c) retaining an auctioneer that has a very good recording system; (d) freeing district employees from having to help on the day of the auction, and; (e) requiring the auctioneer to do all advertising. Good auctioneers will usually have a following and bring that following with them. This will add to the district's profit.

Experience indicates that auctions are best held on an annual basis. This allows building administrators to plan the disposal of obsolete equipment. It also gives the community an idea when the auction will take place. In fact, once the community realizes an auction is held annually, they look forward to the sale. Spring is the ideal time for an auction. The weather is usually cooperative and people are ready to get out-of-doors and spend some money.

In cases where the school district does not have space to store surplus property, it may be possible to have a joint auction with another district. This provides more equipment to auction and may bring in a larger crowd.

Book Give-Aways. A book give-away may be a useful way to dispose of obsolete or surplus textbooks or library books. If the occasion is organized and advertised, many parents will bring children to the give-away. This provides some educational advantage and allows the district to dispose of books in a positive way. Once the give-away has been completed, there are paper salvage companies that will take the remaining books and recycle them. It is unwise to take books that are stamped with the school name to the local landfill. Patrons may see this as "money" being thrown away.

Maintenance of Equipment

The care and upkeep of equipment (office and instructional) is sometimes the responsibility of the purchasing administrator. Because the cost of maintenance over time can exceed the initial cost of a piece of equipment, the initial cost should never be the only consideration in the awarding of any bid. The cost of upkeep is a major factor in determining when a sound purchase has been made.

Not only is repair maintenance important to the life and performance of equipment, but so is preventive maintenance. A good program of preventive maintenance of equipment can save the district hundreds of dollars each year. It is wise to have annual preventative service maintenance done for equipment such as typewriters, copiers, duplicating equipment, microcomputers, and sewing machines.

Bidding for Maintenance

The bidding for equipment maintenance is critical and specifications should be written to protect the district to the fullest. If purchasing administrators are not toally confident with writing such specifications, they should seek assistance from colleagues at other districts. The district legal counsel should also be sought to provide for assistance in preparing both the bid specifications and the contract language. Purchased services such as trash removal, contracted repair of equipment, and student accident insurance are areas where the purchasing administrator may need assistance in bid specification writing.

CONCLUSION

The purchasing administrator serves the educational enterprise by ensuring that personnel who request supplies, equipment, or service receive the right material or service at the right place and time, and at the best price. For this to happen, the purchasing administrator must coordinate and facilitate the activities of a number of individuals—from requestor, to vendor, to delivery person. The person with this responsibility must possess a variety of professional skills, human relation skills, and a reputation for courtesy and fairness. For many publics, the purchasing department will be the only point of contact with the school system. Whatever reputation the purchasing administrator establishes, the school district will bear.

REFERENCES

Aljian, G. W. 1966. 2nd ed. *Purchasing Handbook.* New York: McGraw-Hill.

Call, R. V. 1968. "Purchasing in the Academic Institution." *Journal of Purchasing* 4, no. 2: 72.

Caswell, G. G. 1961. *What Price School Supply Warehousing.* Chicago: National School Supply and Equipment Association.

Council of State Governments. 1975. *State and Local Government Purchasing.* Lexington, Kentucky.

England, W. 1970. *Modern Procurement Management,* 5th ed. Homewood, Ill.: Richard O. Irwin, Inc.

Gensemer, B. L. 1981. "School District Responses to Variations in the Cost of Purchasing Resources." *Journal of Education Finance* 7 (Fall): 137–148.

Jaret, F. and M. Jaret. 1982. "The Error of the Bidding Process." *School Business Affairs* 48, no. 3 (March): 124.

Lehman, G. O. 1973. "The Development of a Mathematical Purchasing Model to be Utilized in the Procurement of Consumable Supplies in School Systems." Ph.D. Dissertation, Purdue University.

Macaluso, J. 1982. "Model Procurement Code Allows Flexibility in University School Purchasing Quotations." *School Business Affairs* 48, no. 3 (March): 16–17.

Marsh, R. H. 1971. "Specialized Buying Techniques: The Development of a Conceptual Model for Public School Systems." Ph.D. Dissertation University of Wisconsin-Madison.

Munsterman, R. E. 1978. *Purchasing and Supply Management Handnook for School Business Officials.* Chicago: Association of School Business Officials.

National School Boards Association. 1969. *Who Makes Buying Decisions in The Public Schools.* Evanston, Ill.: NSBA.

Temkin, K. and P. Shapiro. 1982. "Computerizing Your Annual Purchasing." *School Business Affairs* 48, no. 3 (March): 184.

Wallace, George. 1971. "Purchasing Procedures." In *School Finances, Croft Leadership Action Folio* 34, edited by Neild B. Oldham. New London, Conn.: Croft Educational Service, Inc.

Westing, J. H., I. V. Fine, and G. J. Zenz. 1969. *Purchasing Management*, 3rd ed. New York: John Wiley & Sons.

Young, J. 1971. "Purchasing Thoughts." *School Business Affairs* 37, no. 5 (May): 107.

12 USE OF COMPUTERS IN SCHOOL BUSINESS MANAGEMENT

E. Ronald Carruth and Gayden F. Carruth

INTRODUCTION

Few authorities would dispute the fact that the United States is in the midst of a technological revolution and rapidly changing from an industrial to an information society. Today nearly 65 percent of the American workforce is employed in information/service jobs, and very few successful businesses or school districts are operating the same way they did in the 1950s (Westrend Group 1983).

More specifically, the silicon chip has revolutionized the computer industry, thereby dramatically expanding the availability of low-cost, powerful computer equipment. Managers and employees in the workforce, who ten years ago had no access or limited access to computer resources, now have newfound opportunities. The dramatic change in the affordability of computer equipment has been accompanied by the emergence of the commercial software industry. Application software packages, designed for the small business user, are the focal point of major growth in quality software. Finally, the marketing of computer hardware and software through local computer stores, combined with the media and advertising blitz, has further heightened the awareness of most local school business managers.

Concurrently, the expanded utilization of information tools in private business, combined with a new public awareness of the potential of technology, is increasing the information demands placed on school business managers. School superintendents request more sophisticated information for planning and decision support. School boards and community groups expect more exhaustive trend and alternative analyses to accompany major recommendations in the financing and management of school districts. Prior to the early 1970s, a very small percentage of school business managers had access to computer facilities, limited mainly to the larger metropolitan school districts in the United States. During the 1970s and early 1980s, more school business officials gained access to computer facilities (with data-base management systems operating on large-scale computers supported by shared-cost technical staff) through cooperatives or consortia established in a number of states or geographic areas. Many of these cooperative computer service agencies have provided for their users an array of mainstream business applications, including financial accounting, payroll, personnel, inventory, and transportation systems. However, the emergence of a new computer technology since 1980 offers every school business manager, regardless of the size of the district, direct local access to some level of computer capability and commercially available software packages to address their information requirements. Additionally, for those school districts that already have access to large-scale data-base management systems, the new technology and software offers significant opportunities for the local school business manager to assume the initiative in addressing unique local information needs not yet provided by computer service centers.

This chapter reviews the major information requirements of the school business manager and the potential applications of the computer. It also identifies key areas where school business managers will need to prioritize their information initiatives and the guidelines for selecting and implementing the tools of information technology. Finally, the chapter highlights future concerns and issues for which superintendents and business managers should take cognizance as they assess their information requirements and implement their plans.

INFORMATION REQUIREMENTS AND POTENTIAL APPLICATIONS

Systematic approaches to gathering data, analyzing that data, and reporting results existed in all school districts prior to the advent of computers. Setting priorities for information requirements and selection of key areas for application of computerized information systems is a local prerogative.

A note of caution—the ongoing function of data collection and maintenance is a constant in the use of both computerized and manual systems. The computer obviously does not generate or update raw data. The feasibility of any potential data-processing application is founded in the following considerations:

1. Are the data available?
2. Can the data be collected in an efficient manner?
3. Can the data be adequately maintained and updated?

The computer can facilitate the data-gathering process, for example, through the use of techniques such as the electronic scanning of pre-encoded information. The computer also can facilitate the maintenance of data through the automatic mass updating of certain fields of information. However, the human resources required to collect and maintain data to support any information process should not be overlooked or underestimated.

This section provides a brief overview of potential school business management applications such as financial forecasting; budget preparation, accounting, and control; investment and cash-flow management; purchasing and inventories; capital outlay and debt service; payroll; personnel; facility and equipment management; transportation management; food service; reporting; and office automation. Our treatment is not intended to be exhaustive, nor is the intent to identify priorities or recommend software for the local school business manager.

Financial Forecasting

Financial forecasting has become an essential responsibility of the school business manager. In today's environment of limited fiscal resources and reemphasis on long-range planning, the computer is an invaluable tool for enrollment, revenue, and expenditure projections. It is particularly helpful in rapid-volume recalculation of the column/row results from changes in variables and assumptions. The raw data and assumptions, upon which a local school district forecast is based, are unique to the local setting. The interrelationship between enrollment data and revenue forecasts is also unique, within states, due to interstate differences in educational funding. Electronic spreadsheets (e.g., Visicalc and Lotus 1-2-3) can assist the school business manager in this area. The best resource for assistance in using spreadsheets for forecasting is from other administrators in the same state. However, school business managers tend to rely too heavily on column/row presentation of forecast information. Commercially available graphics and color reprographics software should be explored.

Budget Preparation, Accounting, and Control

Budget preparation, accounting, and control represent the classic application of the computer to school business management. The high degree of computation, data accumulation, sorting, and analysis required in the budgeting, accounting, and control process have tended to make computerized systems popular with school business officials and audit firms. Many business-oriented budgeting and accounting software packages are available on the market today. However, the uniqueness of school district accounting, brought on by unique state accounting regulations and the absence of federal standards, reduces the applicability of much commercial software designed for general business use. While local districts may employ certain features of commercially available software, such as accounts payable/receivables packages, few local school districts will ever have the individual resources to develop comprehensive program budgeting and accounting systems or to keep those systems in congruence with the changes in accounting practice and reporting requirements imposed by state legislatures. School districts can, however, meet this need through shared investment cooperatives. Otherwise, states requiring uniform accounting and budgeting systems must assume responsibility for making software available that meets their standards.

Investment and Cash-Flow Management

Investment and cash-flow management has taken on new dimensions of importance for the school business manager. A restrictive economic climate encourages optimal investment earnings from all levels of government. Today, state and local units of government, which have traditionally flowed funds immediately to local school districts, are closely managing their cash flow to assure improved investment earnings. The local school business manager can utilize commercially available investment management software to improve earnings and thus offset the effects of this trend. Most investment packages are designed as stand-alone applications for the microcomputer and are, in most instances, not fully integrated with computerized accounting systems. However, since the raw data required for investment management are principally summary-accumulated disbursements, revenue receipts, and investment transactions, the application can be efficiently maintained and modified at the local level.

Purchasing and Inventories

Many tasks associated with purchasing and inventory functions are logical applications for the computer. Systems to process quantity-bid requisition data for the preparation of supply- and equipment-bid specifications can be custom designed to meet needs at the local level and need not be integrated with a financial accounting system. On the other hand, since both the issuance and payment of purchase orders create accounting transactions, those tasks should most logically be integrated within the financial accounting system employed by the school district.

Supplies-inventory and fixed-asset-inventory software is available commercially and can be operated as stand-alone systems for inventory management on local computers. However, since both supplies-inventory and fixed-asset transactions do affect the balance sheet, many school business managers prefer those systems to be linked also with the financial accounting system. Such linkage allows depreciation costs for fixed assets and supplies inventory on hand, as reflected on the balance sheet, to agree with summary totals from the inventory systems. Also, inventory-system requirements can be unique to specialized applications within the school district operation (e.g., food services, media and libraries) and thus a generalized-inventory software package may not be applicable.

Today's technology allows for interesting options in the purchasing area if systems are sufficiently integrated. For example, it is possible for a principal to issue a purchase order for supplies on a microcomputer that will automatically create an encumbrance transaction to be transmitted to a financial accounting system operating at the central office or a service center. Then when the principal receives the supplies, a building-level transaction can be generated for accounts payable, removing the encumbrance, updating the inventory, and adjusting the reorder point.

Capital Outlay and Debt Service

Capital outlay and debt service fund management are other possible applications of the computer. Usually, the management of these funds is an integrated feature of the budgeting and accounting system employed. Since the methods of accounting for capital investments vary significantly between the taxpaying private sector and the public sector, school business managers should not anticipate significant help from commercially available products in this area.

Payroll

Like financial accounting, payroll is another universal business application of the computer. Many payroll software packages are available commercially for both the microcomputer and larger computer equipment. School district payroll requirements are not unique. Many systems designed for business are applicable. In some states, banks or other local agencies have made this service available to school districts at a reduced cost. Traditionally, most computerized payroll systems provide for the production of payroll checks, a payroll register, a record of insurance and withholding deductions, a leave subsystem, and the production of W-2 forms. A minimal personnel data base is required for the payroll application. Additional personnel information required by larger districts should be approached as a separate application.

While payroll can be computerized as a separate system, some thought should be given to the convenience of a link between payroll and financial accounting. Since 70 to 80 percent of school district expenditures are for personnel costs, the accounting transactions generated by payroll should automatically enter the accounting system. The larger the district, the more this automatic transfer of payroll transactions becomes a necessity.

Personnel

The number of school district employees should be the primary criterion in determining the need for a more comprehensive personnel data base than that required by payroll. Larger districts will likely require an automated personnel information system with capabilities to manage recruitment, salary schedule placement, assignment, position control, certification, seniority lists, professional development credits, leaves, and substitutes. Smaller districts may prefer to manage these personnel functions manually.

Salary and fringe benefits package cost simulation is a universal application that can be utilized by all school business managers in forecasting the effect of alternative staff compensation plans on district finances. Access to a salary and fringe benefits package simulation is particularly useful in the negotiations process.

Few personnel or salary and fringe benefits package simulations that meet the unique needs of local school districts are available commercially. However, systems developed by school districts or computer service cooperatives can be adapted to local needs elsewhere.

Facility and Equipment Management

Building, grounds, and equipment maintenance is a broad area where potential computer applications could provide valuable information on maintenance schedules and cost. Energy management is a highly specialized field within this area that is enjoying popularity. Computerized monitoring and control of HVAC systems, energy sources, and lighting have proven to be a cost-beneficial application in most plant operations. Due to the highly specialized nature of energy management and computerized security systems, commercially available equipment and software should be the only alternative considered. However, developing specifications and selecting energy and security systems can be complex (Hansen 1983). Computerized custodial and maintenance schedules and other record-keeping functions can be developed locally using a standard data-base software package. The need for sophistication in these systems and the resulting cost benefits will vary depending on the size of the district.

Transportation Management

Transportation routes, bus stops, pupil assignment, bus fleet maintenance, fuel consumption, and other tasks associated with the management of a school district transportation system are candidates for computerized application. A recent study in California (Edwards 1983) finds that significant savings in fuel, as well as other operating and capital expenses, could be achieved if computer management were applied to fleets of twenty or more buses. Comprehensive transportation software usually requires extensive work by local district personnel or a contractor to complete geocoded mapping of residences within the district; integration of that data with information from the school census and attendance zones; and the identification of safe bus stops.

A few transportation system software packages or services are available commercially. Others have been developed by school districts or computer services cooperatives. The payoffs on the use of such systems will vary significantly from district to district. Some of the information can be used for other purposes, for example, simulation of changes in school attendance zones. Care should be exercised in the decision to computerize and in the selection of a system or service. Districts that contract for their transportation service may not realize benefits unless the district plans and manages the routing and can change the service parameters required without significant delays or penalty costs.

Food Service

Food service is another area where significant potential exists for computerized management systems. Food service needs include menu planning (nutritional and cost-based), participation data, free/reduced-price program data, food management, and comparative cost data for marketing the service to the consumer. There is a scarcity of software in this area presently.

Reporting

Special attention should be given by the school business manager to the reporting capabilities of software designed to meet information service requirements in the aforementioned application areas. School business responsibilities for reporting to district administrators, the school board, the community, the state, and the federal government will continue to increase. Recent technological advances in graphics software provide new opportunities for summarizing lengthy reports in understandable, graphic form. New software techniques allow flexible, customized report generation at the local district level without costly specialized programming. School business managers should not be satisfied with uniform, inflexible report modules in software packages.

Office Automation

School business managers must not overlook the area of general office support. Computer-based office systems, with sophisticated word-processing capability, offer tools to improve both office productivity and the quality of written materials throughout the district. Computerized telephone and communication systems offer opportunities to transfer work tasks and data files electronically from data bases located elsewhere to a school work station. Electronic mail or messages within the district is a reality of today's technology, as is the electronic storage of information, thereby replacing the paper and file cabinet era.

Office technology and software are commercially available from numerous vendors in today's marketplace. A long-range plan for office automation, accompanied by the development of specifications, should be seriously considered by the school business manager as an added area of districtwide responsibility.

Other Information Requirements

Many other school district information requirements and computerized applications, such as student or instructional systems, can provide data to the school business manager for program-based budgeting and cost accounting. Such systems, however, require a comprehensive, data-base systems approach within which data from a number of subsystems can be integrated. Such systems are often accompanied by complex documentation and uniform standards that can limit the flexibility of the system to meet unique information needs at the building or functional level if not properly planned and designed.

MEETING YOUR INFORMATION NEEDS: SOME GUIDELINES

Having reviewed the potential computer applications for meeting the information requirements of school business management, including those listed in the preceding section, the inevitable question arises, "Where do I go from here?" Obviously the methodology or guidelines for answering that question will vary greatly depending on the already existing level of usage of computerized information systems by various school business managers. In some cases the manager already has access to a sophisticated data-base information system within the district or from an outside service agency and wishes merely to explore the new software packages available for the microcomputer, as an enhancement or alternative to existing service. At the other end of the spectrum, many school business managers have little or no access to computer equipment or software and are beginning for the first time to investigate alternatives for meeting their information needs.

Regardless of what is already in use in the district, a few practical guidelines should be followed by each school business manager as new applications are investigated (Sharp 1983; Talley 1983). The following section will identify and discuss each of these guidelines.

Identifying the Priority of Local Information Needs

Perhaps the most important guideline in investigating new information applications is to identify clearly, and in as much detail as possible, priority information that the local district wishes to address in the business management area. Whenever possible, a committee approach should be employed, which provides an opportunity for personnel at various working levels within the district to participate in this identification process. A phased, priority approach to addressing key information should be employed. In other words, define and prioritize the key information objectives in workable or manageable terms and apply each of the guidelines set forth in this section to each component or subobjective. If better financial forecasting is a priority of the district, break that process down into its logical components. In the case of revenue projection, this would involve identifying the key areas in which the accuracy of forecasting each source of revenue could be improved.

Reviewing Software or Service Alternatives

Once the areas of priority concentration have been identified, the next logical step is to review the service and software alternatives that could potentially meet your requirements. Some experts today will recommend that one should disregard hardware considerations at this point and concentrate solely on software. Such advice, however, does not take into account the fact that the district may already have a significant investment in hardware or receive service from a vendor or computer service agency. In either case, the only practical software options may be hardware-specific.

Any review of available software or service alternatives should begin as close to "home" as possible. If computer service is already available within the district, begin by investigating local options first. Then proceed to contact other school business managers within the same geographic area as well as local service or software vendors. Also, published directories of software can be consulted. The Association of School Business Officials (ASBO), the Association for Educational Data Systems (AEDS), and professional persons in the area can recommend directories.

As a special note, the alternative of developing applications software at the local school district level should be addressed at this point. Unless the district has an ongoing commitment to software development and maintenance (i.e., a willingness to employ and competitively retain professional systems analysts and programmers), the "do-it-yourself" alternative is not a viable one. The alternative of planning local changes to software, developed elsewhere, that involve modifications to source code at the program level is inadvisable for the same reason. Advertisements for many general-utility software packages today suggest that nontechnical users can meet their own local needs with no special programming. School business managers should approach this option cautiously unless they have some access to software consulting.

Narrowing the Choices

Once the alternative service or software options for meeting a specific information requirement have been identified, the next step is to narrow the choices. First, seek out written reviews and professional articles dealing with each of the alternatives or options. Second, construct a list of key questions regarding each software product or service that needs to be addressed in a demonstration. Third, arrange for a demonstration by the vendor. An onsite demonstration in your district is always preferable, since it allows other district personnel to view the product. Finally, if the results of the initial demonstration appear to warrant continued investigation, contact other users. Preferably other-user contact should be made locally with school business managers, since the experience of users in the private sector may not always have direct applicability.

If the initial demonstration produces questionable results, a second demonstration by an actual user at the user's site may be helpful in validating the vendor's claims and promises. Jones (1983: 35) has suggested the following questions that could be helpful during a user demonstration:

1. What limitations have you found in this system?
2. Did the product live up to its advertising?
3. How did you decide on this product?
4. Did you have to get additional hardware (printers, disc drives, memory, etc.) to make implementation of this software successful?
5. What would you do differently if you were to do this again from the beginning?

Following the above investigation, deliberately narrow the alternatives still under consideration to no more than three software packages or service options.

Making the Final Selection—Criteria

In making the final selection of a software package or service alternative, numerous criteria can be considered. A few key factors are mentioned frequently. However, the final weighing of these criteria, as well as others that the local school business manager or selection committee might identify, should be determined locally. At a minimum, the following criteria should be considered.

User Friendliness. Does the program offer a menu of selected options or program alternatives that allow the user to access a specific part of the program immediately with a minimum of unnecessary steps? Does the information on the display device communicate with the user in English rather than symbols or technical jargon, which require continuous reference to glossaries of terms and detailed instructions? Does the program logically sequence and facilitate the work of the user? Does the program provide proper editing to minimize user error?

Documentation. Does the documentation contain sample screens, sample printouts, and a complete explanation of error messages? If these first tests are met, does the user manual also contain an overview, a tutorial section, a command summary, a technical section, a troubleshooting section, and an index? (Brummit 1983).

User Training. Does the software vendor or service agency provide training? Are the training sessions structured and sequenced according to sound principles of instruction? Are qualified instructors available locally? Are follow-up training sessions available on short notice for replacement personnel? Are programmed instructional materials or interactive computer-assisted training materials available? Will the district receive notices on new or improved training sessions and materials as they become available?

Software Support. Does the software product have a warranty? Will enhancements or updates to the software be made available under the original agreement? Are there procedures for submitting suggested improvements to the vendor or service agency? How does the vendor or service agency communicate regarding software bugs and how are the resultant program changes released to users?

User Support. Are user-assistance services available to the user locally or through a toll-free hotline? Can onsite assistance be made available on a same-day or next-day basis?

Flexibility to Meet Local Needs. Does the software package or service provide the user with optional report formats? Will the system interface with a standard communications software package, thereby allowing the transfer of data and integration with other information system components?

Cost. What are the components of the total cost of the service or software package? Are training, documentation, and user support included within the basic price? Will new service options or software versions require added cost? What additional or new hardware requirements are necessary to implement the service or software package? What is the projected life expectancy of the software and the additional hardware?

Implementing and Evaluating

Once the final service or software product is selected, an implementation plan should be developed. The implementation plan should be in writing, but its complexity will vary depending on the nature of the software product or service being implemented. At a minimum, the plan should detail the tasks, responsibilities, and timelines of both the vendor or service agency and key local district personnel. Finally, the plan should clearly define expected outcomes and improvements in information to be derived from the use of the new service or software.

Once the new service or software product is in place for a full cycle in the targeted information area, the effort should be evaluated on the basis of "return on investment." Return on investment in this instance can be determined by assessing whether the costs allocated to equipment, software, services, and personnel time were justified by the information derived and its consequent improvement in the decision-support capability of the local school business manager and the superintendent.

THE FUTURE: CONCERNS AND ISSUES

A number of general concerns and issues with respect to the use of computerized information systems will continue to confront management in the future. School business managers, like others in management, will address these concerns and issues differently, based on their level of awareness and their experience with computerized information systems. Continued advances in information processing by both hardware manufacturers and software developers could produce new concerns and issues. However, to some degree most of the concerns and issues discussed below are likely to be with the school business manager into the next century.

Comprehensive, Long-Range Information Needs Assessment

Today's new information processing technology (i.e., microcomputers and narrowly structured, stand-alone application packages) has created a strong tendency for school business managers to focus on a short-sighted definition of the information needs of the school district. While a sharp focus is usually an appropriate initial step in exposing school business managers and other personnel to the potential benefits of information processing, it is also devoid in most instances of any attempt to define longer range information needs. Superintendents, like other top management in private industry, will have to provide leadership to assure that a comprehensive, long-range definition of both the data and information needs of the organization is eventually developed, including a commitment to review and update information needs continually.

A corollary issue relates to the question of whether districts should also develop a long-range technology utilization plan, which addresses the types of technology and software to be employed in meeting the district's information needs. The rapidly changing nature of today's technology makes such planning complex at best. However, as the district makes decisions and investments in technology, the "how-to" aspects of planning will take on a narrower and less complex dimension.

Who Will be the Users?

The issue of who the actual users of information technology should be will continue to be a major point of discussion into the future.

Advertisements today suggest that everyone in the school district from the clerk to the superintendent should learn to operate information technology. This question must inevitably be addressed within the context of local personnel resources and district information policy. The practical consideration of how much time school business managers have available to devote to training and actual detailed operation of software packages on the computer is likely to be the major determinant. Once the initial fascination of being an actual operator of the system has waned, combined with the increasing availability of information for decisionmaking, the delineation between information system operators and information users will be clearer.

Ultimately, most school business managers will choose to be solely an information user, who asks questions and defines parameters, while relying heavily upon other district support staff for the expertise to actually operate systems. The notion suggested by today's futurists that the personal computer will replace the attaché case as the constant companion of tomorrow's manager is more likely to be determined by individual preference and the human tendency to delegate routine tasks.

The "Micro" Phenomenon

Technological trends today clearly indicate a long-term exposure to the phenomenon of packing more processing power and data storage capacity into smaller and smaller physical space. The psychological effects of this reality upon school business managers, as they engage in information planning, can lead to the assumption that the information needs of every individual working in the school district can be met in a self-contained manner at their individual work station. The tendency to overemphasize the "micro" approach clearly ignores the realities of the interrelatedness and interdependence of data and information derived at various points throughout the school district organization. The emphasis in the future is more likely to be on integrated data bases and more sophisticated data-base systems, as we move from a data explosion to information- and knowledge-processing systems. A clear and present concern, with which every school business manager must maintain awareness, is the requirement to counterbalance the influence of microtechnology with the "macro" data-base information needs of the district.

Telecommunications

One solution to maintaining a balance between the potential of microtechnology and macroinformation needs lies in the future of the telecommunications industry, which is lined closely to the future of computing. Telephone communication has become an essential tool of the modern school business manager. Likewise, the ability for computers at individual work stations to communicate and transfer data, as well as to access other data bases outside the district, will become an ingredient of the future information system. School business managers must therefore ensure that future telecommunications capability in the district recognizes the long-range importance of electronic data and information transfer in addition to voice communication.

The Human-Machine Interface

Increasing emphasis by both computer equipment manufacturers and medical researchers into ergonomics is being placed on the design considerations and possible harmful side effects of the extended time that members of the workforce will spend at electronic work stations. While solutions to this problem are principally within the purview of computer equipment and office furniture manufacturers, the school business manager should maintain increasing sensitivity to the specifics of this growing problem, for example, display screen color, screen glare, and work station design. Managers should rely heavily upon the product evaluations of those personnel who will have actual operation responsibility.

Security

As school business managers and school districts become increasingly reliant upon computerized information systems, and as more personnel in the district have access to both data and computer programs, the issues of data privacy and potential computer crime become more real. Assuring that proper security measures are in place to prevent unauthorized access to physical areas within each school plant, to specific computer systems, to individual data bases, and to the information derived from that data is a complex task. Both the superintendent and the school business manager should ensure that someone in the school district has specific responsibility for security procedures. Information will increasingly be regarded as a valuable resource and a source of power within every organization. The financial resources and confidential data on students are maintained by the school district as a public trust. Potential illegal electronic access and misuse of those resources or data constitute a major security risk that could erode that public trust.

Contingency Planning

As school districts and school business managers become increasingly reliant upon computerized data and information-processing systems, based on increasingly reliable technology, there may be a tendency to ignore or overlook a very practical consideration, that is, What do we do when the system doesn't work? School business managers should develop and maintain contingency plans, which assure access to an alternative computer resource when computer equipment becomes inoperative. Major computer installations maintain "back-up" agreements with other computer sites for such purposes. As the local school district decentralizes and diversifies its use of the computer across many work stations and types of computer equipment, a contingency plan that assures computer equipment back-up for each work station and critical application should be in place. Additionally, since each critical application is equally reliant upon the operational expertise of specific staff members, the business manager should ensure that key personnel responsibilities for these applications are adequately backed up by other trained personnel.

Information Processing

Many of today's computer applications can best be described as data processing rather than information processing. The typical data-processing system today is built on the foundation of a data base containing data elements that the user inserts into the system. The user then constructs programmed instructions by which the computer sorts, calculates, compiles, and reports the results. These systems provide data-processing service and some decision-support information. Currently, major investments in human and financial resources are being made in the United States and Japan to produce a fifth-generation "supercomputer," which will allow the achievement of true information, knowledge-based processing (Kinnucan 1984). Plans for these systems of the future are based on the growing science of artificial intelligence (AI). They will potentially allow users access to automated decisionmaking capability. These computer systems will have access to large knowledge bases stored in their own memory, as well as "dial-up" access to other data banks. The system will further have the ability to define options and recommend solutions, based on principles already stored in the system, as well as new principles derived from the computer's learning experience. The software design of these systems will more nearly simulate the functions of the human mind.

The Cost

Predictably, school business managers will initially target their attention on start-up capital costs for computer and office automation equipment, as well as the increased personnel costs associated with training and data-base construction. Then attention will be given to ongoing costs for technology and software maintenance, as well as capital replacement costs. Changes in technology and software will give increasing visibility to the issue of rapid obsolescence.

Attention will later turn to efficiency studies that will attempt to measure the cost benefits of improved productivity in the office and improved information flow in the administration of the school district. The benefits will be described as a return on investment in managing the information resource.

The issue of longer-range cost, however, will focus more sharply on the projected cost detriment of insufficient information. School business managers will increasingly face a single question from superintendents, school board members, and in their own thinking, that is, "What would it cost the district if the proposed information resource is not available?" The detrimental effects of short-sighted information planning and management on costs will become all too obvious in the future. Public awareness in the availability of more powerful information tools for revenue and expenditure projection, cash-flow management, investment management, and inventory management will gradually try the patience and understanding of superintendents and school board members with "margins of error" that might have been acceptable in the past.

The cost of human resources, including the time of the school business manager, to manually perform information tasks associated with numerous alternative scenarios constitutes a major argument for initial investment. In the future, however, school business managers must be prepared to address the real cost of a failure to utilize and expand the district's automated information system.

As one case in point, school superintendents and school business managers will consider the direct and associated costs of using computerized graphics to present major points more understandably in their communication with the school board and the community. If passage of an additional mill levy hangs in the balance, the real cost of failure to utilize every available information and communication tool becomes readily apparent.

A FINAL THOUGHT

The use of computers in school business management is not a prospect. It is a reality in many school districts today and an immediate opportunity for all others. The school business manager is responsible for managing the assets and resources of the school district. Information is a major asset of every organization in today's world, one that will become more valuable in the future.

School business managers should assume a leadership role in planning for and implementing computerized information systems. Responsible management of the resources of school districts can be a key to maintaining confidence in public education. Public education is big business. Its constituents and supporters have a right to expect the financial resources of those institutions to be well-managed with modern information technology.

REFERENCES

Brummit, B. 1983. "What To Know About Software Documentation." In *Administrative Uses for Microcomputers, Vol. I: Software*, edited by F. Dembowski, pp. 55-60. Park Ridge, Illinois: Association of School Business Officials.

Edwards, James C. 1983. "California's Computerized Pupil Transportation Systems." *School Business Affairs* 49 no. 7 (July): 48-49.

Hansen, Shirley. 1983. "Selecting and Specing Energy Management Systems." *The School Administrator* 40, no. 10 (November): 10-14.

Jones, B. 1983. "Selecting Microcomputer Software: Administration." In *Administrative Uses for Microcomputer, Vol. I: Software*, edited by F. Dembowski, pp. 32-37. Park Ridge, Illinois: Association of School Business Officials.

Kinnucan, Paul. 1984. "Computers That Think Like Experts." *High Technology* 4, no. 1 (January): 30-37.

Sharp, David R. 1983. "Stalking the Business Computer." *Small Business Computer* 7, no. 4 (September/October): 36-38.

Talley, Sue. 1983. "Selection and Acquisition of Administrative Microcomputer Software." *AEDS Journal* 17, nos. 1 and 2 (Fall and Winter): 69-82.

Westrend Group. 1983. "Restructuring of the Education Delivery Systems." *Learning Trends* 1, no. 2 (September): 1.

INDEX

Abramson, P., 116
Academic quality, 7-8, 10, 82. *See also* Access; Achievement test scores; Competency testing; Curriculum standards; Equity
Access, 2, 7-8, 15, 25, 82
Accountability: for financial management, 1, 8, 29, 31; for student outcomes, 8, 59, 64, 221
Accounting: 29-57; use of computer in, 249-50
Accrual basis (accounting), 32, 35
Achievement awards, 22
Achievement test scores, 7-8, 82. *See also* Scholastic Aptitude Test
Action for Excellence, 7, 22
Adopt-a-school, 129, 137
Advisory Committee on Intergovernmental Relations, 112
Advisory committees, 19, 75-77, 212
Aged population, 3, 13, 82, 184
Alabama: elective course fees, 134
À la carte service, 193-95
Aljian, G. W., 226
Allegheny (Penna.) Conference for Community Development, 138
Allocative decisionmaking. *See* Budgeting

Amador Valley (Calif.) Joint Union High School District, 137
American Bar Association, 234
American Institute of Certified Public Accountants, Auditing Procedures, 40
American Municipal Bond Assurance Corporation (AMBAC), 121
American School Food Services Association (ASFSA), School Food Services Foundation, 189
Anderson, Arthur, and Co. (study), 44-46
Anderson, B. D., 102
Appleton Area (Wis.) School District, 132, 135-36
Apprenticeships, 138
Arbitrage bonds, 123
Arizona Teachers' Retirement System, 106
Artificial intelligence (AI), 265
Asset management, 46-48, 70, 147-62
Assessment, Improvement, and Monitoring System (AIMS), 181, 187-88
Association for Educational Data Systems (AEDS), 257

269

Association of School Business Officials of the United States and Canada (ASBO), School Accounting Research Committee, 33, 53, 147, 239, 257
Athearn, James L., 150
Auctioning, 243
Audit guidelines, federal, 45
Auditing, 29, 38-46
Augenblick, John, 170
Automation, 222-25, 249, 255

Baby boom, 2, 81-82, 204
Back-to-back routing, 172
Baltimore City Foundations, Inc., 131
Bargaining, 20-21, 69, 77-78. *See also* Collective bargaining
Barger, Robert N., 5
Barr, W. Monfort, 115
Bartages, Paul, 147
Bartlesville (Okla.) Public Schools, 132-33, 139
Basic skills, 77, 138
Beloit (Wis.) Public Schools, 130, 135
Bidding, 104, 173, 222, 225, 229, 233-34, 244
Bidding insurance, 160, 162
Bilingual education, 4, 72
Blanket ordering, 222, 225-26, 228-29
Block grants, 45-46. *See also* Grant programs
Boles, Harold, 209
Bond attorneys, 125
Bond banks, 112
Bond Buyer 20 Bond Index, 118
Bond default, 119-20, 127
Bond elections, 4, 116-17
Bond ratings, 30, 119-20, 127. *See also* Moody's Investor Service, Inc.; Standard and Poor's Corp.
Bond redemption, 124
Bond registration, 124
Bonds, municipal, 114-27
Book give-aways, 243-44
Booster clubs, 131-32
Bork, Alfred, 5
Borrowing, 50, 60, 94
Boyer, Ernest L., 22
Brackett, John, 74
Bracstrup, Peter, 9
Brames, Fred, 135

Brown Brothers Harriman and Co., 105
Brown, Oliver, 216
Brown, Richard, Jr., 159
Brummit, B., 259
Bryan, E. L., 198
Budget: definition of, 60; types of, 60, 62
Budget adoption, 62, 69
Budget amendment, 63
Budget cycle, 61; overlap, 63; phases of, 61
Budgeting, 59-85; computers and, 6, 31, 249-50; orientation, 63-68; political process and, 64, 68; rational, 64, 68, 71-74, 84
Building authorities, 112, 127n
Building reserve funds, 114
Burbank, C. William, 133
Buses, school: fueling of, 175-77; longevity of, 172-74; maintenance of, 174, 178
Bussard, R. N., 103

California: insurance administration in, 155-56, 158, 161; transportation study in, 254
California Business Roundtable (CBRT), 23
Call, R. V., 222
Callable bonds, 125
Camp, William E., 112
Campbell, Ronald F., 11
Candoli, Carl, 31, 155, 160
Capital management, 33, 60, 80, 113, 115, 249-52
Career development programs, 138
Career guidance programs, 12, 138
Carter, Jimmy, 43, 45
Carnegie Foundation, 7
Cash basis accounting and reporting, 35
Cash flow: chart, 49, 97, 100, 102; patterns, 99-100; uncertainty of, 99
Cash management, 29, 33, 48-50, 60, 87, 94-102, 249-51
Caswell, G. G., 226
Center routing, 172
Centralization, compared to (budgeting) decentralization: 16, 18-19, 75-80, 85
Certificate of Conformance (MFOA), 53

Certificate of deposit (CD), 48, 51, 88, 96
Certificate of Excellence in Financial Reporting in School Systems (ASBO), 53
CETA, 45
Chambers, Jay, 74
Child Care Food Program, 183–84
Child Nutrition Act (CNA), 182, 200
Chino (Calif.) Unified School District, 136–37
City of Baltimore (Md.) School District, 131
Civil rights, 69
Clark County (Nev.) School District, 135
Class size, 23
Closure, school, 2, 211–213. *See also* Retrenchment
Coalition building, 83
Coinsurance, 152–53
Collective bargaining, 1, 11, 18, 20–21, 79–80
Colorado, school transportation services in, 168
Committee on Economic Development (CED), 23–24
Commodity Food Program, 181–82, 190–91
Commodity study (USDA), 185
Commodity Supplemental Food Program, 184
Community support: consolidation and, 212; control, 18–20; erosion of, 2; facility management and, 204
Comparative budget theory (Wildavsky), 64, 66
Compensatory education, 4
Competency testing, 7–8
Compliance audit, 45–46
Comprehensive annual financial report (CAFR), 36–37
Computer crime, 263–64
Computer education. *See* Computer literacy
Computerization: facility management, 205, 253; financial management, 71, 75, 247–52; purchasing, 222–23, 225; school business management, 247–66; transportation services, 172, 254
Computer literacy, 5–6, 12

Condition of Teaching, The, 7
Connecticut, property tax in, 169
Consolidation, 16, 204, 207, 212, 215. *See also* Retrenchment
Consortiums, 52–53
Constitutional rights, 77
Construction, facility, 113, 116, 204
Contingency planning, 264
Contracting, food service, 192–93
Control Data Corporation, 138
Control, financial, 29–31, 33, 41, 79, 249–50
Cooperative programs: of purchasing, 222, 230–33, 235; with business and industry, 137–39; with higher education, 135–36
Corporate gifts, 130
Cost avoidance, 140
Council of Educational Facilities Planners, 134
Counselor intern programs, 138
Coupon bond, 53
Courts, influence on education of, 11, 77
Current revenues, 113–14, 126
Curriculum: changes, 7; development, 22, 138; evaluation, 22; standards, 7; state prescribed, 76

Dade County (Fla.) Public Schools pool investment program, 51–52
Dallas (Tex.) School District, 131
Data collection, 248–49, 256–57
Data privacy, 263
Data processing, 248–49, 264–65
Davies, Don, 12, 19, 21
Day care, 5
Day, C. William, 217
Debt service: payments, 33, 249, 252; programs, 113, 115
Decentralization, 25, 55, 75; compared to (budgeting) centralization, 75–80, 85; public school tradition of, 9–10, 18–20
Decision packages, 72–73
Deductibles, high, 152–53, 157
Default: bond, 119–20, 127; fear of social security, 148
Deficit spending, 63
Delaware, school transportation services in, 170
Deliveries, equipment and supply, 241

Delsol, Louis, 157
Dembowski, Frederick L., 93-95, 97-98, 101-3
Denver City (Colo.) Schools, 133
Deregulation, 148
Deriso, Jerald L., 205
Desegregation, 169
Detroit (Mich.) Public School System, 132, 138
Direct deposit, payroll, 101
Disaster area populations, 184
Dismissals, teacher, 7
Diversity, 9-10
Donated Food Distribution Program, 185-86
Donations: food, 185-86; funds, 13-32; goods, 130, 132-33; services, 130, 132
Double-entry accounting, 31
Drebin, Allan R., 32, 48
Driver education, 134
Dropout rate, 2
Dual occupancy, 126. *See also* Joint occupancy
Durham County (N.C.) School District PTO, 132

Eaton (Colo.) School District, 176
Educating Americans for the 21st Century, 22
Educational opportunity, 6, 77, 169
Education Commission of the State, 7
Education mismatch, 8
Edwards, James C., 254
Efficiency, production, 42
Elderly Feeding Program, 184, 186
Elective courses, 134
Employment year, teachers', 22
England, W., 226-27
Energy: conservation, 210-11; management, 206, 210-11, 253
Enrichment fund, 131
Enrollments: declining, 2, 13-14, 82, 85, 134, 165, 177, 195, 211-15, 218; increases in, 3, 165, 207, 212
Equalization aid, 112
Equipment, 22, 249, 253
Equity, 7-8, 14-15, 25, 74, 80
Escondido County (Calif.) Union High School District, 131
Evanston (Ill.) School District, 133

"Examination of the Types of Nontraditional Financing Methods and Their Present and Potential Impact on Public School Districts, An" (Meno), 140-43
Excellence: commitment to, 10, 25; financing, 13, 15; planning and managing, 203-4
Expenditure planning, 60, 69-70
Expenditures, 14-16, 63, 70, 129

Facilities, educational: adaptive reuse of, 212-15; construction of, 113, 116, 204; designing, 217-18; increased utilization of, 206-7, 211-18; interagency use of, 215-16; long-range plans for, 298-9; modernization of, 206-10, 218; proposed annual survey of, 208; purposes of, 205-6
Facility management: 203-18, 249, 253; community support and, 204; computers and, 205-6, 208, 249, 253; operational funds and, 208
Fall River (Mass.) Public Schools, 123
Family structure, 4, 25
Federal National Mortgage Association, 96
Federally funded projects, 49
Financial Accounting Foundation, 55
Financial reporting, 29-56. *See also* Auditing
Fine, I. V., 228
Fiscal control budgeting, 70, 84
Fiscal federalism, 15
Fiscal period, 60
Fixed assets, 32
Fleeing to quality, 120
Florida: government pooling federations in, 104; transportation bidding in, 173
Food and Nutrition Service (FNS), 187, 191
Food Distribution Programs, 184-85
Food programs, 179-89, 198-99
Food services, 179-200; computers and, 249, 254; contracting, 133, 192; director training and certification, 189; management and operations, 193-98; survey, 185-87
Food storage, 196-97

INDEX

Forecasting, financial, 48, 61, 63, 67, 249–50
Foreign language education, 8. *See also* Bilingual education; Trilingualism
Foundation grants, 130
Fox, G. Thomas, Jr., 9
Fraud: detection, 41, 47; deterrence, 47, 241; liability for, 120
Friedlob, G. T., 198
Friese, J. C., 197
Fringe benefits, 253
Frost & Sullivan, Inc., 199
Full disclosure, 31
Fund accounting systems, 32, 35–36, 60, 63
Fund balance forecasts, 63
Funds, federal, 35–36

Gander, Peggy, 151
Gara, Robert, 157
Garms, Walter, 4, 11, 20, 75
Gates Foundation, 131
General Motors, 138
Generally accepted accounting principles (GAAP), 35, 56, 63
General obligation bonds, 115, 117–18
General purpose financial statement (GPFS), 36–37
Gensemer, B. L., 221
Gifted education, 12
Gilroy, S. K., 190
Gloucester Township (N.J.) School District PTO, 132
Goals, educational, 9–10, 13
Goldberg and Marchesano and Associates, 138
Goodlad, John, 7, 18
Governance, school, 10–11, 19; changes in, 10–13; decentralization of, 25, 195; participation in, 12–13, 25. *See also* Community support; School site management
Governmental Accounting Standards Board, 55
Government securities. *See* U.S. Treasury bills and notes
Graduation requirements, 7, 74
Grant programs, 112, 170; auditing of, 43–45. *See also* Block grants
Graphics software, 255

Greenville (S.C.) School District, 52
Griffin-Spaulding County (Ga.) School District, 130, 139
Guthrie, James W., 20, 75

Haig, Robert M., 169
Handicapped education, 8, 12, 69, 77, 80, 169, 173. *See also* Special education
Hanes, Carol E., 170
Hansen, Shirley, 253
Harmer, Gary, 55
Harroun, Leon E., 157–58
Hartford (Conn.) City School District, 130
Hawaii, school transportation legislation in, 168, 170
Hazelwood (Mo.) School District, 134, 137
Head Start program, 45
Health insurance, 155, 159, 161
Henke, Cliff, 174–76
Hester, Dwight, 151
Hill, Thom, 148
Hispanic population, 4
Home computers, 6
Homework, 7
Horry County (S.C.) School District, 137
Hough, Wesley C., 53
Hoyle, John R., 5
Hunt, Allan, 156
Hutton, E. F. and Company, Inc., 106

Idle funds, 33, 93–94, 99, 101
Illinois: government pooling federations in, 104; medical self-insurance programs in, 157; school transportation in, 168; textbook rental in, 134
Illiteracy, functional, 8
Incrementalism, 67
Indiana, textbook rental in, 134
Indian reservations, 184
Industrial orientation programs, 138
Information processing, 247–49, 264–65
In Search of Excellence, 17
Institute for Educational Development, 138
Instruction, computerized management of, 5–6

Instructional hours (minimum), 77, 79
Insurance: alternatives to, 148, 151; costs of, 148, 152, 161; market competition, 148-49; reserves, 151; and risk management, 147-67. *See also* Coinsurance; Deductibles; Pooling, Self-insurance; Stop-loss coverage; Unbundling
Insurance Institute of America, 60
Interest groups, educational, 10, 21, 75, 83, 213
Internal control, 29, 41; MFOA definition of, 46-47
Internal Revenue Service (IRS): Code of Federal Regulations, 123; Final Arbitrage Regulation, 50, 123-24
Inventories, 196-97, 249, 251-52
Investment: cash management and, 33, 48, 94-96; computer use in, 249-51; definition of, 88; management, 87-107, 108n; types of, 88
Iowa, textbook rental in, 134

Jaret, F., 234
Jaret, M., 234
Jenkins, Harvey L., 157-58
Job placement programs, 138
Johns, Roe L., 114, 170
Johnson, Lyndon, 64
Johnson, Ronald W., 61
Joint occupancy, 212-15, 218
Joint ventures, governmental, 53-55
Jones, B., 258
Jordan, K. Forbis, 170

Kannwischer, M. D., 189
Kansas, elective course fees in, 134
Kavulla, T. A., 195
Keenan, John R., 155-56, 158, 161
Kelly, James A., 15
Kentucky, Model Procurement Code, 234-35
Kern County (Calif.) maintenance coop, 174
Kinnucan, Paul, 265
Kirst, Michael W., 4, 11, 23, 80-81
Klein, Ken, 158
Knezevich, Stephen J., 64-65
Kuhn, 48

LaChance, P. R., 198-200
Lane, C. Jerome, 205
Larson, William A., 159
Laser communications, 6
Lease-purchase agreements, 126
Leasing: of school facilities, 133-34, 212-14, 216; of school services, 133
Lee County (Fla.) School District, 158
Lee, Robert D., Jr., 61
Lehman, G. O., 230
Lenz, Matthew, 150
Levine, Marsha, 7, 12, 22
Liability, school district, 148, 151, 161
Life insurance, 159, 161
Loan funds, 112
Loaned executives, 129
Local banks, 48
Local education authorities (LEAs), 187
Local Planning and Budgeting Model (LPBM), 74-75, 84-85
Local preference, 68-70, 84
Loss prevention and control, 148-49, 151-52. *See also* Risk management
Lotus 1-2-3, 250

Macaluso, J., 234
Mac-Phail-Wilcox, Bettye, 101
Malconado, R. M., 102
Maeroff, Gene I., 131
Maintenance, equipment, 244
Maintenance, facility, 206-8, 218
Marsh, R. H., 226
Martin County (N.C.) School District, 136
Massachusetts: early school transport legislation, 165, 168; property tax financing of education, 169
Mathematics, 8, 22
Mazzoni, Tim L., Jr., 11
McLawhorn, Charles W., 52
McMurrin, Lee R., 5
McNett, Ian E., 23
Memphis (Tenn.) Public School System, 137
Meneffe, Gerald R., 155-56, 158, 161
Meno, Lionel R., 130-31, 133-34, 140-45
Merced City School District (Calif.), 136

Merger. *See* Consolidation
Merit pay, 7
Meulder, W. R., 102
Michigan: pooling federations in, 104, 107
Microcomputers, 261
Microtechnology, 262
Migration, differential, 3, 25
Millard (Omaha, Neb.) School District, 171
Minnesota, revenue pooling in, 79
Minnesota Business Partnership, 23
Minority population, 2-4, 8, 25, 77
Moody's Investors Service, 117-19
Moore, Francis E., 47
Moyer, Linford, 103
Moyer, Ralph W., 147
Multiple reporting, 34
Municipal bond failure, 119-20
Municipal Bond Insurance Association (MBIA), 121
Municipal bonds. *See* Bonds
Municipal Finance Officers Association (MFOA), 30, 32, 37-38, 40, 46, 53; Certificate of Conformance, 37
Munsterman, R. E., 237
Murry Bergtraum High School for Business Careers Lower Manhattan Area (New York City), Program, 138

Naisbett, John, 6, 8
Natale, Joseph, 151, 159
National Academy of Sciences, 181
National Association for the Exchange of Industrial Resources (NAEIR), 133
National Center for Education Statistics, 3, 165-67
National Commission on Excellence, 7
National Council on Governmental Accounting, *Governmental Accounting and Financial Principles* (Statement 1), 35-37, 54-55
National Highway Traffic Safety Administration, 173
National Commodity Processing System, 185, 190-91
National Research Council, Food Nutrition Board, 181
National School Lunch Program (NSLP), 180-82, 184, 186, 195

National School Board Association (survey), 236
National School Resources Network, 138
National Science Board, 22
Nation at Risk, A, 7
Natural Gas Policy Act, 177
Nebraska, school transportation in, 168, 170-71
Needy Family Program, 184
Negotiated contracts, 20-22
New Mexico, school transportation in, 170
New York City Educational Construction Fund, 126
New York (state) School System, 156, 169
"No insurance," 152-53
Noncertified school employees, 21
Nontraditional financing methods (NTFM), 129-39
North Carolina, elective course fees in, 134
North Glenn (Colo.) School District, 131
NOW accounts, 96
Nutrition education, 186-88, 198-99
Nutrition Education and Training Program, 186
Nutrition programs, child, 179-84. *See also* National School Lunch Program; School Breakfast Program; Special Milk Program

Oakland (Calif.) City Schools cooperative programming, 138
Oatman, Donald W., 54
Obsolescence, technological, 5
Obsolete property, disposal of, 242-43
"Offer versus serve" food service plan, 181, 193-94
Older American Act, 184
Omnibus Reconciliation Act, 45
Orphanages, school lunch program and, 181

Palley Simon Associates, 156
Parent advisory councils, 19
Parental involvement, 10, 15, 18-19, 21-22, 25, 76, 131

Parochial schools, transportation services and, 161
Parrish, Thomas, 74
Pavline, Lawrence, 213
Payroll, 104, 249, 252
Pennsylvania: pooling federations in, 104, 107, 156
Pennsylvania School District Liquid Asset Fund (PSDLAF), 104-7
Peoria (Ill.) Public School District, 136
Percentage-matching grants, 112
Performance budgeting approach, 70-71, 84
Personnel costs, 6, 212, 265
Peters, Thomas J., 17-18
Phoenix Union (Ariz.) High School District, 134-35
Pierce, Lawrence C., 20, 75
Pitruzello, Philip, 213
Place Called School, A, 7
Planning: expenditure, 69-70, 75-78; program, 69, 75-77; revenue, 69-70, 75-76, 79. *See also* Budgeting
Plewes, M. S., 199
Pluralism, public school tradition of, 9-10
Pogrow, Stanley, 6
Pogue, G. A., 103
Policymaking. *See* Governance
Politics, education and, 80-84
Pollution control, 175-76
Pooling, 49, 51-52, 104, 152, 155-57, 161
Poor population, 6, 8
Population, U.S.: shifts in age and racial composition of, 3-4, 25
Preemployment training, 138
Prentiss, B. R., 189
Pre-refunding, 123, 125
Principals, 20, 22, 26
Private business, 22-24, 137-39
Private schools, transportation to, 169
Productivity accounting, 53-54
Program plan. *See* Budget
Program budgeting. *See* Performance budgeting
Program-oriented budgeting. *See* Performance budgeting
Program Planning Budgeting Systems (PPBS), 59, 64-65, 71-72, 84
Property coverage, 155, 159, 161

Property tax, 79, 112, 169
Proposition 2½ (Mass.), 112
Proposition 13 (Calif.), 112
Public Law, 92-142, 169
Public Law, 94-105, 182
Public Risk Insurance Management Association, 160
Purchasing: cooperative, 225, 230-32; cost effectiveness and, 222; development of, 221-45; ethics in, 239-40; evaluation of, 237-39; small order, 225-26, 229-30; stockless, 225-26; traditional framework for, 223-24; use of computer in, 222-23, 225, 233, 240, 249, 251-52
Purchasing handbook, 236-37, 240
Pure risk, 149, 152
Pyhrr, Peter A., 72
Pyramid reporting, 36-38

Quotations, purchasing, 233-35

Rakich, Ronald, 150-51, 158, 160, 162
Ravitch, Diane, 10
Recognition certificates, 53-54
Recommended dietary allowance (RDA), 181
Reform, 6-10, 13, 15-16, 18, 25-26, 69, 81
Reisler, Raymond F., 4
Remedial education, 8, 138
Repetitive budgeting, 67
Repurchase agreement, 96
Resource-Cost Model (RCM), 74
Retarded children, 181
Retraining, technological, 6
Retrenchment, 211-16
Revenue anticipation notes, 96-97
Revenue development, 129-44
Revenue planning, 60, 69-70, 75-76, 78-79
Revenue sources, traditional, 111-27. *See also* Property tax
Revenue sources, alternative, 129-44
Revzan, Henry A., 152, 161
Rialto (Calif.) Unified School District, 133
Ricks, J. F., 189
Risk avoidance, 148, 151, 154, 162
Risk evaluation, 150
Risk exposures, 155; audit of, 150

INDEX

Risk management, 53, 147–62
Risk Management Society, 160
Risk retention, 148, 151–59
Risk transference, 151–52, 160–62
Ritter, L. S., 102
Rocky Mountain (Colo.) School Study Council, 231
"Rolled-over" financing, 122
Routing, school bus, 171–72, 178
Rowan County (N.C.) School District, 132
Runaway shelters, 181

Sacramento (Calif.) City Schools, 136
Salaries, 7. *See also* Payroll
Sale/lease-back principle, 135
San Francisco (Calif.) School District, 131
Santa Barbara (Calif.) School District, 134
Satellite communications, 6
Satelliting, 193–94
Scanning, 61
Schergens, Becky, 138
Scholastic Aptitude Test, 8
Schomp, Katherine, 133
School access, sale of, 134–35
School boards: negotiated contracts, 22; policymaking, 16; purchasing policies, 236–37
School boards association, 11
School Breakfast Program, 182–84, 186, 195
School Bus Fleet, The (survey), 176
School Business Affairs, 198
School-based management. *See* School site management
School days, lengthening of, 7, 23
School site management, 1, 18–20, 55–56, 75–78; basic components of, 20; pilot grants for, 78
School year: lengthening of, 7, 23; minimum length of, 69
Schultz, Rachel W., 179n
Schwartz, Lee, 103
Scott, Charles, 132
Science, 8, 22
Seattle School District v. the State of Washington, 170
Secular humanism, 77
Self-insurance, 53, 152–59, 161
Self-monitoring, 93

Separation of powers, 61
Sex education, 72, 77
Shapiro, P., 225
Sharp, David R., 256
Short-term financing, 122
Single audit, 29, 38, 45–46
Small order purchasing, 225–26, 229–30, 234
Social security, 148
Software, computer, 247; capabilities of, in school business management, 248–56; selection of, 257–60
Sole sourcing, 225, 227–28
South Carolina, state insurance program, 159
Southfield (Mich.) Public Schools, 134
Space sharing, 214. *See also* Dual occupancy, Joint occupancy
Spataro, Anthony, 156
Special education, 4, 8, 77, 80, 169
Specialized schools, 23
Special Milk Program, 183, 186
Speculative risks, 152
Staff development programs, 8–9
Staff reductions, 2–3
Standard and Poor's Corporation, 119, 121
Stanford University, Institute for Research on Educational Finance and Governance, 74
State Board of Education Investment Pool, 49
State education agencies (SEAs), 187–188
Stettler, Howard F., 47
St. Louis (Mo.) City Schools, 138–39
Stockless purchasing, 225–27
Stollar, Dewey H., 168
Stop-loss coverage, 152–56, 158–61
Strayer, George D., 169
Stubbs, Donald R., 157
Student activity funds, 50–52
Student internship programs, 138
Student pictures. *See* School access
Subcontracting, 152
Subsidized food programs, 180–86
Summer Food Service Program, 184, 186
Summer school education, 134
Sumner, S., 102
Supercomputer, 265
Superintendents, 11, 16, 22

INDEX

Supplementary income, teachers', 22
Surety bonds, 152
Surplus property, 242-43
Sweeney, James, 147
Swimming instruction, 134
Systems analysis, 71
Systems contracting, 222, 225-27

Talley, Sue, 256
Task Force for Economic Growth, 22
Taxes, education and, 2, 14, 49, 79, 82. *See also* Property tax
Tax-exempt securities, 96, 119, 121
Taxpayer backlash, 22
Teacher organizations, 11-12, 21
Teacher performance, 7-8, 23
Teacher training, 7-9
Technology: curriculum development in, 22; and education, 2, 5-6, 15, 25, 247-66
Telecommunications, 5, 263
Temkin, K., 225
Test scores. *See* Achievement test scores, Scholastic Aptitude Test
Texas (state) Permanent Fund, 106
Textbook rental, 134
Third-party insurance, 120-21
Thornton Township (Ill.) High School District, 136
Trade-ins, equipment, 243
Training, technological, 5
Transfer payments, 31, 33
Transfer techniques, 152. *See also* Insurance, Subcontracting, Surety bonds
Transportation, 165-78; costs of, 165-67, 177-78; financing of, 169-71, 178; fuels and, 175-78; management of, 171-77, 249, 254; numbers served by, 165-67, 177; provision of, 168-69
Trilingualism, 6
Tucker, Marc S., 6
Tuition tax concessions, 18, 82

Unbundling, 152, 158-62
Uncertainty, fiscal, 63
Unions, 12, 20, 22
Universal public education, 82
University of Denver, Bureau of Educational Research, 232

Upper Merion Area (King of Prussia, Penna.) School District, 132
U.S. Department of Agriculture (USDA), 182, 184-85, 188, 190, 194, 197-99
U.S. Department of Defense, 64
U.S. Department of Education, 46, 64
U.S. Department of Health and Human Services, 46
U.S. Department of Housing and Urban Development, 46
U.S. Department of Labor, 5
U.S. News and World Report, 5
U.S. Office of Management and Budget (OMB), 45-46, 63; "Uniform Requirements for Grants to State and Local Governments," 45
U.S. Treasury, 49
U.S. Treasury, bills and notes, 96
User fees, 91, 133-34

Van Egemond-Pannell, D., 194
Vaughn, Emmet J., 150, 152, 160
Vehicles. *See* Buses
Vending machines. *See* School access
Vendor payment, 242
Vendors, visits to, 222, 232-33
Vigo County (Ind.) School District, 136
Virginia: insurance management study, 147; state building authority in, 127n
Visicalc, 250
Vocational Foundation, Inc., 138
Volunteer tutorial programs, 22
Voter approval, 76, 114-16, 127, 127n
Voter backlash, 22
Vouchers, 18, 82

"Walk-in" distances, 171, 178
Wallace, George, 232
Warehousing, 196-97, 226
Washington, D.C. School District, 131, 138
Washington Public Power Supply System, 120
Washington: school transportation in, 170; state-funded transportation maintenance coop, 174

Waterman, Robert H., Jr., 17-18
Wayne Central (N.Y.) School District, 134
Webb, L. Dean, 152
Weisbrod, Burton A., 142
Westran, Roy A., 153
Westerville (Ohio) School District, 135
Westing, J. H., 228
Wichita (Kan.) City Schools, Dental Prevention Model, 131
Wildavsky, Aaron, 64, 67, 80
Wilson Quarterly, 9
Winawer, H. H., 187-88
Wirt, Frederick M., 80-81

Wisconsin: elective course fees in, 134; government pooling federations in, 104; state bargaining rights legislation, 20-21
Women's movement, 8
Workers' compensation, 155-56, 161
Work/study programs, 138-39
WTS Consulting Services, Inc., 106

Yield curve, 122
Young, J., 229

Zenz, G. J., 229
Zero-based budgeting (ZBB), 59, 64, 72-74, 84-85

ABOUT THE EDITORS

L. Dean Webb is Professor of Educational Administration at Arizona State University. Formerly a public school teacher and administrator, she has participated in numerous state and local school finance studies. She has served on the board of directors of the American Education Finance Association (AEFA), the editorial advisory board of the *Journal of Education Finance*, and was co-editor of the 1984 AEFA yearbook, *School Finance and School Improvement: Linkages for the 1980s*. Dr. Webb has written extensively in the area of school finance and school law and is coauthor of several texts, including *Educational Administration: An Introduction* and *School Business Administration*.

Van D. Mueller is Professor of Educational Administration at the University of Minnesota. He has served on the Board of Directors of AEFA and the National PTA, and as a Minnesota representative to the Education Commission of the States. He has participated in several state school finance studies (Indiana, Missouri, Minnesota) in addition to chairing a legislatively established commission studying the impact of declining school enrollments in Minnesota. He currently serves on the Advisory Committee on Higher Education Relationships for AASA and directs the Minnesota site of the Education Policy Fellowship Program of the Institute for Educational Leadership.

ABOUT THE CONTRIBUTORS

E. Ronald Carruth is Executive Director of the Minnesota School Districts Data Processing Joint Board in St. Paul. His professional experience includes computer service cooperative director, assistant superintendency and secondary teaching. He has served as Secretary of the American Federation of Information Societies and as President of the Association for Educational Data Systems. His fields of interest include educational management information systems and instructional systems.

Gayden F. Carruth is Assistant Superintendent for the Inver Grove Heights, Minnesota school district. Her professional experience includes the assistant superintendency, research director, elementary principal and teacher. She received the AEFA dissertation award for outstanding research in the field of educational finance in 1981. Her fields of interest include educational finance, planning and instructional effectiveness.

C. William Day is Associate Professor and Program Head-School Administration at the School of Education, Indiana University. Day has published over sixty articles dealing with educational facilities, and has conducted field service work in twenty-seven states. He is serving his sixth term as President of the School Facility Council, a major division of the Associates of School Business Officials in the United States and Canada.

Joyce E. Ferguson is Supervisor of Purchasing for Aurora (CO) Public Schools. She is chairperson of the Association of School Business Officials and the Purchasing and Supply Management Research Committee, and former chair of the Rocky Mountain School Study Council Cooperative Purchasing Committee.

Lloyd E. Frohreich is Professor of Educational Administration at the University of Wisconsin–Madison and specializes in school business administration, educational finance and education facilities. Currently he serves as a faculty associate with the Wisconsin Center for Education Research and is conducting research on resource utilization and its effects on students. Prior to that time he was a teacher and school business manager in Indiana.

Dr. Robert Gresham is the Director of Transportation Services for the Adams County School District 12 in Northglenn, Colorado, having served in that capacity since 1979. Previous to this assignment he had served as Assistant to the Superintendent in District 12, Assistant Superintendent for the Albuquerque Public Schools and assistant Superintendent for the Manhattan, Kansas Schools. He is currently Vice-Chairperson for Program, Transportation Management Research Committee of the Association of School Business Officials and President of the Colorado State Pupil Transportation Association. Two books came from his tenure as Director of the Future Schools Project, a Title III Project of the Albuquerque Public Schools—*The Albuquerque Story* and *Financing Elementary and Secondary Education in New Mexico*.

Guilbert Hentschke is Associate Professor in the Graduate School of Education and Human Development and Graduate School of Management, University of Rochester, and is the author of *Management Operations in Education* and *School Business Administration: A Comparative Perspective*. Professor Hentschke is currently serving as Acting Dean of Education at Rochester and has held administrative and academic positions in the Chicago Public Schools and at Teachers College, Columbia University.

Bettye MacPhail–Wilcox is Assistant Professor of Educational Administration at North Carolina State University, where she teaches Educational Finance, Principles of Educational Administration, Program Evaluation, and other practitioner courses. She is Associate

Editor of the *Journal of Education Finance* and Program Coordinator for Elementary/Secondary Administration. Her most recent research in educational finance concerns investments in teacher education and salary and supply levels.

Lionel R. Meno is Superintendent of Schools in the City School District of Syracuse, New York. In addition to the normal duties as superintendent of a large urban school district, he has developed a special interest in nontraditional financing methods for school districts. Dr. Meno received his Ed.D. from the University of Rochester, in New York State.

Suzette S. Pope is the Chief Accountant in the Dade County (FL) Public Schools' Bureau of Business Management. She holds B.B.A. and M.B.A. degrees from the University of Miami, and has served as an official county representative at various state, regional, and national level organizations relating to finance, accounting, and business management.

Richard G. Salmon is Associate Professor and Program Leader of Educational Administration at Virginia Tech University. He has conducted research studies in the areas of school finance and business management for local, state, and federal agencies. He has published articles in several journals and is serving currently as managing editor of the *Journal of Education Finance*.

Charles H. Sederberg is Professor of Educational Administration and director of the Center for Educational Policy Studies in the College of Education, University of Minnesota. He teaches courses in budgeting, financial management, and management information systems. Research activities focus on school finance policies, staffing, and rural education. Professional experiences include secondary teaching, the principalship, and district level administration.

Stan Tikkanen is the Executive Director of Finance and Business Services for Independent School District No. 284, Wayzata, Minnesota. He previously served as the Director of School Financial Management for the Department of Education. He holds a Masters of Accounting Degree in School Business Administration from the College of St. Thomas, St. Paul, Minnesota.

William R. Wilkerson is Professor of School Administration at Indiana University. Previous professional experience was as a public school teacher, and as an administrator and faculty member at Eastern Illinois University and Indiana State University. His research interest areas are school construction financing and school debt management, and he has conducted studies for several states, the U.S. Office of Education, and many local school districts.

AMERICAN EDUCATION FINANCE ASSOCIATION OFFICERS 1984-85

Officers

President	G. Alan Hickrod
President-Elect	James Phelps
Secretary Treasurer	George R. Babigian
Immediate Past President	Nelda H. Cambron-McCabe

Directors

M. David Alexander	Kathleen Maurer
John Augenblick	Kent McGuire
Carla Edlefson	Van D. Mueller
Lloyd E. Frohreich	Lawrence C. Pierce
Thomas L. Johns	Mary Frase Williams
Suzanne Langston	Arthur E. Wise
Bettye MacPhail-Wilcox	

Editor, Journal of Education Finance

Kern Alexander

Sustaining Members

American Association of School Administrators
American Federation of Teachers
National Education Association